The Political Thought
of Frederick Douglass

The Political Thought
of Frederick Douglass

In Pursuit of American Liberty

Nicholas Buccola

NEW YORK UNIVERSITY PRESS
New York and London

NEW YORK UNIVERSITY PRESS
New York and London
www.nyupress.org

First published in paperback in 2013

References to Internet websites (URLs) were accurate at the time of writing.
Neither the author nor New York University Press is responsible for URLs
that may have expired or changed since the manuscript was prepared.

Library of Congress Cataloging-in-Publication Data
Buccola, Nicholas.
The political thought of Frederick Douglass : in pursuit of American liberty / Nicholas
Buccola.
p. cm.
Includes bibliographical references and index.
ISBN-13: 978-0-8147-8711-3 (cl : alk. paper)
ISBN-13: 978-1-4798-6749-3 (pb : alk. paper)
1. Douglass, Frederick, 1818-1895 — Political and social views.
2. Douglass, Frederick, 1818-1895 — Philosophy.
3. Liberty — Philosophy. I. Title.
E449.D75B83 2011
973.8092 — dc23   2011043494

New York University Press books are printed on acid-free paper,
and their binding materials are chosen for strength and durability.
We strive to use environmentally responsible suppliers and materials
to the greatest extent possible in publishing our books.

Manufactured in the United States of America
10 9 8 7 6 5 4 3 2 1

To the memory of
Catherine Martinet, my cousin and my friend
(June 3, 1961–June 5, 2006)

Contents

Acknowledgments

The completion of this book would not have been possible without the support of many people. First, I am grateful to the incredible group of people that surrounded me as a graduate student at the University of Southern California. Many colleagues and professors at USC—especially Howard Gillman, Judith Stiehm, Sharon Lloyd, Jonathan O'Hara, Dave Bridge, Jillian Medeiros, Amy Below, Jesse Mills, and Art Auerbach—provided vital intellectual and emotional support as I began my research on Frederick Douglass. Alison Renteln and Jim Kincaid read and commented on early versions of this manuscript. Thanks to Alison for teaching me that the formulation of a research agenda is, and ought to be, an exercise of mind and heart. Thanks to Jim for his thoughtful feedback on this project and for inspiring me to think about the vocation of a scholar in a new light. The greatest gift I received while I was at USC was the opportunity to work with Mark Kann. Mark went above and beyond the call of duty as my advisor and mentor. Without Mark's wisdom, encouragement, and responsiveness, this project would not have been possible. He has taught me so much about writing, teaching, and the history of American political thought.

When I left USC I was fortunate enough to secure my dream job at Linfield College in McMinnville, Oregon. Although Linfield is a small liberal arts college where one's performance as a teacher matters more than anything else, it has proven to be a wonderful place to do research. I am grateful to all the folks in the Office of Academic Affairs—especially Barbara Seidman, Victoria McGillin, Meridith Symons, Nancy Drickey, and Liz Atkinson—for supporting this project. Faculty Development Grants and Summer Collaborative Research Grants from that office as well as grants from the Institute for Humane Studies, the Acton Institute, and the Jack Miller Center for Teaching American Founding Principles and History have allowed me the time and resources to finish this book. I owe a great debt of gratitude to my colleagues in the Linfield Department of Political Science—Dawn Nowacki, Patrick Cottrell, and Howard Leichter—who have provided much-needed intellectual and moral support. In addition to my marvelous colleagues, I have had the great fortune to work with some fantastic students at Linfield. While teaching them, I have learned much about Frederick Douglass and so many other things. My Linfield research assistants—especially T. Craig Sinclair, Mike Stead, Aila Wallace, and Braden Smith—have been invaluable.

I am also grateful to Robin Condon and her colleagues at the Frederick Douglass Papers Project at Indiana University-Purdue University Indianapolis in Indianapolis, Indiana. During a visit to the Douglass Papers Project in the summer of 2009 I was able to read many of Douglass's unpublished letters, speeches, and editorials and I had many great conversations with Robin and her staff. I thank everyone at the Douglass Papers Project for their kindness, professionalism, and assistance.

I would also like to thank Thomas Spragens of Duke University and two anonymous reviewers who read the manuscript for NYU Press. Their thoughtful comments improved this manuscript in innumerable ways. Thanks also to Ilene Kalish, executive editor at NYU Press, and to Aiden Amos, an editorial assistant at NYU Press, who have been incredibly supportive from the proposal stage of this project through to the book you hold in your hands.

Finally, I would like to thank my family and friends. My mom and dad, Kathy and Tony Sr., have been sources of constant support and encouragement. My brothers Tony Jr., Craig, and Scott and my sister Michelle as well as my many aunts, uncles, cousins, nieces, nephews, and friends have provided me with so much love and reminded me of what really matters. And thank you to my wife Emily for listening to me ramble about Frederick Douglass and for being such a great source of love and wonder in my life.

"From this little bit of experience—slave experience—I have elaborated quite a lengthy chapter of political philosophy, applicable to the American people."

Frederick Douglass,
"Sources of Danger to the Republic,"
February 7, 1867

The Facts and the Philosophy

Frederick Douglass as Political Thinker

Introduction

By 1860, Frederick Douglass's patience was wearing thin. After spending nearly two decades as an antislavery activist and enduring the many setbacks of the 1850s—the congressional compromises, the *Dred Scott* decision, the execution of John Brown—he admitted to reaching a "point of weary hopelessness."[1] The American people, he wrote, claim to accept the "civic catechism of the Declaration of Independence" and yet with three million people held in bondage around them, they are not moved from "the downy seat of inaction." Douglass argued that the persistence of this "terrible paradox" was not due to a "failure to appreciate the value of liberty," but rather because the American "love of liberty" was "circumscribed by our narrow and wicked" selfishness.[2]

Douglass devoted his near six decades as an orator, writer, and public official to convincing his fellow Americans to purge this narrowness and selfishness from their love of liberty. His aim, in short, was to persuade the American people to accept a new liberal creed that would replace narrowness with egalitarianism and selfishness with humanitarianism. His life's mission, he said in 1888, was "to hasten the day when the principles of liberty and humanity expressed in the Declaration of Independence and the constitution of the United States shall be the law and the practice of every section, and of all the people of this great country without regard to race, sex, color, or religion."[3] This book is about the political philosophy that animated his mission. I argue that Douglass believed his goals could only be accomplished if the classical liberal commitment to individual rights was coupled with a robust conception of mutual responsibility. Two ideas were at the core of his political thought: a belief in universal self-ownership and a commitment to a doctrine he called "true virtue." According to the idea of universal self-ownership, every human being is the *"original, rightful, and absolute owner of his own body,"* and according to the doctrine of true virtue, each individual has extensive obligations to stand up for the rights of others.[4] Douglass's embrace of these foundational ideas was rooted in the experience of slavery and his quest to abolish it. His hatred of the cruelties of slavery led him to an acute appreciation of the importance of individual rights, and the challenges he confronted as an abolitionist led him to believe that an ethos of "each for all and all for each" was necessary to secure these rights.

I believe an exploration of Douglass's political thought is worthwhile for two major reasons. First, Douglass was a prominent and unique voice in one of the most important periods in American political history. The problem of slavery raised fundamental questions about the nature of the American polity. What are the foundations and limits of democratic authority in the United States? What rights do individuals possess? Are individual rights universal? What obligations do individuals have to one another? By drawing on his experiences as a slave, Douglass was able to offer a distinct perspective on these and other basic questions of political philosophy. He set himself apart from most of his contemporaries by defending a far more inclusive and morally demanding liberalism. Unlike so many of his predecessors and contemporaries, Douglass's natural rights philosophy was truly universal in its application and his "outsider" status pushed him to articulate a much more urgent view of the obligations individuals have to one another. Second, I believe the spirit of Douglass's ideas continues to be relevant to contemporary debates about political theory and practice. We are confronted, as Douglass was, with problems that cannot be addressed by the language of liberty alone. Instead in discussions of public philosophy and policy, contemporary citizens and statesmen are grappling with how to balance our commitment to rights with a greater sense of the obligations we have to others. As we confront the myriad challenges of our age, we would do well to reflect on the ideas of Frederick Douglass, who in the face of some of the biggest political crises this country has ever confronted, attempted to show that the promises of freedom are more likely to be realized in communities of responsible individuals.

Frederick Douglass: A Life of Agitation and Service

Although relevant moments in Douglass's life will come up again and again in what follows, this is not a work of biography and my analysis proceeds thematically rather than chronologically. The details of Douglass's life have been ably described by Douglass himself and by a number of excellent historians.[5] Before discussing Douglass's political thought, though, I would like to provide a brief description of his life. He was born into slavery in Tuckahoe, Maryland, in 1818. Over the course of the next twenty years, he experienced the full spectrum of slavery from the relative freedom of life as a "city slave" in Baltimore to the horrors of life on a plantation run by the infamous "slave-breaker" Edward Covey.[6] At age 20, Douglass escaped from slavery and spent a brief period working as a common laborer in Massachusetts. Within a few years of attaining his freedom, he was "discovered" by the abolitionist leader William Lloyd Garrison and joined the abolitionist lecture circuit. Soon after joining the circuit, he faced a problem: his oratorical skills so impressed his audiences that many began to doubt whether or not he truly was "a graduate of the peculiar institution." This (among other things) led his Garrisonian mentors to attempt to rein in their new colleague. "Give us the facts," John A. Collins instructed Douglass, "we will take care of the philosophy."[7] Douglass did not take this advice, and the American political tradition is all the richer for it.

Douglass spent the 1840s and 1850s agitating on behalf of abolition. He lectured widely, authored autobiographies describing his life as a slave, and edited abolitionist newspapers—*The North Star* from 1847 to 1851, *Frederick Douglass' Paper* from 1851 to 1860, and *The Douglass Monthly* from 1860 to 1863. In his speeches and writings, Douglass drew on his experiences as a slave and his study of natural rights philosophy in an attempt to convince his listeners and readers of the evil inherent in the slave system. In addition, Douglass lent his skills of persuasion to other progressive causes such as women's suffrage, temperance, the abolition of capital punishment, equal rights for immigrants, and universal public education.

During the Civil War, Douglass used his voice and his pen to push President Abraham Lincoln and other Republican leaders to acknowledge that the conflict was about slavery and could not be resolved without the abolition of that institution.[8] In addition, once he felt that the war was being waged for the right reasons and when he became convinced that black soldiers would be granted equal pay and treatment by Union commanders, he used his influence to recruit on behalf of the Union cause. After the war, Douglass continued his work as a progressive reformer, turning his attention to achieving equal citizenship for freedmen as well as continuing to speak and write in favor of the causes listed above.

During the 1870s and 1880s, Douglass established himself as a staunch supporter of the Republican Party. His support was rewarded with several opportunities to serve in Republican administrations. First, in 1871, he was selected by President Ulysses S. Grant to serve as secretary to a commission charged with the task of investigating the annexation of Santo Domingo. Then, in 1874, Douglass was again called into service by President Grant, this time to serve as the president of the Freedman's Saving and Trust Company, an institution established to provide financial assistance to freed slaves. In 1877, Douglass was appointed by President Rutherford B. Hayes to serve as U.S. Marshal in the District of Columbia before he was appointed to become Recorder of Deeds for the District in 1880. Douglass's last appointment came when he agreed to serve as American consul-general to Haiti from 1889 to 1891. Douglass continued to agitate on behalf of progressive causes until the day he died. On February 20, 1895, he attended a meeting of the National Council of Women in Washington, D.C. Shortly after he returned home to prepare to lecture that evening, he collapsed and died instantly.[9]

Like many other important figures in the history of American political thought, Douglass never published a comprehensive treatise of political philosophy. Over the course of his public career, though, he did produce three autobiographies, thousands of speeches and editorials, and volumes of correspondence from which we can cull a fairly coherent picture of his answers to many central normative questions in politics. In this book, I attempt to reconstruct that picture. In so doing, I have tried to be mindful of the fact that Douglass was not, first and foremost, a philosopher. Instead, Douglass is most often viewed, quite rightly, as a reformer and statesman. When interpreting his writings and speeches, then, it is necessary to keep in mind that he was a political actor who was attempting to achieve particular objectives. As such, although my analysis proceeds thematically instead of chronologically, I have tried to be mindful of the contexts in which Douglass was writing and speaking. While it is vital to keep these contexts in mind, my primary aim in this book is to explain the core commitments of Douglass's political philosophy, which I contend was remarkably consistent over time. I invite the reader, then, to think of Douglass as a sort of philosophical statesman. He was a political actor whose ideas were to some extent conditioned by the demands of the politics of his time, but he was an actor who remained faithful to a set of core ideas. My hope is that this book will provide readers with a deeper understanding of those core ideas. I am not the first to offer an interpretation of Douglass's political thought; so before proceeding to my argument, it is appropriate to say something about the interpretations offered by others.

Situating Frederick Douglass in the American Political Tradition

In *The Political Philosophy of Thomas Jefferson*, Garrett Ward Sheldon describes three approaches to the study of political ideas:

> (1) the historical approach, which examines the language used by a society to discuss political problems; (2) the political science approach, which studies the role of political language in political activity; and (3) the approach of political philosophy, which, more abstractly, examines the concepts in past political ideas and their relation to other theories found throughout the history of Western political thought.[10]

This study of Douglass's political thought draws on all three approaches, but relies most heavily on the third. When I began this project I was motivated, at least in part, by a desire to address what I took to be a glaring lack of scholarly attention to Douglass as a political philosopher. The canonical interpretations of the American political tradition failed to even mention Douglass and, at the time I began this project, there had not been a book-length study of Douglass published by a political theorist.[11] Sometimes gaps in the literature are there for good reason, but I did not believe this was the case for Douglass. [12]After all, how could it be that one of the most prominent Americans of the nineteenth century, a man who was deeply engaged in the most important moral and political battle of that century, was so ignored by political theorists?

Although Douglass had been ignored in the canonical interpretations of American political thought produced in the twentieth century and did not become the subject of a book-length study by a political theorist until almost a decade into the twenty-first, the cupboard of research on Douglass as a political philosopher is not completely bare. Indeed, like many other iconic figures in American political history, his political philosophy has been a matter of interpretive dispute. As you will see in my argument in chapter 3, in one sense the categorization of Douglass's political philosophy is simple: he was a liberal. This is only noncontroversial, though, if we adopt a general definition like the one offered by political theorist Judith Shklar. "Liberalism," Shklar wrote, is a "political doctrine" with "only one overriding aim: to secure the political conditions necessary for the exercise of personal freedom."[13] If we adopt this sort of broad definition, then it is fair to say that most American political thinkers are within the liberal tradition.[14] As numerous scholars of

American political thought have pointed out, it is precisely for this reason that we must dig deeper into the liberal tradition in order to appreciate the diversity that exists within it.[15] Scholars of American thought have divided the liberal tradition in a variety of ways, but perhaps the most basic division is between "classical" and "reform" liberalism. According to political theorist Kenneth Dolbeare, classical liberals emphasize self-reliance, natural rights, private property and limited government intervention in social and economic affairs.[16] Returning to the language used in Shklar's general definition above, classical liberals believe the conditions are met for the exercise of personal freedom when a limited government protects the rights of individuals to life, liberty, and property. Reform liberals share the classical liberal belief in individual rights, but worry about whether or not genuine freedom can be exercised under conditions of economic and social inequality. Reform liberals contend that true liberty can only be realized in communities that empower individuals to fulfill their potential. This empowerment, reform liberals contend, comes from individuals feeling a greater sense of obligation for one another's well-being than classical liberalism seems to demand, and from a willingness to accept government intervention in social and economic life in order to promote greater equality.

Interpreters are divided on how to classify Douglass, but the majority identifies him with the classical liberal tradition.[17] Interpreters in this majority connect him to the contemporary political spectrum by contending that he is best thought of as the founding father of black conservatism in the United States and hear his arguments echoed on the contemporary right from thinkers like Thomas Sowell, Shelby Steele, and John McWhorter.[18] According to this reading, the defining features of Douglass's political morality are his commitments to natural rights, limited government, and a self-help individualism that would later be popularized by Booker T. Washington in the early twentieth century, and celebrated by Supreme Court Justice Clarence Thomas in our own time. Another set of interpreters identifies Douglass as a thinker who was keenly aware of the myriad forms of inequality that threaten the exercise of personal freedom and, as such, embraced a political philosophy that departed significantly from the core tenets of classical liberalism. Before proceeding, I would like to provide brief sketches of each side of this interpretive divide.

In her short book *American Citizenship*, political theorist Judith Shklar offered an interpretation of Douglass as a classical liberal. Douglass is a central figure in Shklar's arguments throughout the book, but of particular interest for my purposes is her discussion of Douglass in the context of the late-twentieth-century "ideological conflict" over social welfare programs.

One side accuses its opponents of being a paternalistic elite who want to eliminate poverty by paralyzing the helpless poor. The second group charges the other side with being harsh populist achievers who blame the victims unfairly, and who in disregard of actual conditions and needs simply want to put everyone to work for a tiny wage and to no good end.[19]

Shklar calls the latter group "the defenders of the helpless poor" and the former group the "party of individual effort." The defenders of the helpless poor, representing the left of the political spectrum, view the poor as "social victims who are being denied racial equality, opportunities for decent work and education, and access to normal public goods." Douglass's ideas, Shklar contends, are on the other side of the divide: "The opposing party of individual effort, like Frederick Douglass, hopes that the government will do nothing more than ensure fair play for all. Anyone who truly wants to work, they argue, can find employment, and with it will come standing and self-respect." Douglass's party, Shklar says, sees the "defenders of the helpless poor" as a "threat" to "the values of work and independence."[20]

In *On Hallowed Ground*, intellectual historian John Patrick Diggins reaches a conclusion similar to the one reached by Shklar. In his analysis of "Black America and the Liberal Tradition," he describes two "policy positions" that we can see in American thought from the Reconstruction era to contemporary American politics. One position, "stretching from Frederick Douglass to Booker T. Washington to our contemporaries Shelby Steele and Thomas Sowell, emphasizes liberal individualism based on initiative in the private sphere, self-development, work and thrift, the rationality of economic life, personal responsibility, and integration with the larger white society."[21] The other position, "which stretches from W. E. B. DuBois to Martin Luther King Jr. to our contemporaries Henry Louis Gates and Cornel West" emphasizes such things as "race as a collective experience, power as residing in groups rather than individuals," and "the necessity of civil disobedience and non-violent coercion."[22] Diggins brings this reading into a contemporary ideological context by contending that Douglass's individualism is an alternative to the "mystique of difference" celebrated by the political left: "At a time when many Americans are told that their identity lies in being recognized as some kind of ethnic subspecies, it may be helpful to remember that Lincoln and Douglass could share a national identity and a common historical foundation in American liberalism."[23] These claims leave little doubt that Diggins situates Douglass's legacy on the right wing of contemporary political discourse.

In *Creative Conflict in African American Thought,* Wilson Jeremiah Moses contends that Douglass accepted "Free the slaves and leave them alone" as his "motto" after the failure of Reconstruction convinced him of "the unreliability of government as defender of political rights." After the Civil War, Moses argues, Douglass "settled into a doctrine of laissez faire, in which greed was to be regulated only by the invisible hand of moral sentiments."[24] Moses concludes that Douglass is best described as a "laissez faire liberal." It is worth noting that unlike Diggins, Moses does not celebrate this interpretation of Douglass. In other words, while it is clear that Diggins prefers the classical liberalism he finds in Douglass to the "mystique of difference" offered by contemporary progressive liberals, Moses finds Douglass's laissez faire liberalism to be deeply problematic.[25]

Some scholars who embrace the classical liberal reading of Douglass are more ambivalent. Intellectual historian Waldo E. Martin, for example, identifies both laissez faire and humanitarian elements in Douglass's political thought.[26] Similarly, political theorist Gayle McKeen emphasizes the centrality of self-help in Douglass's thought, but contends that his philosophy does not fit neatly into either the classical or reform categories.[27] The most sustained treatment of Douglass as a political thinker is Peter C. Myers's recent book, *Frederick Douglass: Race and the Rebirth of American Liberalism.* Myers contends that Douglass is "unequaled in his articulation of the first principles of natural rights liberalism in their application to racial justice in America."[28] Although Myers's account is nuanced and complex, the crux of his argument is that Douglass is best understood as an advocate of natural rights and that his argument "lives on" in the writings of black conservatives like Thomas Sowell, Shelby Steele, and John McWhorter and in what might reasonably be called the "conservative" writings of black writers situated on the contemporary left such as Juan Williams and Orlando Patterson.[29] It would be unfair to conclude that Myers's interpretation fits neatly on the classical liberal side of the divide I am describing here. Myers calls Douglass a Hamiltonian nationalist who embraces an active federal government and he is careful not to overstate the connection between Douglass's ideas and the ideas of contemporary black conservatives. Rather than saying that Douglass clearly fits into the contemporary conservative camp, Myers contends that he shares the contemporary black conservative rejection of the "culture of alienation" that he believes pervades the thinking of several other black thinkers.[30]

As you will see in the chapters that follow, I believe those who interpret Douglass as a classical liberal capture part of the truth about his political philosophy. He was indeed an ardent defender of self-ownership, self-reliance, and several other lodestars of the classical liberal tradition. But a pure libertarian he was not. As an alternative set of interpreters has made clear, Douglass was a thinker who was acutely aware of the problem of inequality and whose remedy to this problem departed in significant ways from the core tenets of classical liberalism. Douglass, more so than most, was cognizant of the vulnerability of individuals in isolation and he appreciated the myriad ways in which human beings need one another to survive and flourish. Rather than offering a purely classical liberal politics of rights and interests, these interpreters contend, Douglass offers us a politics of fraternity and obligations. His legacy lives on not in the individualist ideas of Clarence Thomas and his ilk but in the ideas of thinkers like Martin Luther King, Jr., Thurgood Marshall, and contemporary progressives. This alternative set of interpreters sees Douglass as something other than an ardent individualist. According to these interpreters, Douglass's project forced him to transcend the bounds of individualism to a set of ideas that emphasize the language of community and obligation. As you will see in my analysis in the chapters that follow, these interpreters capture an important part of the truth as well.

The classic expression of this view is found in Wilson Carey McWilliams's *The Idea of Fraternity in America,* a text in which the author examines an "alternative tradition" that emphasizes interdependence and obligation that has existed alongside the classical liberal tradition's emphasis on rights and interests in American political history. McWilliams argued that Douglass's experience as a slave led him "close to a true recognition of human weakness and dependence" and to an understanding "that what is really to be feared in human affairs is isolation." Douglass, McWilliams argued, was "devoted to the ideal of human fraternity" and saw that the "principal antagonists" of this ideal are "those who accept individualism and the doctrine of self-reliance, for these must necessarily be fearful of their fellows."[31]

Political scientist J. David Greenstone and historian Daniel Walker Howe have offered interpretations of Douglass not far from the reading offered by McWilliams. Prior to his untimely death, Greenstone had planned to write a chapter on Douglass and the abolitionist Lydia Maria Child in his classic text on American political thought, *The Lincoln Persuasion,* in which he would argue that Douglass was a reform liberal—a term Greenstone defined as a philosophy that held "individuals have an obligation . . . to cultivate and develop their physical, intellectual, aesthetic and moral faculties," and who believe this obligation "extends to helping others do the same."[32] Greenstone associated the reform liberal view with a more activist state that supports increased funding for educational and cultural programs. In his book *Making the American Self*, historian Daniel Walker Howe agrees with this interpretation: "Douglass's political thought illustrates beautifully David Greenstone's conception of reform liberalism as a philosophy dedicated to national regeneration."[33] Howe takes this interpretation a step further by recruiting Douglass into the cause of contemporary progressive politics: "Douglass can speak to the issues of today if we want him to: compensatory education, head start, measuring how far students have come instead of what point they have reached—these contemporary issues find an advocate in Frederick Douglass."[34]

In addition to this reform liberal interpretation, some scholars have taken this alternative reading even further by suggesting that Douglass is best understood as part of the civic republican tradition. Although this tradition is varied and complex, its core is described by political scientist Alan Gibson as "beliefs that virtue (defined as the voluntary subordination of self-interest to the public good) is necessary to the preservation of republics and conversely that corruption (the pursuit by citizens and rulers of private gain at public expense) must be avoided."[35] Historian Daniel McInerney has argued that Douglass and other abolitionists adopted the republican language of corruption as the core of their case against chattel slavery.[36] In a similar vein, Michael Sandel identifies Douglass with the civic republican "political antislavery" strand of thought that defined freedom as empowerment (as opposed to the liberal "abolitionist" strand of William Lloyd Garrison and others who defined freedom as noninterference).[37] Most recently, political theorist Robert Gooding-Williams has argued that "Douglass's politics of reconstruction" often "appears to belong to a tradition of Roman and republican political theory." Gooding-Williams contends that Douglass relied on a republican "narrative of decline" in the years prior to the Civil War in order to make the case that the country was in need of a virtuous rededication to the principles of the Declaration of Independence.[38]

As you will see in the second half of this book, I believe the advocates of these alternative readings are on to something. McWilliams is right to point out that Douglass's experience at the margins of the political community led him to a distinct appreciation of the perils of isolation. Greenstone is right to suggest that there are ways in which Douglass's conception of liberty goes beyond the purely negative view of freedom as absence of interference. Howe captures something important about the spirit of Douglass's project, which was truly regenerative in nature.[39] Douglass was attempting to fashion a refounding of the American republic in a way that vindicated the first principles expressed in the Declaration of Independence and purged it of beliefs and practices offensive to those principles. In the words of philosopher Derrick Darby, the "true genius of Frederick Douglass's political philosophy" is his calling of "our attention to the blatant inconsistencies" between American ideals and practices. In the language of Gooding-Williams, Douglass's central message to all Americans was to "reenact their fathers' founding commitment to the principles of the Declaration" by purging the practice of slavery. [40] Furthermore, Howe's attempt to enlist Douglass in the contemporary progressive cause is not without merit. Douglass was acutely aware of the severe inequalities that existed around him and he envisioned an active role for government to combat those inequalities.

In sum, the scholarly literature on Douglass's political thought leaves us with an interpretive puzzle to be solved. Before proceeding, a word must be said on why making sense of this interpretive puzzle matters. There are two interrelated reasons why this is worthwhile: one scholarly and one political. As a scholarly matter, the divergent interpretations of Douglass's thought present us with a dispute to be resolved. A careful analysis of his words with due consideration to the contexts in which he communicated them can provide us with a better sense of what counts as a legitimate reading and what does not. Making sense of Douglass's legacy is significant for political reasons as well. Douglass, like Abraham Lincoln and the American Founders, comes down to us as an almost mythic figure in our political history. He has become perhaps the most recognizable symbol of American abolitionism and one of our country's earliest defenders of equal rights for all. Douglass's symbolic significance has led to contemporary appropriations by scholars and politicians from across the ideological spectrum. These scholars and politicians sometimes argue and more often assert that Douglass's ideas are supportive of their own positions in contemporary debates. It is not surprising, for example, that in recent political discussions Douglass's name was invoked by prominent members of both the Republican and Democratic parties and that he has been celebrated by figures as divergent as Glenn Beck and Angela Davis.[41] The explicit or implicit suggestion that Douglass is "on our side" in a contemporary philosophical or policy debate may carry some significance for political elites and citizens. If Douglass's ideas are being misappropriated, it is the duty of scholars to set the record straight. My hope is that this book contributes to this task.

Plan of the Book

In the chapters that follow, I reconstruct Douglass's political thought. As noted above, because my aim is to explain the core principles of his political philosophy, my argument proceeds thematically rather than chronologically. In the next two chapters, I demonstrate that the core of his thought was liberal. In chapter 2, I explore how Douglass drew on the experience of slavery to defend the classical liberal idea of self-ownership. A political community is only just, he argued, if each individual's right to control his or her own life is respected. In chapter 3, I draw out the political consequences of this belief in self-ownership by describing Douglass's commitments to individual rights, toleration, and limited, representative government and by demonstrating that he rejected anarchist, socialist, perfectionist, and radical democratic alternatives to liberalism. My aim in chapter 3 is to establish that the basic framework of Douglass's politics is liberal.

After establishing Douglass's liberal credentials, I move in a slightly different direction. As a progressive reformer, Douglass had to confront the fact that most of his contemporaries accepted the liberal ideas that made up the core of his thought while being simultaneously committed to ideologies of exclusion such as sexism, racism, and xenophobia. American liberalism was, in short, incomplete. In order to close the gap between the promises of liberalism and the realities of American life, Douglass infused his political philosophy with an egalitarian ethos of inclusion and a robust conception of mutual responsibility. He had to convince his listeners that all human beings—regardless of race, sex, or origin—ought to be *included* in the promises of liberalism, and he had to convince his listeners that they should feel *obliged* to take the steps necessary to make this happen. I will show that Douglass believed each individual has an obligation to stand up for the rights of others when they are being violated or are under threat, to treat others fairly, and to stand up against unfair institutions and practices. Furthermore, he believed that citizens and statesmen have obligations to cultivate a "moral ecology" that will encourage individuals to make responsible choices.

In chapter 4, I show how Douglass's experience as an abolitionist led him to articulate this philosophy of mutual responsibility and I examine the sorts of arguments he offered in defense of the claim that free men have obligations to liberate slaves. From this discussion of the mutual obligation in Douglass's thought, I proceed to a discussion of the consequences of these ideas for the behavior of individuals and institutions. In chapter 5, I examine two ideal types central to Douglass's political philosophy—the Reformer and the Self-Made Man—in order to capture a sense of how he believed individuals ought to behave in order to achieve and maintain a just political community. The Reformer directs individuals to feel a strong sense of responsibility for the realization of justice and fairness in the basic structure of the political community, and the Self-Made Man directs individuals to work hard and behave virtuously in order to achieve personal, familial, and neighborhood well-being. In chapter 6, I examine Douglass's understanding of the proper role of the state in educating its citizens in a way that is supportive of freedom and virtue. I contend that through coercion, law-making, rhetoric, and the establishment of educational institutions the state can promote what Douglass called a "humanitarian culture."[42]

In chapter 7, I conclude by offering some reflections on debates over Douglass's legacy. I contend that most interpreters have oversimplified Douglass's views and that all attempts to draw contemporary conclusions from his nineteenth-century arguments should be chastened by a heavy dose of humility. With this in mind, I contend that while it is hard to know what conclusions Douglass would come to in the philosophical and policy debates of today we can say something about how the spirit of his thought might shape the lens through which we view contemporary political questions. Fundamentally, he directs us to think about the ways in which the liberal goal of securing the conditions necessary for the exercise of personal freedom depends upon the prevalence of a robust sense of mutual responsibility.

"Every Man Is Himself
and Belongs to Himself"

*Slavery and Self-Ownership as the
Foundations of Douglass's Liberalism*

Introduction

Frederick Douglass developed his views of political morality in the shadow of slavery. Born into bondage, he spent the first twenty years of his life experiencing the perils of an existence dominated by the arbitrary whims of those who claimed him as property. Douglass's hatred of slavery cannot be overstated. To be enslaved, he said, is to be subjected to "the greatest injury this side of death" because to enslave a man is to "blot out his personality, degrade his manhood, and sink him to the condition of a beast of burden."[1] In this chapter, I contend that Douglass's arguments against slavery have significance far beyond his critique of the institution. Indeed, I believe his abhorrence of slavery provides the foundation for the two principles at the core of his political thought: it led him to embrace the liberal idea of self-ownership and his desire to see the institution abolished led him to an acute appreciation of the ways in which the achievement of universal freedom depends upon the development of a strong ethos of mutual responsibility.

In what follows, I retrace a crucial part of Douglass's intellectual journey that took place after he made the physical journey from slavery to freedom. I begin, as he did, with the experience of slavery. In the next section, I examine his definition of slavery, what he believed to be its origins in human selfishness, and explain why he thought the institution was so cruel. Then, I reconstruct Douglass's case for self-ownership, which he believed was the foundation for individual rights to life, liberty, property, and equal citizenship. I focus in particular on his use of the idea to defend the abolition of slavery and universal suffrage. I conclude by arguing that the egalitarianism at the core of his philosophy of self-ownership is an important contribution to the liberal tradition and that the morally robust foundation of his liberalism is intimately connected to the philosophy of mutual responsibility explored in later chapters.

In exploring these matters I hope to accomplish several goals. First, I want to show *how* Douglass grounded his liberal politics. I argue that he rooted his politics in the idea of self-ownership, which he believed provides the physical and metaphysical freedom necessary to pursue a variety of human ends: love, friendship, intellectual development, moral excellence, spiritual striving, and material comfort. Second, I want to show *why* Douglass grounded his liberalism in this way. I contend that his case for self-ownership is rooted in the "negative" claim that slavery is morally wrong as well as the "positive" claim that personal freedom is morally good.[2] Third, I make the case that there is something distinctive and important about Douglass's articulation of liberal foundations. It is fair to say that Douglass spent most of his life outside and at the margins of American citizenship. His understanding of the promises and shortcomings of liberalism was rooted in this outsider status. Douglass's account has particular moral force because it is grounded not only in his personal experience but in the nation's experience. Slavery and its aftermath were the major moral and political problems at the center of American life during Douglass's career. This is important because the problem of slavery led to a national crisis that compelled political thinkers and actors to grapple with first principles. The Civil War was a moment of great destruction and, at the same time, great possibility. As political theorist Sheldon Wolin has pointed out, during periods of turmoil the "range of possibilities appears infinite, for now the political philosopher is not confined to criticism and interpretation; he must reconstruct a shattered world of meanings and their accompanying institutional expressions; he must, in short, fashion a political cosmos out of political chaos."[3] In 1864, Douglass captured the essence of Wolin's insight when he identified the Civil War as a moment of refounding: "The public mind is now everywhere grappling with fundamental principles. We are looking for solid rock, upon which to rest the foundation of the state. . . . Four years of war arising out of old political and moral errors, must induce [citizens] to inquire diligently for the true path to permanent peace and prosperity."[4] In sum, it was in the context of the personal and national experience of slavery that Douglass developed his understanding of the moral foundations of liberalism.

"The Greatest Injury This Side of Death": Douglass's Summum Malum

Political theorist Sharon Krause has written that behind every "political theory stands a *summum malum*, the one thing in political life its author most fears or despises."[5] There is little question about the *summum malum* in the political thought of Frederick Douglass. "The greatest injury this side of death," he wrote, "which one human being can inflict on another, is to enslave him."[6] Because Douglass formulated his understanding of self-ownership and other natural rights in the shadow of his experience as a slave, it is appropriate to begin this chapter with an examination of his reflections on the institution of slavery. In the next three sections, I provide a detailed account of Douglass's reflections on the meaning of slavery, the root of slavery in human selfishness, and the nature of slavery's cruelties.

What Is Slavery?

Douglass defined slavery as "one man claiming and exercising an uncontrolled right over the body and soul of another."[7] On another occasion he defined it as the "granting of that power by which one man exercises and enforces a right of property in the body and soul of another."[8] There are many important ideas packed into these short definitions. First, slavery is a system in which one person claims to have a property right in another. Douglass compared the nature of this rights claim to the status of property rights in livestock.

> The condition of a slave is simply that of the brute beast. He is a piece of property—a marketable commodity in the language of the law, to be bought or sold at the will and caprice of the master who claims him to be his property; he is spoken of, thought of, and treated as property. His own good, his conscience, his intellect, his affections are all set aside by the master. He is as much a piece of property as a horse. If he is fed, he is fed because he is property. If he is clothed, it is with a view to the increase of his value as property.[9]

The transformation of free man into slave is constituted by the individual "losing his manhood and being converted into a merchantable commodity."[10] Elsewhere, Douglass said, "The first work of slavery is to mar and deface those characteristics of its victims which distinguish *men* from *things*, and *persons* from *property*."[11] The first part of Douglass's definition of slavery, then, is the idea that it is a system that treats persons as if they were property.

Second, it is worth noting the unlimited nature of the slave master's claim. According to Douglass, the relationship between master and slave knows no law higher than the will of the master. "The law," Douglass said, "gives the master absolute power over the slave. He may work him, flog him, hire him out, sell him, and, in certain contingencies, *kill* him, with perfect impunity."[12] The absolute nature of the master's right over the slave is the reason Douglass rejected defining slavery as "a system whereby a man is compelled to work."[13] The point is not that the slave is compelled to *work*, but rather that the "law of slavery" says that the slave can be compelled to do *anything* the master wishes.

Third, the claim of the master is to both body and soul. Not only is the slave denied the physical rights of bodily integrity and locomotion, but he is denied rights of mind and soul such as the freedom to pursue an education and worship God according to the dictates of his conscience. This fact of slavery follows from the absolute nature of the master's claim over the slave. Although the acceptability of baptism and religious instruction for slaves underwent some liberalization over the course of history, the will of the master was always the ultimate arbiter of these matters.

It is worthwhile to point out some of the things that did *not* qualify as slavery in Douglass's mind. During the 1840s, he traveled the United States and Great Britain lecturing a great deal on the meaning of slavery. Douglass thought it was necessary to provide a precise definition of the institution because there seemed "to be a great want of information regarding it," and it bothered him when the term was used in ways that deviated from its "real and intrinsic meaning."[14] The misuse of the term was problematic, Douglass argued, because it diluted its rhetorical power. The relationship of slave to master, he contended, was unlike *any* other human relationship and for this reason Douglass thought use of the term slavery to describe any other phenomenon was "an awful misnomer."[15] In an 1854 address at the Chatham Court in Canada, he discussed why he thought this was so problematic.

> No term is more abused, or misapplied, than that of *Slavery*. It is frequently connected with drunkenness, hard-working, legal disabilities, and many other things. Men are said to be slaves of their propensities, passions, or of circumstances; but none of those are applicable to slavery in the strict sense in which [I] would bring it before [you].[16]

The four "misapplications" of slavery discussed by Douglass most frequently are the use of "slavery" to describe hard work, the deprivation of a particular political right or privilege (such as the right to vote), poverty, and intemperance.

Although it is natural to associate the idea of hard work with the condition of slavery, it is not hard work itself that constitutes slavery. Difficult physical labor was a central part of the lives of most slaves, but Douglass thought it was crucial to point out that hard labor does not, by itself, qualify as slavery. It was not the labor itself, but rather the *relations* of labor that concerned him. He believed hard work was often necessary and could be laudable if undertaken for noble ends. Indeed, Douglass said the two things are not only distinct, but in a sense, antithetical. He often told audiences that he worked much harder as a freeman than he did as a slave.[17] Soon after escaping from slavery in 1838, Douglass began to work as a "dollar a day laborer."[18] In *My Bondage and My Freedom*, he described the significance of the transition from slavery to hard work in this way.

> I found employment, the third day after my arrival in New Bedford, in stowing a sloop with a load of oil for the New York market. It was new, hard, and dirty work, even for a calker, but I went at it with a glad heart and a willing hand. I was now my own master— a tremendous fact— and the rapturous excitement with which I seized the job, may not easily be understood, except by some one with an experience something like mine. The thoughts—"I can work! I can work for a living; I am not afraid of work; I have no Master Hugh to rob me of my earnings"—placed me in a state of independence, beyond seeking friendship or support of any man. That day's work I considered the real starting point of something like a new existence.[19]

As a slave, Douglass had no hope of reward or personal advancement. So he worked only hard enough to avoid punishment. As a free laborer, however, he knew his labor could go toward "benefiting those he loved, his wife and child. In these circumstances there was no work too low, too dirty, too menial for him."[20] In his mind, one is not a slave simply because one is engaged in hard work.

The second rhetorical abuse challenged by Douglass was the attempt to describe the deprivation of a particular political right or privilege as slavery. In an 1846 address on slavery, Douglass disputed this use of the term when he said: "Slavery is not to be deprived of any political privilege. It is not to be deprived of the right of suffrage, otherwise all women were slaves, because they were universally deprived of this right."[21] Slavery, rather, "consisted not in taking away any of the rights of man, but in annihilating them all."[22] Although Douglass was a staunch opponent of all forms of invidious discrimination, he did not believe the condition of an average free woman or child was analogous to the condition of the average slave.

A third misuse of "slavery" was its equation with poverty. Defenders of slavery often argued, for example, that "the condition of the people of Ireland is more deplorable than that of the condition of the American slaves."[23] Although Douglass sympathized with the plight of the poor in Ireland and elsewhere around the world, he argued that poverty and slavery should not be confused.

> The Irishman is poor, but he is *not* a slave. He *may* be in rags, but he is *not* a slave. He is still the master of his own body, and can say with the poet, "The hand of Douglass is his own." . . . The Irishman has not only the liberty to emigrate from his country, but he has liberty at home. He can write, and speak, and co-operate for the attainment of his rights and the redress of wrongs.[24]

According to Douglass's reasoning, a poor Irishman is not a slave because he is free *from* the restraints of slavery. Unlike the slave, the poor man is at least formally free to emigrate and agitate for political rights.

The fourth and final common misuse of the term slavery was its frequent use in connection with drunkenness and other manifestations of moral weakness. Temperance advocates were fond of comparing the condition of the intemperate man to that of the slave. Even though Douglass spoke on behalf of temperance throughout his career, he came to reject the conflation of intemperance and slavery. According to Douglass, slavery is, properly speaking, a *social* phenomenon. An individual cannot, then, be a slave to himself.

"The Very First Element of Slavery": The Spirit of Selfishness in Human Nature

In order to gain a full understanding of slavery in Douglass's thought it is necessary to provide some explanation of what he thought moved one human being to enslave another. His assessment of this question is important because it provides the foundation for his belief in the inherent precariousness of human freedom, a central theme in his political thought. Douglass believed the phenomenon of slavery was a manifestation of the spirit of self-ishness in human nature. Because he believed this spirit is an essential part of human nature, it has foundational importance for his moral and political thought.

Douglass believed the spirit of selfishness in human nature makes men "constantly liable to do evil."[25] He held that although reason, conscience, and revelation direct man to respect the rights of others, the spirit of selfishness has the potential to morally blind him and make him unwilling to respect any authority other than his own will. The omnipresence of selfishness in human nature, Douglass argued, is evident from both "the facts of human nature, and by the experience of all men in all ages."[26] At an 1847 commemo-ration of the abolition of slavery in the West Indies, Douglass said:

> From the earliest periods of man's history, we are able to trace manifesta-tions of that spirit of selfishness, which leads one man to prey upon the rights and interests of his fellow-man. Love of ease, love of power, a strong desire to control the will of others, lay deep-seated in the human heart. These elements of character, over-riding the better promptings of human nature, [have] cursed the world with Slavery and kindred crimes.[27]

The love of ease creates a temptation to exploit the labor of others rather than laboring for oneself. For Douglass, the most nefarious manifestation of this tendency was the institution of slavery, under which the slave "toils that another may reap the fruit; he is industrious that another may live by idle-ness."[28] Slavery was not, however, the only avenue available for the exploita-tion of others. After the Civil War, Douglass continued to identify ways in which the love of ease led men to act unfairly. In his 1871 essay on "The Labor Question," which is discussed at length in the next chapter, Douglass argued that it was the "selfishness" of economic elites rather than an inherent defect in the market-based economy, that caused the vast disparity between rich and poor in "our industrial civilization."[29]

Douglass contended that human beings are also tempted by a love of power and a desire to control the will of others. Man, he argued in an 1886 address on women's rights, has a "disposition to trample upon the weak and play the tyrant."[30] Again, Douglass said that one need not engage in abstract speculation to reach this conclusion because human history provides all the evidence one needs. "No fact is more obvious," he said, "than the fact that there is a perpetual tendency of power to encroach upon weakness, and of the crafty to take advantage of the simple."[31] The facts of human history make clear that there will always be "hardened villains" who "will cheat, steal, rob, burn and murder their fellow creatures."[32] Although Douglass pointed to hardened villains as particularly blatant manifestations of the spirit of self-ishness in human nature, he did not believe these habitual offenders had a monopoly on evil in humanity. Instead, Douglass argued that the capacity to do evil resides within every human heart.

In order to demonstrate the existence of the selfish tendency in human nature, Douglass pointed to what he thought were the most obvious man-ifestations of it in human behavior. "The very first element of Slavery," he said in an 1856 antislavery address, "is selfishness, extreme and bitter selfish-ness—selfishness that destroys the happiness of one man, to increase that of another."[33] In an 1873 address on the U.S. policy toward Santo Domingo, Dou-glass argued that the idea of "manifest destiny" was rooted in "the low, the selfish, the ambitious and rapacious side of human nature."[34] A third example of the spirit of selfishness operating in human nature is the late-nineteenth-century resistance to Chinese immigration. Between 1848 and 1882, more than 300,000 Chinese immigrants came to the United States. Many Ameri-cans reacted harshly to what they perceived to be a "Yellow Peril."[35] In 1882, Douglass said, "I have no sympathy for the narrow, *selfish* notion of economy which assumes that every crumb of bread which goes into the mouths of one class is so much taken from the mouths of another class; and hence, I cannot join with those who would drive the Chinaman from our borders."[36] One need not develop a sophisticated theological or philosophical theory to demonstrate that there is a selfish streak in human nature. All one needs to do, Douglass said, is look around.

Douglass believed the spirit of selfishness emanated from the human heart. By this, he meant that the will to power has its roots more in our pas-sions than in our reason. He referred to selfishness as a "tendency" and a "propensity."[37] Reason is, though, an important tool that can be put to use by those who desire to exploit, control, and dominate others. Those who are animated by the spirit of selfishness seldom act without justification for their evil deeds. Douglass pointed out, for example, that selfish individuals often attempt to justify their behavior by appealing to widely held prejudices. Racial, religious, ethnic, and gender prejudice have been ready weapons for those wishing to satisfy their selfish desires at the expense of others. Preju-dice is, in Douglass's view, an *instrument* of subordination, not the *cause* of subordination. The philosophical, political, economic, and pseudo-scientific construction of racial hierarchy, for example, served as a means by which individuals could satisfy their natural desire to dominate others. "Pride and selfishness," Douglass said in a famous 1854 address responding to popular justifications of racial hierarchy, "combined with mental power, never want for a theory to justify them."[38]

The existence of selfish tendencies in human nature was, to Douglass, as obvious as it was regrettable. Selfishness can blind men to morality and make them capable of acting like hardened villains. There is no clearer manifestation of this fact than the existence of human slavery. Under the institution of slavery, one human being disregards the humanity of another and seeks to subject him to his will. What remains to be seen is why Douglass thought this was morally wrong. It is to this question that we now turn.

The Annihilation of the Self: The Physical and Metaphysical Cruelties of Slavery

With Douglass's definition of slavery and what he thought to be its causes in mind, we can now turn to his critique of the institution. Douglass's deep commitment to individual rights was rooted, in part, in his deep hatred of slavery. It is fair to say that slavery serves as the "state of nature" at the foundation of his liberal political values. Slavery is a profoundly illiberal institution in two senses. First, slavery authorizes some individuals to *restrain* other individuals. Slaves are held, in effect, by the command, "your liberty or your life." This is a violation of the traditional liberal notion of freedom as the absence of restraint. Second, slavery is profoundly illiberal in the sense that it authorizes some individuals to *control* others. To be a slave is not only to be restrained, but also to be controlled by the will of another. Slaves are deprived of their liberty and they are forced to do things commanded by the master.[39]

Slavery served as the antithesis to Douglass's fundamental liberal commitment to personal freedom. Whereas liberalism exalts the individual and makes his freedom the overriding aim of politics, slavery permits the annihilation of some individuals by others. Under the institution of slavery, the selfhood of the enslaved individual is obliterated. Douglass's arguments *against* slavery are, in a very important sense, arguments *for* liberalism. I believe Douglass's case against the cruelties of slavery is an important contribution to the tradition of liberal political philosophy.

The language employed by Douglass in his condemnations of slavery is striking and, upon reflection, it is clear why the idea of self-ownership became the foundation of his liberalism. The "paramount evil" of the institution, Douglass said in a number of speeches delivered during his tour of the United Kingdom in the late 1840s, is that it denied the individual's right to "look upon himself as his own."[40] Because it denied the significance of the slave's reason, conscience, affections, and will, it is fair to say that the institution was an attempt to destroy "his identity."[41] In an 1846 address on "The American Temperance Movement, Slavery, and Prejudice," he said:

> Only look at the condition of the slave: stripped of every right—denied every privilege, he had not even the privilege of saying "myself"—his head, his eyes, his hands, his heart, his bones, his sinews, his soul, his immortal spirit, were all the property of another. He might not decide any question for himself—any question relating to his own actions. The master—the man who claimed property in his person—assumed the right to decide all things for him.[42]

In short, the very selfhood of the slave is crushed by the "absolute power" the master has over him.[43] In Douglass's words, "The will and wishes of the master are the law of the slave," who has "no voice whatever in his destiny."[44]

The "denial of [the slave's] personality" ranged from the mundane to the profound.[45] On a day-to-day basis, the master decided for the slave "what he should eat and what he should drink, what he should wear, when and to whom he should speak, how much he should work, how much and by whom he is punished."[46] In addition to these day-to-day matters, slaveholders had control of aspects of the slave's destiny of more lasting importance such as familial bonds, intellectual and moral development, and religious aspiration. In an 1846 address Douglass delivered in Paisley, Scotland, he said:

> Slaveholders determine when a man shall marry, how long he shall continue married; they also claim the right of tearing the babe from the arms of the frantic mother. Conscience, which God has planted in the heart of man, all his religious aspirations, all his hopes, are subject to the will of him who dares claim man as his property.[47]

The slave is a human being who "having a mind, he may not cultivate and improve it; having a soul, he may not call it his own; having moral appreciations, he may not be guided by them; having a conscience, he may not walk by its admonitions; having an immortal spirit and a soul to aspire, he may not aspire, humbly as his Master did."[48] Under the institution of slavery, all of those matters which an individual might consider to be constitutive of his or her identity—family bonds, association with friends, religious commitments, moral choices, intellectual cultivation, and so on—are controlled by the will of another. For Douglass, the annihilation of the slave's selfhood was the core of the moral criminality of slavery.

Douglass believed slavery was at war with the nature of man. Slavery attempts to deny the rationality, the capacity for moral understanding, sociality, and the inclination to liberty of its victims. Because the institution of slavery is in direct conflict with these aspects of human nature, it can only be maintained through extraordinarily cruel measures. According to Douglass, "Cruelty marks every part of the system. The slave cannot be held without cruelty."[49] Cruel means are necessary to establish and maintain the system because "man was not made for [the] condition [of slavery], nor did he ever like to submit to that condition."[50]

> Slavery is a cruel system, because the slave is held by no power but physical force. The slave does not go voluntarily and take the condition of a slave. He is a man and has the feelings of a man. As a man he is not only conscious of the right to liberty, but deep down in his own soul is planted a love of liberty which is ever awake in his bosom; and loving liberty he can never be kept in the condition of a slave without force.[51]

Because human beings have a natural desire to be free, slaveholders "are forced to resort to all the unnatural means we have associated with slavery as its necessary concomitants."[52]

The unnatural means employed by slaveholders took on both physical and metaphysical forms. The physical cruelties of slavery are well-known. Perhaps the most memorable scenes from Douglass's autobiographies are his descriptions of the physical brutality of slave masters and "overseers." In *My Bondage and My Freedom*, for example, Douglass described the brutal beating of a slave named Esther at the hands of Douglass's "old master" Captain Anthony. Esther and a slave named Edward had fallen in love, but Captain Anthony, probably motivated by jealousy, ordered her to stop seeing him. "This unnatural and heartless order," Douglass wrote, "was, of course, broken. A woman's love is not to be annihilated by the peremptory command of any one, whose breath is in his nostrils."[53] One morning, the young Douglass awoke to this scene.

> Esther's wrists were firmly tied, and the twisted rope was fastened to a strong staple in a heavy wooden joist above, near the fireplace. Here she

stood, on a bench, her arms tightly drawn over her breast. Her back and shoulders were bare to the waist. Behind her stood old master, with cow skin in hand, preparing his barbarous work with all manner of harsh, coarse, and tantalizing epithets. The screams of his victim were most piercing. He was cruelly deliberate, and protracted the torture, as one who was delighted with the scene. Again and again he drew the hateful whip through his hand, adjusting it with a view of dealing the most pain-giving blow. . . . The whole scene, with all its attendants, was revolting and shocking, to the last degree; and when the motives of this brutal castigation are considered, language has no power to convey a just sense of its awful criminality. After laying on some thirty or forty stripes, old master untied his suffering victim, and let her get down. She could scarcely stand, when untied.[54]

Scholars have identified the beating of Esther as a crucial moment in the development of Douglass's thought. Jenny Franchot argues that the image of Esther became "the emotional center of his critique of slavery."[55] Peter C. Myers contends that the story is significant for several reasons, the most important of which is the fact that it provoked "natural anger" in Douglass in response to the blatant violation of Esther's rights.[56] In addition to these findings, the Esther story is illustrative of the ways in which physical cruelty was used to punish slaves who attempted to establish independent identities. Captain Anthony attempted, if you will, to beat the personality out of Esther. In this case, a desire to prevent two slaves from pursuing a romantic relationship seems to have been the justification, but there were several other reasons offered by slave masters and overseers for physical beatings. According to Douglass, the most common reason given for the physical punishment of a slave was "impudence," which "may mean almost anything, or nothing at all, just according to the caprice of the master or overseer, at the moment."[57] The point is that no matter what the slave did, his bodily integrity was constantly under threat. Through this regime of physical intimidation and systematic torture, masters and overseers attempted to "blot out his personality, degrade his manhood, and sink him to the condition of a beast of burden."[58]

As terrifying as these depictions of physical brutality are, Douglass did not believe they constituted the "paramount evil of the infamous institution."[59] Instead, he argued that the greatest cruelties of the slave system were metaphysical in nature.

There is still a deeper shade to be given to this picture. The physical cruelties are indeed sufficiently harassing and revolting; but they are put as a few grains of sand on the sea shore, or a few drops of water in the great ocean, compared with the stupendous wrongs which it inflicts upon the mental, moral, and religious nature of its hapless victims. It is only when we contemplate the slave as a moral and intellectual being that we can adequately comprehend the unparalleled enormity of slavery, and the intense criminality of the slaveholder.[60]

According to Douglass, the first work of slavery is to dehumanize the slave. There is a systematic attempt to deny the existence and development of the characteristics that distinguish human beings from other animals. Slaves are deprived of the opportunity to develop their intellectual faculties, to "decide what is morally right and wrong," to cultivate "filial affection," and so on.[61] In other words, the "first aim" of slavery is to reduce "man to a mere machine."[62]

Douglass described many forms of metaphysical cruelty. First, there is the obvious emotional cruelty of tearing families apart at a moment's notice. Some of the most powerful imagery of antislavery literature, including Douglass's autobiographies and Harriet Beecher Stowe's *Uncle Tom's Cabin,* is provided by incidents of familial destruction. In *My Bondage and My Freedom,* Douglass described being introduced to his brothers and sisters at a young age. "We were brothers and sisters, but what of that? Why should they be attached to me, or I to them? Brothers and sisters we were by blood; but *slavery* had made us strangers. . . . [S]lavery had robbed these terms of their true meaning."[63] Of his mother, Douglass wrote, "My poor mother, like many other slave-women, had *many children,* but NO FAMILY!"[64] Many slaves never had the opportunity to develop bonds with their families and those who did had to live in constant fear that those bonds would be shattered by the whims of the master.

Douglass also drew attention to what he believed was the greatest cruelty of slavery: the psychological agony of being in bondage. In an 1855 address entitled "An Inside View of Slavery," he told a Boston audience:

> Whipping is not what constitutes the cruelty of Slavery. To me the thought that I am a slave is more terrible than any lash, than any chain. A slave to-day, to-morrow, next year, all the years of my life,—my manhood denied, ignored, despised,—this being eternally shut up to a single condition, no outgoing, no progress, no future, this is more horrible, more distressing than any whip. . . . The mental agony of a slave is never appeased.[65]

Because human beings have a natural desire to decide for themselves how they will live their lives, the condition of slavery is psychologically terrifying. Not only does the slave know he is in a condition of bondage today, but he has little reason to believe that his condition will improve in the future. The absence of a sense of possibility and hope, the very things that fuel the human desire for freedom, leaves the slave in a condition of deep despair. To Douglass, this agony was the most abominable cruelty of the slave system.

In response to accusations of cruelty, defenders of slavery often claimed that inhumane treatment was the exception and not the rule of the institution. A good master or overseer, these defenders argued, related to his slaves as a feudal baron related to peasants. Rather than relying on a system of fear and intimidation, he relied on feelings of mutual obligation. According to these defenders, benevolent slavery was not only possible, but it was beneficial to both master and slave.[66]

Douglass disputed the possibility of benevolent slavery. First, he contended that physical cruelty was often necessary because slaves did not desire to be in bondage. As such, there was a natural desire to attempt to escape and, because there was no hope of reward, there was a natural desire to avoid work. In order to combat these natural tendencies, masters and overseers often relied on physical abuse to break the will of the slave. Furthermore, Douglass believed that even if a slave master was somewhat humane, moral corruption would follow from the possession of absolute power. The inevitability of this corruption followed from the unnaturalness of the master-slave relationship.

> Cruelty was inseparable from the system, and it could not be otherwise. The most humane man in the world—aye, if they could conceive of an angel from heaven becoming a slaveholder, he would be compelled to be cruel because he would have to keep man in the condition of a slave. . . . Man was not made for that condition, nor did he ever like to submit to that condition. His tendencies were to freedom—his happiness was dependent upon progress, elevation, and improvement.[67]

In other words, the relationship between master and slave is by definition a cruel one. Even a totally benevolent slaveholder who takes great care of his slave's physical being perpetrates a great act of cruelty. In "An Inside View of Slavery," a speech delivered in Boston in 1855, Douglass made this point clear: "Kindness is no substitute for justice. Care for the slave as property is no compensation for *denial of his personality*. You may surround the slave with luxuries, place him in a genial climate, and under a smiling and cloudless sky, and these shall only enhance his torment, and deepen his anguish."[68]

Attending to the slave's physical needs, whether done out of compassion or desire to increase his value as property, is not genuine kindness. Either way, Douglass argued, the master fails to respect the humanity of the slave: "To talk of *kindness* entering into a relation in which one party is robbed of wife, of children, of his hard earnings, of home, of friends, of society, of knowledge, and of all that makes life desirable, is most absurd, wicked and preposterous." [69]

According to Douglass, slavery, which is the exercise of an uncontrolled right to the body and soul of a person, is rooted in the selfishness of human nature and it is unjust because it violates the physical integrity and annihilates the personality of the slave. Just as many late-twentieth-century political thinkers are best understood when it is remembered that they wrote in the shadow of totalitarian mayhem, Douglass is best read as a thinker animated by the horrors of slavery. [70] Read in this way, I believe his critique of the physical and metaphysical cruelties of slavery constitute an important chapter in the history of liberal ideas.

A Life of One's Own: Douglass's Case for Self-Ownership

In this section, I examine Douglass's belief that each individual is the rightful owner his or her own person. According to historian Eric Foner, for Douglass and other abolitionist thinkers, "freedom meant self-ownership." [71] It is fair to say that freedom and self-ownership were synonyms in Douglass's vocabulary. He believed slavery was morally criminal because it is the very antithesis of the deepest yearning of the human soul: the desire to be free.

Douglass's case for freedom was rooted in natural law. According to political theorist Paul Sigmund, natural law thinkers are distinguished by "a belief that society should be restructured in a way that is more in keeping with the requirements of human nature." [72] Douglass drew on his belief that human beings are naturally freedom-loving to make the case that slavery was a profoundly unnatural institution and the realization of slavery's opposite, self-ownership, was required by natural law. He supported this claim by appealing to two aspects of human nature: human desires and human capacities. Human beings want to direct their own lives and they have capacities—reason, moral judgment, and free will—that make them fit to do so. Self-ownership, Douglass contended, is the foundation for individual rights to life, liberty, and property as well as the right to participate in democratic governance. If we respect that an individual owns himself, he argued, we should refrain from depriving him of his life, we should resist interfering unduly with his liberty, we should not violate his legitimate claims to property, and we should treat him as a political equal.

I argue that Douglass's case for self-ownership is interesting and important for a number of reasons. First, Douglass rooted his moral arguments in the experience of slavery and this gives his articulation of liberal principles an added moral force and persuasive power. These personal and contextual factors inspired Douglass to offer what Sheldon Wolin calls an "imaginative recovery" of previously articulated ideas.[73] Second, his formulation of and reliance on the idea of self-ownership as the basis for the right to liberty differs in emphasis from other thinkers in the liberal tradition. Rather than emphasizing the economic dimension of self-ownership, Douglass offered a version of the idea that is comprehensive and deeply moralistic. Third, as you will see later, Douglass blended his quintessentially liberal commitment to self-ownership with a robust philosophy of social responsibility. Understanding why and how Douglass attempted to combine these ideas are the central tasks of this book.

Discussions of self-ownership rarely address the formulations of abolitionist thinkers. The typical history of self-ownership is captured by political theorist Robert S. Taylor who says that Locke "effectively launched the literature of self-ownership" and the concept "did not come to play a major role in political theory again until the publication of Robert Nozick's *Anarchy, State, and Utopia*."[74] When we reduce the idea to the classical formulation of Locke and the late-twentieth-century formulation by Nozick, we ignore a crucial period when the idea was at the center of a "language of insurgent popular politics."[75]

Abolitionists were often described as "men of one idea." This may be true, Douglass responded, but our "one idea was immensely comprehensive, and capable of manifold applications."[76] The "one idea" Douglass had in mind was self-ownership.

[There] was one idea, rule or principle, call it what you will, which entirely took possession of me, even in childhood, and which stood out strongly, invincible against every argument drawn from nature and scripture in favor of slavery. What was the idea, rule, or principle? This it was: Every man is the *original, rightful, and absolute owner of his own body;* or in other words, every man is himself, is *his* self, if you please, and belongs to himself, and can only part from *his* self ownership, by the commission of a crime.[77]

It is important to note that Douglass's embrace of self-ownership cannot be understood outside of the context of natural law. He believed that each individual belongs to himself and that he cannot surrender his self-ownership without violating natural law. Rather than embracing the view that the individual is the source of his own moral laws, Douglass sided with natural law thinkers who contend that transcendent moral law limits the sovereignty of the self. In other words, there are certain things, Douglass thought, that are immoral, even if the individuals involved consent to them.

Douglass said the claim to self-ownership contains within it "a whole encyclopedia of argument."[78] Indeed, he relied on the doctrine of self-ownership to champion a range of progressive causes, including the abolition of slavery, universal suffrage, women's rights, immigration reform, and religious liberty. Although he believed that no "simpler proposition, no truth more self-evident or more native to the human soul, was ever presented to human reason or consciousness," he recognized that argument was necessary because "against prejudice, custom, and superstition, nothing is self-evident."[79] It was for this reason that Douglass believed it was incumbent on friends of freedom to explain why self-ownership was required by natural law.

Although Douglass's writings and speeches are replete with references to self-ownership, there is no formulation more powerful than the one offered in an open letter he wrote to his former master, Thomas Auld. I will use this formulation as the basis for the explanation provided in this section. In the letter, Douglass relied on self-ownership to defend his decision to escape from slavery.

> The morality of the act, I dispose as follows: I am myself; you are yourself; we are two distinct persons, equal persons. What you are, I am. You are a man, and so am I. God created both, and made us separate beings. I am not by nature bound to you, or you to me. Nature does not make your existence depend upon me, or mine depend upon yours. I cannot walk upon your legs, or you upon mine. I cannot breathe for you, or you for me; I must breathe for myself, and you for yourself. We are distinct persons, and are each equally provided with faculties necessary to our individual existence. In leaving you, I took nothing but what belonged to me, and in no way lessened your means for obtaining an *honest* living. Your faculties remained yours, and mine became useful to their rightful owner. I therefore see no wrong in any part of the transaction.[80]

This passage is extraordinarily powerful because it reveals the real-life importance of self-ownership for Douglass. His arguments were not merely abstract musings—to the contrary, they were offered in defense of his decision to escape from slavery. In addition, this passage contains the central claims that constitute Douglass's contention that each individual belongs to himself: each human being is separate and distinct from every other, an individual's selfhood or personality is unique to him, all human beings are equal in morally relevant ways, and each individual is provided with the faculties necessary to maintain his individual existence. Let us consider each of these claims in turn.

First, Douglass emphasized that he and Auld were "distinct" and "separate" persons. This may seem like a rather innocuous ontological claim, but it is an essential part of Douglass's case for freedom. His focus on the physical separateness of human beings is similar to other thinkers within the liberal tradition who have assumed the truth of "atomism."[81] According to this doctrine, society is best viewed as a collection of separate individuals, not an organic whole. Like other liberals, Douglass relied on the atomistic ontology as a starting point for a political morality that emphasizes the primacy of individual rights and responsibilities.

When Douglass declared that he and Auld were separate and distinct beings, he was making a claim about the separateness of their bodies *and* the distinctiveness of their personalities. In other words, his case for self-ownership rested on beliefs in both physical and metaphysical individuality. When Douglass defended self-ownership, he discussed both "form and features"—physical individuality—and "thought and feeling"—metaphysical individuality.[82] Indeed, as noted earlier in the chapter, the violation of physical integrity was less revolting to him than the violation of metaphysical dignity. It is precisely because each human being is rational and capable of moral choice that deprivation of self-ownership was so utterly appalling to Douglass. During the debates over slavery and suffrage, he repeatedly asserted that the "selfhood" of each individual is "absolute" and "complete," in the sense that each human being has a personality that is unique. Each individual's personality—his intellectual faculties, sentimental capacities, and will—is separate and distinct from every other's. Douglass understood that the recognition of physical and metaphysical separateness, while an important foundational step, does not necessarily lead to the acceptance of a right to self-ownership. In order to make the case for this right, it was necessary for Douglass to argue that human beings have a special dignity that entitles them to respect.

This leads us to the second major claim made by Douglass in his letter to Auld: "[W]e are two . . . equal persons. What you are, I am. You are a man, and so am I."[83] Douglass's argument for self-ownership rested not only on the separateness and individuality of human beings but also on a belief in universal human equality. According to his understanding of equality, *all* individuals possess rights by virtue of their "natural dignity" as human beings.[84] Human beings, Douglass believed, possess dignity above the rest of creation because they have "natural powers" that distinguish them in morally relevant ways.[85] More specifically, Douglass thought the capacity of human beings to reason and to distinguish right from wrong dignified their existence. The natural dignity of human beings provides the basis for their rights. Because humans are intellectual and potentially moral beings, there are certain things that should not be done to them. Most fundamentally, Douglass believed that because human beings possess natural dignity, they should not be deprived of the right to direct their own lives.

Douglass believed the equal right to self-ownership has its source in two aspects of human nature: desires and capacities. First, Douglass argued that personal freedom is rooted in human desires. He said this is "self-evident" in the sense that it is obvious that most human beings exhibit a natural desire to be free. "Human rights," he said in his famous "Claims of the Negro Ethnologically Considered" speech, "stand upon a common basis . . . all mankind have the same wants."[86] Douglass argued that the "existence of [the natural right to liberty] is self-evident. It is written upon all the powers and faculties of man. The desire for it is the deepest and strongest of all powers of the human soul."[87] Douglass explained the idea of self-evidence in this way: "I have said the right to liberty is self-evident. No argument, no researches into moldy records, no learned disquisitions, are necessary to establish it. To *assert it, is to call forth a sympathetic response from every human heart*, and to send a thrill of joy and gladness around the world."[88] When an individual reflects on his own nature, Douglass thought, he is able to recognize his own desire to be free. The recognition of this desire in oneself, Douglass hoped, would provide the basis for sympathy with others who claim these rights. But he recognized that human beings are often reluctant to "apply the same rules and maxims" to others that they apply to themselves.[89]

Douglass did not believe the right to self-ownership was rooted in human desires alone. He recognized that grounding rights in "wants" lacked moral force. His more compelling argument for self-ownership was that human beings are *fit* to be free. In other words, because human beings have intellectual and moral capacities, they are capable of directing their own lives. Because human beings are capable of free choice and moral responsibility, it is a moral crime to deny them the opportunity to direct their own lives. Douglass's argument from human capacities is a distinctively moral one. Rather than embracing liberalism as merely the best means to channel human desires and keep the peace, he relied on the requirements of natural law to make the case that universal freedom is a moral imperative.

Douglass applied the moral imperative of self-ownership to a number of political controversies. Most obviously, he relied on the moral argument for self-ownership in support of the abolition of slavery. Douglass went beyond saying that abolition was appropriate because slaves *wanted* to be free, to say that abolition was morally required because slaves were *fit* for freedom. Prior to emancipation, Douglass responded to the anxiety many whites felt at the prospect of the slaves being "turned loose." In an 1862 address on "The Black Man's Future in the Southern States," he offered this in response to their anxiety:

> We are asked if we would turn the slaves all loose. I answer, Yes. Why not? They are not wolves nor tigers, but men. They are endowed with reason—can decide upon questions of right and wrong, good and evil, benefits and injuries—and are therefore subjects of government precisely as other men are.[90]

Slaves are fit to be free because they are endowed with reason, possess the ability to tell right from wrong, and have free will to choose how they will act. Douglass believed that although slaves were raised in extraordinarily inhumane conditions, they retained their humanity and would, once liberated, be fit for self-government.

Douglass's case for self-ownership is also illustrated by his arguments in the debate over women's suffrage. Douglass was present at the Seneca Falls Convention of 1848 and he agitated on behalf of women's rights until (quite literally) the day he died.[91] The foremost leader of the women's suffrage movement, Elizabeth Cady Stanton, said of Douglass: "He was the only man I ever saw who understood the degradation of the disenfranchisement of women."[92] His responses to two common arguments against female suffrage are fine examples of how he used self-ownership as the basis for his progressive political goals. First, those opposed to female suffrage often said that women did not need to participate in politics because they were virtually represented by their fathers and husbands. In an 1886 speech on women's rights, Douglass responded to this argument by appealing to self-ownership:

> If man could represent woman, it follows that woman could represent man, but no opponent of woman suffrage would admit that woman could represent him in the government, and in taking that position he would

be right; since neither can, in the nature of things, represent the other, for the very obvious reason that neither can be the other. The great fact underlying the claim for universal suffrage is that every man is himself and belongs to himself, and represents his own individuality, not only in form and features, but in thought and feeling. And the same is true of woman. She is herself, and can be nobody else than herself. Her selfhood is as perfect and as absolute as is the selfhood of man. She can no more part with her personality that she can part with her shadow.[93]

The separateness and individuality of women was not the only basis for their rights. Douglass was also confronted with a second argument against female suffrage: they are not entitled to an equal right to participate because they "cannot perform military service." His response reveals how he relied on the intellectual and moral capacities of all human beings to make the case for natural rights. Setting aside the validity of the claim that women cannot perform military service, Douglass argued that it ought to be rejected because it "founds one of the grandest intellectual and moral rights of human nature upon a purely physical basis. According to it, the basis of civil government is not mind, but muscle; not reason, but force; not right, but might; it is not human, but bestial. It belongs to man rather as a savage, than as a civilized being."[94] Douglass contended that the very idea of individual rights and civil government are rooted in human intellectual and moral capacities. In an 1855 speech on "The Present and Future of the Colored Race," he said: "The foundation of all governments and all codes of law is in the fact that man is a rational creature, and is capable of guiding his conduct by ideas of right and wrong, of good and evil, by hope of reward and fear of punishment."[95]

Douglass believed self-ownership should be respected and protected because human beings have a natural *desire* to be free and because their rational and moral *capacities* make them fit for freedom. He thought the obligation to respect the natural rights of others is "easily rendered appreciable to the faculty of reason in man, and that the most unenlightened conscience has no difficulty in deciding in which side to register its testimony."[96] He recognized, though, that the human ability to comprehend the truth of this obligation does not, by itself, lead to social peace and harmony. The difficulty is this: "In whatever else men may differ, they are alike in the apprehension of their natural and personal rights. The difference between abolitionists and those by whom they are opposed, is not as to principles. All are agreed in respect to these. The manner of applying them is the point of difference."[97]

So far, I have discussed Douglass's appeal to human separateness, individuality, and equality as the bases for the claim to self-ownership. The other claim made by Douglass in the letter to Auld is that nature "does not make your existence depend upon me, or mine depend upon yours" and that we "are each equally provided with the faculties necessary to our individual existence."[98] At first glance, this seems like a rather radical view of human independence. It may appear that Douglass was suggesting that individuals are self-sufficient. It would, however, be a mistake to read Douglass's assertion of independence from Auld as an embrace of cold-hearted individualism. Instead, as I will show in detail in later chapters, Douglass's commitment to independence existed alongside a belief in the natural sociality and interdependence of human beings.[99] What Douglass rejected was any understanding of interdependence that violated his core commitment to personal freedom.

It is easier to understand Douglass's view of independence and interdependence when we consider these ideas in context. He denounced the idea of human interdependence when it was used to rationalize slavery and other oppressive practices. Violation of the natural rights of minorities and women, for example, was often justified by their alleged dependence on white men. When Douglass argued that "independence belongs to our nature," he was attempting to combat the notion that some types of people are more dependent than others. [100] All human beings, he believed, are endowed with the capacities that enable them to be *as independent* as their fellows. This view of independence should not, however, be equated with the position that individuals are completely self-sufficient as some critics of liberalism have claimed.[101] Douglass understood that individuals need one another to survive and to flourish, but he refused to accept the notion that interdependence justified excessive interference with individual liberty.

Douglass's view of independence is illuminated by a consideration of the theoretical alternative offered by defenders of slavery. The ideas of George Fitzhugh, a Virginian who practiced law and wrote extensively in defense of the "Southern social system," stand out as precisely the sort of thinker Douglass rebelled against. According to political scientists Arnaud Leavelle and Thomas Cook, Fitzhugh "represented in all its force the reaction of the Civil War South away from the liberalism and individualism of Thomas Jefferson, particularly the elements derived from Locke and the Enlightenment.[102] In *Sociology for the South*, Fitzhugh rejected liberal individualism in favor of an organic, collectivist theory.

Some animals are by nature gregarious and associative. Of this class are men, ants and bees. An isolated man is almost as helpless and ridiculous as a bee setting up for himself. Man is born a member of society, and does not form society. Nature, as in the cases of bees and ants, has it ready formed for him. He and society are congenital. Society is the being—he one of the members of that being. *He has no rights whatever, as opposed to the interests of society; and that society may very properly make any use of him that will redound to the public good.*[103]

Douglass rejected the idea that individual rights are subordinate to "the interests of society" or "the public good." Individuals need one another to survive and flourish, Douglass argued, but they ought to interact on cooperative, not coercive, terms.

Before concluding this section, it is worthwhile to emphasize the deontological basis of Douglass's case for self-ownership. "Rights," he argued in an 1888 address on women's suffrage, "do not have their source in the will or grace of man. They are not such things as he can grant or withhold according to his sovereign will or pleasure."[104] Douglass believed individuals have an obligation to respect the natural rights of others regardless of the consequences. Rather than embracing a consequentialist justification for rights, Douglass was, one might say, a "Hell or High Water" liberal. In the late 1850s, when many abolitionists were beginning to lose faith in the idea that slavery could be abolished peacefully, he said:

> Whether men should be slave or free, does not depend on the success or failure of freedom in any given instance. Some things have been settled independently of human calculation and human adjudication. One of these things is, that man has by nature a right to his own body, and that to deprive him of that right is a flagrant violation of the will of God. This is settled. And if desolation and ruin, famine and pestilence should threaten, Emancipation would still be the same urgent and solemn duty that it ever was. When the God of all the earth ordained the law of freedom, He foresaw all its consequences. Do right though the Heavens fall. We have no right to do evil that good may come, nor to refrain from doing right because evil may come.[105]

Human beings are bound by the fundamental law of nature because individual rights are not social experiments, as pragmatists might describe them, but rather moral truths rooted in the nature of human beings. "Liberty," Douglass contended, "is not a device or an experiment, but a law of nature dating back to man's creation, and if this fundamental law is a failure, the responsibility is not with the British Parliament, not with the British people, but with the great author of this law."[106]

In this section, I have made the case that Douglass's commitment to self-ownership was rooted in his beliefs in ontological individualism, individuality, universal human equality, and independence. He justified each of these beliefs by appealing to human nature. Douglass's natural law case for self-ownership can be summarized in the following way: he believed the desires and capacities of human beings entitle them to ownership of their selves. Respect for the principle of self-ownership requires that other individuals refrain from depriving one another of individual rights to life, liberty, property, and to participate in democratic governance. An individual who owns himself has all the rights that are denied to a slave: the right to physical integrity, the right to locomotion, the right to form a family, the right to acquire property, the right to pursue an education, the right to worship God, and the right to participate in self-government.

What Is Special about Douglass's Theory of Self-Ownership?

Now that I have offered a detailed description of Douglass's view of self-ownership and how he justified it, I would like to say a brief word about how his account differs in emphasis from other formulations of the idea. The differences in his formulation are important because they direct us to the ways in which he makes important contributions to the liberal tradition. Douglass's account is remarkable in three important ways: his grounding of self-ownership in the experience of slavery, the comprehensiveness of his formulation, and the universality of his application.

First, Douglass was able to buttress his normative arguments for self-ownership with real-life illustrations from the experience of slavery. As pointed out earlier in this chapter, he viewed slavery as the total annihilation of the selfhood of slaves. In order to support this claim, he drew on his personal experiences. When he spoke of the criminality of being "robbed of wife, of children, of his hard earnings, of home, of friends, of society, of knowledge, and of all that makes life desirable," he was not speaking in the abstract.[107] Furthermore, Douglass's personal experience was reflective of the national problem of slavery. As he attempted to articulate the "fundamental principles" which should be the "solid rock, upon which to rest the foundation of the state," he drew on the lessons drawn from the personal and national experience of slavery. This foundation provided Douglass's case for self-ownership with extraordinary moral force and persuasive power.

Second, Douglass formulated and defended the idea of self-ownership in a way that differed in emphasis from other liberal thinkers. Both Locke and Nozick, for example, emphasized the economic dimension of self-ownership. Locke introduced the idea in his discussion of the labor theory of value and Nozick discussed the idea in his arguments against economic redistribution. The focus on the economic aspect of self-ownership provides critics of liberalism with fodder for the claim that the idea is nothing more than a justification for possessive individualism.[108] Douglass did not privilege the economic aspect of self-ownership. Instead, he discussed several aspects of human life that are impacted by the deprivation of self-ownership: physical integrity, sexual integrity, marriage, family life, intellectual development, moral flourishing, religious striving, and economic independence. The comprehensive nature of Douglass's formulation makes him less susceptible to the claim that self-ownership is nothing more than a bourgeois rationalization of possessive individualism. This is not to say that Douglass has been completely spared of the kinds of criticisms that have been directed at Locke and Nozick. Several scholars, most notably Peter Walker, Waldo Martin, and Wilson Jeremiah Moses have accused Douglass of individualist excesses.[109] Martin, for example, argues that at the core of Douglass's individualism was a deep "procapitalist bias" that bordered on the "delusory."[110] Martin's argument seems to be rooted in a belief that, given the depth of Douglass's sensitivity to exploitation, it is disappointing that he failed to embrace socialism. I will return to Douglass's views of capitalism and socialism in chapter 3, but a brief word must be said about how Martin's critique affects what I am saying here. While it is certainly true that Douglass rejected socialism and embraced capitalism, it is also true that his doctrine of self-ownership was not focused on the economic sphere. Given the nature of the tyranny Douglass was confronting—chattel slavery—this is not surprising. What Douglass sought, and what he believed self-ownership had the potential to provide, was a doctrine that established firm "moral fences" that protected the individual's choices—economic and otherwise—from the arbitrary interference of others.[111] In sum, whatever the merit of Martin's critique of Douglass's embrace of capitalism, it is still the case that Douglass offered a conception of self-ownership that was truly comprehensive in character.

Third, Douglass separated himself from most of his predecessors in the liberal tradition by making the case that *all* people ought to be free. "Upon reflection," Joyce Appleby writes, "we can see that the soft underbelly of any society, at least in ideological terms, is the gap between its shared moral commitments and day-to-day fidelity to those unifying principles."[112] The gap in America's liberal society was between the promise of freedom expressed in the Founding documents and the day-to-day exclusion of a vast majority of individuals from that promise.[113] Douglass relied on a universal formulation of the idea of self-ownership to make the case that this gap ought to be closed. By incorporating a truly universal understanding of human equality into his understanding of self-ownership, he broadened earlier formulations of liberalism. As political theorist Anthony Arblaster has pointed out, for example, "it did not occur to anyone except a few radicals and 'extremists' that [the principle of self-ownership] might also apply to female human beings."[114] We can include Douglass among those radicals and extremists who took the important step of declaring that the common nature of *all* human beings provides the basis for a universal right to self-ownership. Indeed, he understood his own project as a kind of radical conservatism. "Radicals," he wrote in 1870, "are the greatest conservatives, for they go to the root of the problem and cut it out, and thus restore the whole body to good health."[115]

The universality of Douglass's case is evident, but it must be acknowledged that in the messy world of politics his egalitarian humanism was sometimes in tension with other commitments. Despite all his proclamations of the universal applicability of his creed, he was the foremost spokesman for African Americans of the nineteenth century and he believed that the most urgent application was to the causes of abolition and reconstruction. This tension is revealed in Douglass's conflict with his allies in the suffrage movement over whether or not to support the Fifteenth Amendment. Elizabeth Cady Stanton and other suffrage advocates opposed the Amendment because it guaranteed the vote only to black men.[116] Douglass admitted that in an ideal world the Amendment would guarantee voting rights to all Americans, but that the cause of black suffrage was too urgent to wait.

> When women, because they are women, are hunted down through the cities of New York and New Orleans; when they are dragged from their houses and hung upon lamp-posts; when their children are torn from their arms, and their brains dashed out upon the pavement; when they are objects of insult and outrage at every turn; when they are in danger of having their homes burnt down over their heads; when their children are not allowed to enter schools: then they will have an urgency to obtain the ballot equal to our own.[117]

We cannot know for sure whether or not Douglass supported the Fifteenth Amendment over the objections of women's rights advocates because his racial loyalties trumped his egalitarian universalism or because he genuinely believed that the cause of black male suffrage was urgent enough that it was necessary to support imperfect legislation. Rather than seeing this prioritizing as a sign that Douglass's universalism was inauthentic, political scientist Leslie Friedman Goldstein encourages us to think of it as a manifestation of prudent statesmanship. According to Goldstein, even though Douglass believed in universal suffrage as a matter of moral principle, his sense of the pragmatism necessary in politics led him to refuse to "have them merged into a single cause" because of the potential that such a merger would "increase the odds against public acceptance" of the Fifteenth Amendment.[118]

Conclusion: From Slavery to Self-Ownership

In this chapter, I have explored Douglass's reflections on slavery and his moral argument for self-ownership in order to demonstrate how he grounded his liberal commitments. I have argued that he is best understood as a part of the natural rights strand of liberal thinking, but that he separated himself from many of his predecessors in this tradition by drawing on the experience of slavery to articulate the commitment to self-ownership in a comprehensive and inclusive way. According to Douglass, slavery deprives individuals of all that makes life desirable: physical security, familial affection, friendship, physical and social mobility, opportunity for intellectual development, access to material comfort, and the space necessary to pursue happiness, moral excellence, religious piety, and other ends. Douglass thought that slavery was wrong because it permitted the annihilation of the human personality and that the recognition of each individual's right to self-ownership was required by natural law. His articulation of an experientially based, universal, and comprehensive theory of self-ownership is an important contribution to the liberal tradition. His hatred of slavery and attraction to self-ownership are at the foundation of his liberal democratic politics. It is to a more detailed explanation of his politics that we now turn.

From Slavery to
Liberty and Equality

Douglass's Liberal Democratic Politics

Introduction

On Monday, August 16, 1841 Frederick Douglass went to Nantucket to attend
the summer meeting of the Massachusetts Anti-Slavery Society. His attendance at this meeting would mark a profound shift in his life; for it was there
that he was first "discovered" by antislavery leaders William Lloyd Garrison,
Wendell Phillips, Parker Pillsbury, and John A. Collins. After standing up at
the meeting and describing some of his experiences as a slave, Douglass's life
would forever be changed as he crossed the threshold into the tumultuous
world of political activism. That night is also significant for other, more symbolic, reasons. At that meeting of the Massachusetts Anti-Slavery Society, we
are able to see some of the ideological diversity that existed in the political world where Douglass would come of age. Whatever the truth of Louis
Hartz's famous contention that liberalism has been a hegemonic force in
American political life, within the circles in which Douglass would run, his
embrace of liberalism was anything but a foregone conclusion.[1] There were
certainly liberals at the meeting that night, but there were other perspectives
represented as well. William Lloyd Garrison, who would go on to become
a crucial figure in Douglass's ascent to the heights of the antislavery world,
was a committed anarchist.[2] John A. Collins, the society's general director,
was a prominent utopian socialist.[3] Throughout his development as a political thinker, Douglass was presented with a series of ideological alternatives
such as Garrison's anarchism and Collins's utopian socialism. In this chapter
I make the case that he consistently rejected these in favor of liberalism.

As pointed out in chapter 1, the liberal tradition is broad and deep, but
there are several "core" commitments that are shared by thinkers within
it. First, liberals believe in the primacy of individual rights to life, liberty,

and property. Second, liberals believe religious and moral diversity ought to be tolerated or even celebrated. Third, liberals reject anarchism as a viable option and endorse limited government to protect individual rights. Fourth, liberals believe that democratic government is most likely to protect individual rights, but stop short of the romantic devotion to majority rule that is typical of radical democrats. In what follows, I describe each of these ideas in a bit more detail before demonstrating that Douglass endorsed the core commitments of liberalism. My aim is to demonstrate that the basic framework of his political vision was liberal and democratic in nature.

The Primacy of Individual Rights

At the center of the liberal universe is the commitment to individual rights. Individuals are thought to be endowed by God, nature, or convention with rights to life, liberty, and property. Governments, according to liberals, are created to secure these rights. The classic formulation of this idea in the American tradition is found in the Declaration of Independence, where it is claimed that "all men are created equal" and that "they are endowed by their Creator with certain unalienable rights," including the rights to "Life, Liberty, and the pursuit of Happiness." More recently, legal philosopher Ronald Dworkin has reasserted the primacy of rights in liberal political morality by describing them as "trumps" that are supposed to protect individuals from illegitimate interference by others.[4]

The central controversy within liberalism is over what rights should be deemed fundamental and which should be subject to limitations by the will of the majority. As political scientist Kenneth Dolbeare has pointed out, "The principal tension within the liberal tradition has been conflict over the assigning of priorities among the natural rights of individuals."[5] Perhaps the most contentious debate within liberalism is over the status of private property rights. On one side, liberals usually classified as "classical" or "libertarian" argue that the right to private property is every bit as fundamental as the rights to life and liberty and, as such, should only be interfered with in rare circumstances. On the other side, liberals usually classified as "progressive" or "reform" argue that property rights are not as fundamental as the rights to life and liberty and, as such, the majority ought to be empowered, in more circumstances than the libertarian is willing to grant, to interfere with these rights.

This controversy within liberal rights theory and practice is not the only one. "Perfectionists" within the liberal tradition, for example, express concern that the right to liberty has been taken to excess, permitting individuals to behave in immoral ways. These controversies within liberalism are worth pointing out because it would not be accurate to say that the liberal commitment to individual rights is a monolithic one.[6] Instead, there are longstanding debates about the meaning and relative value of liberal rights, and these tensions must be acknowledged. These controversies notwithstanding, my main point here is to suggest that individual rights are at the core of liberal political morality. When we seek to determine whether or not a thinker is to be identified within the liberal tradition, it is wise to start with his or her position on the sanctity of individual rights.

The Importance of Toleration

Liberalism was born out of the "cruelties of the religious wars" and, as a result, toleration of religious diversity has always been a core commitment of its adherents. In the words of political theorist Judith Shklar, "liberalism's deepest grounding is in place from the first, in the conviction of the earliest defenders of toleration, born in horror, that cruelty is an absolute evil, an offense against God or humanity."[7] The individual, liberals claim, should be free from coercive meddling with his soul. As liberalism developed during the nineteenth century, particularly in the writings of John Stuart Mill, the case for toleration was extended to the moral sphere, as liberal thinkers argued that toleration of moral diversity also follows from the commitment to personal freedom. In Shklar's words, liberals contend that "social diversity and the burdens of freedom must be endured and encouraged to avoid the kinds of misery" that follow from "organized repression."[8]

The liberal commitment to toleration of religious and moral diversity is obviously related to the primacy of rights. Individual rights, liberals believe, provide individuals with the social space necessary to worship God and pursue happiness according to their own conceptions of the good life. Although the two ideas are related, it would be a mistake to conflate them. As Shklar has pointed out, the philosophy of Thomas Hobbes reminds us that it is possible to emphasize natural rights without believing in toleration, and the philosophy of Michel de Montaigne reminds us that it is possible to defend toleration without advocating a liberal politics of rights.[9] The important point is that liberals have always been skeptical of coercive attempts to enforce religious or moral conformity. There are some matters, liberals contend, that are properly left to the conscience and discretion of individuals.[10] The commitment to toleration of religious and moral diversity is an essential part of the liberal project.

A Commitment to Limited Government

The overriding liberal commitment to personal freedom has led political theorist Benjamin Barber to contend that liberal democratic theory is rooted in an "anarchistic disposition" that is hostile to government and politics.[11] According to Barber, liberals regard the individual as sovereign and as a result they flirt with an anarchist rejection of government and politics, but stop short of taking this step. While it is certainly true that many liberal theorists are attracted to the fantasy of absolute freedom from politics, it is also true that what makes them liberals and not anarchists is their belief that this is not a realistic possibility. Liberals believe that limited government is necessary to secure the conditions necessary for personal freedom.

Locke is a prime example of this phenomenon. As Sheldon Wolin has pointed out, Locke's true ideal was the "perfect state of nature," in which free and equal men interact according to the dictates of natural law without the need for coercive government.[12] But this was not to be, Locke argued, because the state of nature is corrupted by the "viciousness of degenerate men" and, as a result, government is necessary to protect our natural rights.[13] In Madison's language, "if men were angels, no government would be necessary." But men are not angels, the liberal contends, and so we must have civil government limited by the rule of law.[14]

The liberal belief in the need for civil government and their commitment to the rule of law are essentially interrelated. Liberals believe that civil government ought to be limited to specific ends, the most fundamental being the protection of individual rights. In order to limit the power of government, liberals endorse the rule of law, which "is meant to put a fence around the innocent citizen so that she may feel secure" in the exercise of her rights.[15] In other words, the rule of law functions within liberalism to order the actions of both private and public actors. In Locke's famous words, the end of law should be "to preserve and enlarge freedom."[16] The rule of law should embody the liberal commitment to individual rights and serve as a check against the depredations of vicious men inside and outside of government. In Shklar's words, liberalism may seem to be "very close to anarchism," but the rule of law is "the original first principle of liberalism" and "it is not an anarchistic doctrine."[17] In sum, the devotion to personal freedom leads liberals to flirt with anarchism, but their distrust of human nature causes them to pull back and endorse limited government under the rule of law.

The Marriage to Democracy

While it is certainly possible to imagine nondemocratic liberalism and one can find examples in history of relatively robust spheres of freedom under nondemocratic regimes, the fact remains that liberalism and democracy have in theory and practice been wedded together more often than not. This is not a coincidence. Shklar has argued that a liberal society is "of necessity a democratic one, because without enough equality of power to protect and assert one's rights, freedom is but a hope. Without institutions of representative democracy and an accessible, fair, and independent judiciary open to appeals, liberalism is in jeopardy. . . . It is therefore fair to say that liberalism is monogamously, faithfully, and permanently married to democracy—but it is a marriage of convenience."[18]

From the liberal perspective, democracy is usually seen as the form of government most likely to serve the overriding aim of securing freedom. The democratic commitments to free elections, representative and transparent political institutions, checks and balances, and equality before the law are more compatible with the core commitments of liberalism than any of the alternatives.

The union between liberalism and democracy is not without its tensions. As Wolin has pointed out, there is a "liberal-democratic divide" that should be acknowledged.[19] On the one side, there are liberals like Shklar whose primary devotion is to liberty and who view democracy as instrumentally valuable. On the other side, there are democrats like Wolin whose primary devotion is to collective self-government and who define and defend liberty in relation to this primary commitment. Liberal democrats attempt to reconcile commitments to individual liberty and democracy but tend to put their strongest emphasis on defending the liberal side of the divide.

The Liberal Politics of Frederick Douglass

My aim in the next four sections is to demonstrate that Douglass's political commitments place him within the liberal family. First, I will argue that Douglass's primary political commitment was to individual rights to life, liberty, and property. Like many others within the liberal tradition, he demonstrated some ambivalence about the sanctity of private property rights, but he never abandoned liberalism for a socialist alternative. Second, I contend that Douglass was committed to toleration of moral and religious diversity. His was an ideology that accepted moral and religious diversity as natural and inevitable and he was not tempted by "ideologies of agreement" that seek religious or moral conformity.[20] Third, I show that Douglass rejected anarchism in favor of limited government. Although many of his abolitionist colleagues followed their opposition to coercion to its logical conclusion and embraced utopian anarchism, Douglass's first-hand knowledge of human evil made him unable to indulge such fantasies. Fourth, I demonstrate that Douglass embraced a "genuine democratic republic" as the best form of government. I argue that his attitude toward democracy was closer to the instrumental appreciation of a liberal than the romantic devotion of a radical democrat.

Douglass's Declaration: The Primacy of Individual Rights in His Thought

Douglass interpreted the American Founding as an essentially liberal moment in human history and saw his project as an attempt to extend the liberal promises of the Founding to all people. Throughout his writings, we find praise for the liberal principles expressed in the Declaration of Independence. In 1854, soon after the passage of the Kansas-Nebraska Act—a law that repealed the Missouri Compromise of 1820, created the Kansas and Nebraska territories, and permitted settlers in those territories to determine for themselves whether or not they would condone slavery—Douglass delivered a speech in Chicago in order to challenge the consistency of the legislation with liberal principles. "The right of each man to life, liberty, and the pursuit of happiness," Douglass declared, "is the basis of all social and political right," and therefore no law-making body can legitimately grant the majority the power to determine whether or not human beings will be slave or free.[21] The persistence of the central role of the Declaration in Douglass's thought is revealed by the fact that over three decades later at the annual convention of the New England Woman Suffrage Association, he told the audience that "woman's claim to the right of equal participation in government" has its foundation in natural law and in the liberal ideas articulated by the American Founders. "Our Moses and our prophets," he told the audience, "so far as the rights and privileges of American citizens are concerned, are the framers of the Declaration of Independence."[22] These are but two examples of Douglass making the case that the natural rights philosophy at the heart of the Declaration of Independence ought to be the guiding compass of our political life. Douglass's consistent choice of the framers of the Declaration of Independence as "our Moses and prophets" is significant. Like Abraham Lincoln, Douglass viewed the Declaration as the foundation of American political morality. The Declaration, Lincoln said in words that capture Douglass's view as well, is the "apple of gold" and the Constitution is the "picture of silver subsequently framed around it. The picture was made, not to conceal or destroy the apple; but to adorn, and preserve it. The picture was made for the apple—not the apple for the picture."[23]

Douglass argued that the movements for abolition and women's rights were heirs to the revolutionary ideology of natural rights expressed in the Declaration. These movements, he contended, were calling for a "rededication to our founding ideals."[24] In 1855, at a state convention in support of black New Yorkers, Douglass told the crowd that these principles possess truth that transcends time and place.

> The science of government has received no very great alteration, illustration or illumination, since the signing of the Declaration of Independence by the American people. We are not here now to force any new consideration upon the public. We are especially proud to endeavor to carry out the great fundamental principles of the American government—to carry out those great truths long ago uttered by the Fathers of this Republic.[25]

Douglass described his "mission" as an attempt "to hasten the day when the principles of liberty and humanity expressed in the Declaration of Independence and the constitution of the United States shall be the law and the practice of every section, and of all the people of this great country without regard to race, sex, color, or religion."[26]

With the philosophy of the Declaration as his foundation, Douglass embraced the traditional liberal triad of rights to life, liberty, and property as well as the related right to pursue happiness. The first right listed in the traditional triad is the right to life. In an 1858 resolution in opposition to capital punishment he signed, Douglass and his fellow authors described the right to life as "the great primary and most precious and comprehensive of all human rights."[27] In a stinging 1859 critique of "American Civilization," he said that one "of the first features which mark the distinction between a civilized, and a rude nation, is the value attached to human life, and the protection given it by the former."[28] The primary importance of the right to life is easy enough to explain. If the right to life is not secure, then liberty and property cannot be enjoyed and happiness cannot be pursued.

As I demonstrated in chapter 2, the second right in the liberal triad, the right to liberty, was crucially important to Douglass. He claimed that the right to liberty is "self-evident," in the sense that the "desire for it is the deepest and strongest of all powers of the human soul."[29] The right to liberty, Douglass believed, is rooted in the eternal and universal nature of man. In an 1850 address called "The Antislavery Tocsin," he spoke of the right to liberty in this way:

> It existed in the very idea of man's creation. It was his even before he comprehended it. He was created in it, endowed with it, and it can never be taken from him. No laws, no statutes, no compacts, no covenants, no compromises, no constitutions, can abrogate or destroy it. It is beyond the reach of the strongest earthly arm, and smiles at the ravings of tyrants from its hiding place in the bosom of God. Men may hinder its exercise— they may act in disregard of it—they are even permitted to war against it; but they fight against heaven, and their career must be short, for eternal providence will speedily vindicate the right.[30]

Douglass's justification for the right to liberty was discussed at length in the last chapter. What is important for the purposes of this one is to describe how this commitment fit within his liberal democratic politics.

Douglass's understanding of liberty is well within the liberal tradition. He endorsed a view of the legitimate limitations on liberty that is almost identical to John Stuart Mill's harm principle. In 1851, Douglass penned an important essay of political philosophy entitled "Is Civil Government Right?" I will discuss the context of the essay in greater detail below, but at this point it is worth noting that this essay stands out as an example of Douglass attempting to work out his own understanding of fundamental principles of political morality. Among other things, Douglass used the essay to explore the meaning of liberty.

> All admit that the right to enjoy liberty depends upon the use made of that liberty; hence Society has erected jails and prisons, with a view to *deprive men of their liberty when they are so wicked as to abuse it by invading the liberties of their fellows.* We have a right to arrest the locomotion of a man who insists upon walking and trampling on his brother man, instead of upon the highway. This right of society is essential to its preservations; without it a single individual would have it in his power to destroy the peace and the happiness of ten thousand otherwise right minded people.[31]

Douglass, like Mill, suggested that the individual's right to liberty ends where the rights of others begin. While Mill justified this view in the "permanent interests of man as a progressive being," Douglass relied on the idea that men are "free by the laws of nature."[32] Because freedom is rooted in the laws of nature, Douglass thought, it is also limited by those laws. In this respect, it is fair to say that Douglass adopted a view reminiscent of John Locke's "fundamental law of nature," which held that the legitimate exercise of freedom is limited by the lives, liberties, and possessions of others.[33]

Douglass's understanding of liberty is further illuminated by considering how he related it to virtue. The traditional dichotomy between liberal and "perfectionist" thinkers hinges on the precedence of liberty and virtue in their thought. According to political theorist Robert P. George, the perfectionist perspective is rooted in "the belief that law and politics are rightly concerned with the moral well-being of members of political communities," and liberals, who reject the perfectionist aspiration to "make men moral," are "*the* principal" rivals to this perspective.[34] As a philosophical matter, Douglass usually came down on the liberal side of this divide. Rather than agreeing with the perfectionist argument that the state should be authorized to coerce moral behavior, he contended that freedom is a necessary precondition for virtue and religious piety. When asked if money should be spent to send Bibles to slaves, Douglass responded: "The first thing is freedom. It is the all important thing. There can be no virtue without freedom—there can be no obedience to the Bible without freedom."[35] Douglass repeated this argument in his advocacy of women's rights. Many antifeminists defended the exclusion of women from the public sphere by arguing that the denial of equal rights was necessary to protect women from moral degradation.[36]

[I]f seclusion and absence from contact with the outside world were the best protection to womanly dignity, the harem would surpass the home. The caged, veiled, and cushioned women of the East, never allowed to be seen by the vulgar crowd, watched over by eyes as vigilant as the suspicions of despotism, would furnish the highest example of refinement and virtue. But such is not the case. Enforced morality is artificial morality. It is the safety that never drowns because it never goes into the water, the virtue that never falls because never tempted.[37]

After extensive world travel during the late 1880s, during which he witnessed what he thought to be the mistreatment of women in Egypt, Douglass warned Americans not to "enforce this Mahometan idea of woman upon American women—an idea in which woman has no recognized moral, social, or religious existence. . . . She is deemed incapable of self-direction—a body without a soul. No more distressing thing confronted us during our recent tour in Egypt than this social and religious annihilation of woman."[38] In short, Douglass rejected the view that individual freedom ought to be constrained in the name of virtue or religion. Instead, he argued that rather than being in tension with individual freedom, authentic morality and religious piety require it.

These examples may lead us to conclude outright that Douglass rejected the view that individual freedom ought to be constrained in the name of virtue or religion, and furthermore that he accepted the classical liberal or libertarian view that rather than being in tension with individual freedom, authentic morality and religious piety require it. Such a straightforward conclusion is undermined, however, by Douglass's status as a defender of temperance and even prohibition of alcohol. Prior to the Civil War, he joined many abolitionists in supporting the temperance movement—the moral reform advocates who promoted abstinence from alcohol. After the Civil War, Douglass continued to promote temperance and went beyond earlier moral condemnations to embrace legal bans on liquor. In an 1886 letter to *The Issue* magazine of Nashville, Tennessee, Douglass wrote: "For a long time I refused to commit myself to the doctrine of absolute prohibition of intoxicating drinks, because I thought it interfered with the personal liberty of the citizen. But the sober contemplation of the evils of intemperance not only upon the dram drinker, but upon his family, his friends, and upon society generally, has compelled me to go the whole length of prohibition."[39] Douglass's involvement in the temperance cause as a moral reform movement is not inconsistent with his embrace of the liberal view of liberty. Classical liberals have no problem with the idea that individuals can use their skills of persuasion to convince others to refrain from engaging in certain behaviors. Things get complicated from a liberal perspective when individuals attempt to force their moral views on others through the coercive instruments of government. So a full understanding of Douglass's view of the right to liberty is not captured without addressing this apparent contradiction.

There are three major reasons why Douglass drifted away from liberalism toward perfectionism on the issue of prohibition. Perhaps paradoxically, he thought his reasons were rooted in, rather than being in tension with, his devotion to liberty. First, his experience as a slave led him to believe that alcohol was used as a sort of opiate to keep subordinated classes from rebelling. In an address delivered in 1846 in Paisley, Scotland, Douglass said:

> In the Southern States, masters induce their slaves to drink whiskey, in order to keep them from devising ways and means by which to obtain

their freedom. In order to make a man a slave, it is necessary to silence or drown his mind. It is not the flesh that objects to being bound—it is the spirit. It is not the mere animal part—it is the immortal mind which distinguishes man from the brute creation. To blind his affections, it is necessary to bedim and bedizzy his understanding. In no other way can this be so well accomplished as by using ardent spirits![40]

Second, Douglass believed there was a connection between temperance and the fitness for freedom described in chapter 2. You will recall that Douglass's case for freedom was rooted in the claim that human beings want to be free and have capacities—such as the capacity to reason and to tell right from wrong—that make them fit for freedom. When human beings are drunk, Douglass argued, those capacities are diminished and therefore the case for their freedom is weakened. In the Scotland speech cited above, he said:

> The blacks are to a considerable extent intemperate, and if intemperate, of course vicious in other respects, and this is counted against them as a reason why their emancipation should not take place. As I desire, therefore, their freedom from physical chains, so I desire their emancipation from intemperance, because I believe it would be the means—a great and glorious means—towards helping to break their physical chains and letting them go free.[41]

Third, it appears that Douglass believed the negative consequences of alcohol consumption (for the individual and those around him) were potentially so great that prohibition could be justified. Although he does not state this specifically in the passage above, it is reasonable to assume that the violation of rights was central among the negative consequences Douglass had in mind. In other words, Douglass may have held the view that individuals under the influence were more likely to "invade the liberties of their fellows," and therefore, attempts to prevent individuals from getting drunk could be justified by a concern for individual rights.

There is little question that Douglass's views of alcohol reveal that he was not a social libertarian. Furthermore, his embrace of the cause of prohibition, whatever its merits, was illiberal. He took the leap from moral condemnation to state prohibition because he thought this was necessary, first, to achieve emancipation, and second, to secure equal citizenship. Douglass was in most instances a liberty man, but he had his limits.

The last right in the liberal triad is the right to property. In the previous section I noted the controversial status of this right within the liberal tradition. Douglass's ambivalence on the status of private property rights is a manifestation of the complex relationship between property and freedom that has troubled numerous thinkers within and outside the liberal tradition. The key question for my purposes is this: did Douglass's attitude toward private property lead him to leave the liberal family and embrace socialism? In what follows, I argue that Douglass expressed reservations about the inequality that followed from the unregulated free market, but that he rejected the socialist alternative that was adopted by some of his fellow abolitionists.

Douglass's justification of the right to property is nearly identical to the views of John Locke: "The theory of property in the soil," Douglass said, "runs thus: that man has a right to as much soil as is necessary for his existence; and when a human being has incorporated a portion of his own strength and that which belongs to his personality into that soil against the universe."[42] Like Locke, Douglass relied on his theory of self-ownership to argue that individuals are entitled to the fruits of their own labor. Indeed, he even went so far as to say in 1871 that once the government had "secured to its members" the "undisturbed possession of the natural fruits" of each individual's "exertions," there was "very little left for society and government to do."[43] Against this view, Douglass was confronted with many utopian socialists within the antislavery movement, but he consistently rejected their ideas. During the nineteenth century, many activists in various reform movements were attracted to the ideas of Charles Fourier. According to historian Carl J. Guarneri, "Fourierism"—a utopian socialist doctrine offered by a thinker who "rejected liberal capitalism at its takeoff point and championed in its place his 'New Industrial World' of justice, harmony, and personal fulfillment"—was "the most popular and dynamic secular communitarianism of the nineteenth century."[44] American Fourierists proposed to "sidestep politics" by creating utopian cooperative communities in which individuals would share all things in common. These communities, or "phalanxes," would evolve, Fourier said, toward "Harmony," which represents the "full maturity of the race."[45]

Several abolitionists accepted this condemnation of liberal capitalism and argued that the battle against chattel slavery was too narrow. All forms of slavery, including "wage slavery," ought to be opposed as well. Guarneri has demonstrated that there was a split within the abolitionist movement between thinkers who "believed that northern free labor was inherently sound and emphasized the opportunities and openness in American society," and utopian socialists, who "insisted otherwise."[46] On one side there were thinkers like John A. Collins, a close associate of Douglass during his first few years on the abolitionist lecture circuit, who was a prominent promoter of this view. Collins believed "that private property was the root of all evil" and founded a utopian community, Skaneateles, in Western New York.[47] On the other there were thinkers like Douglass, who continued to embrace the right to property in the face of utopian socialist opposition. At a meeting of the Rhode Island Anti-Slavery Society, a speaker attempted "to show that wages slavery is as bad as chattel slavery," and Douglass responded by declaring this argument to be "arrant nonsense" because to "own the soil is no harm in itself. It was given to man. It is right that he should own it. It is his duty to possess it—and to possess it in that way in which its energies and properties can be made the most useful to the human family—now and always."[48]

Douglass's embrace of the right to private property was not absolute, and a strong case can be made that he was closer to the reform liberal view described earlier in the chapter than he was to the classical liberal view. He voiced his concerns about early capitalism in an essay entitled "The Labor Question." The "labor question" was a term that was used as a catch-all for issues such as working conditions and the distribution of wealth. Prior to the publication of this important essay, Douglass had expressed the view that although he was committed to the institution of private property, "the mode of holding" property and "the amount held" were legitimate political questions with respect to which "various opinions may be honestly entertained."[49] Unlike classical liberals committed to putting the right to property on the same level of sanctity with the rights to life and liberty, Douglass believed it was legitimate for the political community to consider the question, "What manner of holding property in the soil is best, which best secures the happiness of the whole human family?"[50]

The essay on "The Labor Question" reveals Douglass's discomfort with the inequality within "our industrial civilization."

> The real object [in addressing the labor question] must necessarily be to arrive at the principles that affect society in its relations to production, and especially to comprehend those laws which govern the distribution of labor's results, and which, it must be apparent to the most superficial thinker, now operate so unequally. The profound truth conveyed in the apparently paradoxical utterance of Jesus, when he said, "That unto every one which hath shall be given; and from him that hath not, even that he hath shall be taken away from him," receives daily and literal illustration in all the operations of our industrial civilization. The non-producers now receive the larger share of what those who labor produce. The result is natural. Discontent culminates in exactly the same ratio that intelligence sustains aspiration.[51]

Douglass's response to the labor question reveals that on this issue he was closer to the reform liberal view than he was to the libertarian view.

> The question, whether civilization is designed primarily for Man or for Property, can have but one direct answer, whatever may be the methods each may think desirable by which to attain that end. The happiness of man must be the primal condition on which any form of society can found a title to existence. The civilization, then, looked at in its material aspect alone, which on the one hand constantly increases its wealth-creating capacities and on the other as steadily leaves out the benefits thereof to at least seven-tenths of all who live within its influence, cannot have realized the fundamental condition of its continuance. That society is a failure in which the large majority of its members, without any direct fault of their own, would, if any accidental circumstances deprived them for a month of the opportunity of earning regular wages, be dependent upon private or public charity for daily bread. Yet such is the actual condition of even favored American labor.[52]

Although Douglass was concerned about the fundamental unfairness and legitimate discontent of the burgeoning industrial capitalist system, he seemed to struggle when searching for "equitable remedies."[53] From the perspective of the Hartzian reading of American political thought, this was probably rooted in an irrational devotion to liberal ideas. It may be the case, however, that Douglass's failure was due to a sincere commitment to both liberty and equality. On the one hand he was committed to the institution of private property and the idea of free labor as pillars of individual liberty. On the other hand he was disturbed by the gross inequalities being produced by "our industrial civilization." I will return to Douglass's thoughts on the labor question later in this book. For now, it is important to note that his concerns about economic inequality did not cause him to abandon the liberal family's devotion to individual rights to private property.

Within the abolitionist movement there were those who looked at the "labor question" and responded by rejecting private property and wage labor in favor of common property and cooperative labor. The split between American Fourierists and apologists for early liberal capitalism has been well documented.[54] Although it is clear that Douglass had reservations about the material inequalities of early capitalism, he defended the institution of private property and the "free labor" system of the North rather than joining the socialists. His consistent defense of the institution of private property and the idea of free labor is further evidence that he is best understood as a member of the liberal family.

Conformity or Pluralism?
Douglass on the Toleration of Moral and Religious Diversity

Several prominent liberals including John Rawls and Judith Shklar have made a compelling case that one of the core commitments of liberalism is to toleration of moral and religious diversity. Shklar has pointed out that liberalism was born in opposition to the cruelty of religious coercion and that, at least since Mill, liberals have extended this logic to the moral sphere and have been committed to the view that "it is in diversity alone that freedom can be realized."[55] Similarly, Rawls made the case that moral and religious pluralism is a fact of social life and that one can respond to this fact in one of two ways. First, there is the liberal response: to tolerate this religious and moral pluralism. Second, there is the illiberal response: to attempt to combat this pluralism and enforce religious and moral unanimity.[56] A thinker's response to the fact of pluralism is very telling.

So where does Douglass come down on the question of moral and religious diversity? Did he adopt a liberal attitude or did he embrace an illiberal ideology of coerced uniformity? There is little question that Douglass adopted an essentially liberal attitude toward moral and religious pluralism. Far from being uncomfortable with moral and religious disagreement, Douglass embraced disagreement as an essential protector of personal freedom. In other words, he was much closer to Mill than he was to Hobbes. In order to make this case, I focus on two manifestations of this commitment: his discussion of moral pluralism in the context of the debate over women's suffrage and the evidence of his religious liberalism.

At the 1886 meeting of the New England Woman Suffrage Association, Douglass spoke to "an immense audience" on the topic "Who and What Is Woman?"[57] In his speech, he responded to common anti-women's rights arguments. Antifeminists often argued that the domestic sphere was (ideally) marked by harmony and that the political sphere was (inevitably) marked by conflict.[58] To invite women into the conflict-ridden political realm was to invite disharmony into the domestic realm. In response to the argument that granting women the right to vote "will introduce strife and division into [the] family," and therefore "peace and tranquility will no longer dwell under the family roof," Douglass went beyond the discussion immediately at hand to draw lessons for society as a whole.[59] He described the conservative view in this way:

> It is assumed that difference of opinion in the State may be more safely tolerated than difference of opinion in the family, bound together by respect,

tenderness, and love, and therefore more able to sustain such difference. It holds that in order to have peace and tranquility in the family, the woman, the wife, the daughter, and the sister, must have no opinions of their own, or must not be allowed to express such opinions if they have them; that they must deny their intellect and conscience, and become moral, social, and intellectual monstrosities, bodies without souls; in fact, like gods of the heathen, have ears, and hear not; have eyes, and see not; and have tongues, and speak not.[60]

Douglass responded by saying that "a principle which requires such self-abnegation, such stultification and self-abasement, cannot be sound, or other than absurd and vicious."[61] His response to this principle reveals much about his attitude toward pluralism.

Douglass did not believe moral disagreement would lead to the dire "consequences" predicted by conservatives.[62] "Husbands and wives," he said, "differ in opinion every day, about a variety of subjects, and yet dwell together in love and harmony. How insufferably flat, stale, and unprofitable is that family in which no difference of opinion enters? Who on earth can want to spend his or her days as a simple echo?"[63] Rather than leading to chaos, Douglass argued that disagreement can lead to a discordant harmony.

A difference of opinion, like a discord in music, sometimes gives the highest effects of harmony. A thousand times better is it to have a brave, outspoken woman by one's side, than a piece of mincing nothingness that is ashamed to have an opinion. For myself, from what I know of the nature of human understanding, I at once suspect the sincerity of the man or the woman who never has an opinion in opposition to mine. *Differing, as human minds do, in all their processes and operations, such uniform agreement is unnatural, and must be false, assumed, and dishonest.* The fact is no family or State can rest upon any foundation less than truth and honesty.[64]

Douglass's language anticipates what Rawls called reasonable pluralism.[65] Like Rawls, he believed that the free exercise of human reason will not lead to universal agreement. Instead, the free exercise of reason is likely to lead to a variety of moral views. Douglass thought moral and religious disagreement should be accepted as a fact of social life. Rather than being a cause for panic, he believed this fact should be celebrated as a natural consequence of human freedom.

Douglass also adopted the tolerant attitude typical of liberalism when confronted with various religious controversies. A number of examples can be cited in support of this view. Early in his public career, Douglass traveled to the British Isles to deliver a series of antislavery lectures. In an 1846 letter written to his abolitionist colleague William Lloyd Garrison, Douglass commented on a number of political developments he observed on the other side of the Atlantic. In addition to telling Garrison about movements against the Corn Laws and in favor of universal suffrage, Douglass offered this support for those agitating for the separation of church and state: "The opposition to the gross injustice of compelling a man to support a form of worship, in which he not only feels no interest, but which he really hates is great and increasing."[66] In the early 1870s, we see Douglass maintaining his liberal attitude toward church-state matters when he took a controversial position in the debate over prayer in public schools. In the context of that debate, he embraced a strict separationist stand on church-state relations: "[M]y command to the church, and all denominations of the church whether Catholic or Protestant is, hands off this Government. And my command to the Government is hands off the church."[67]

A third piece of evidence of Douglass's religious liberalism emerged in his response to accusations from the Bethel Church of Philadelphia that he had not given enough credit to prayer for bringing about the passage of the Fifteenth Amendment to the Constitution. As you will see in chapter 5, Douglass accepted a strongly humanistic view of social change. In other words, rather than believing that God was directing history from on high, Douglass thought the fate of humanity was in the hands of human beings. In response to this view, some religious leaders took offense, contending that Douglass was not giving enough credit to God and the power of prayer for bringing about a Union victory in the Civil War and passage of civil rights laws in its aftermath. In a public letter to the editor of the *Philadelphia Press* in response to the accusations, Douglass defended his humanistic view and added a classical liberal jab at organized religion: "No human institution," he declared, "has been crueler and more malicious than organized religion. It has been ready to persecute those who dissent from its views, and all that it lacks today is the power, not the will."[68] It is worth noting here that Douglass's misgivings of organized religion did not extend to religious belief itself. During the course of one of his many harangues against the hostility of churches to the antislavery cause, Douglass wrote: "[I]n our denunciation of the clergy we might forget to cultivate our piety towards God, and I therefore, commend rigid self-examination to the abolitionists as a means of reviving the early religious enthusiasm which they brought to the Anti-slavery cause."[69] A fourth piece of evidence of Douglass's religious liberalism is found in an

1870 essay on various debates of sexual morality entitled "St. Paul's Bachelor Views." In this essay, Douglass adopted a liberal view when he contended that it was utterly hopeless to try to settle "great social questions with scriptural authority."[70] In 1871, Douglass penned an essay entitled "An Attempt against Religious Liberty" in which he made the case against a proposed constitutional amendment that would enter into the fundamental law of the land a recognition of the existence of a Supreme Being:

> We trust our legislators will ignore this memorial, for our country's strength and prosperity rest in part on the separation of Church and State. We have so far been spared the religious wars and persecutions that have racked countries with State Churches. Our tradition of religious toleration, moreover, not only guarantees freedom of worship of all sects, but also freedom of disbelief for atheists. If a Constitutional Amendment were adopted recognizing the Supreme Being, some of our German friends in this country, who are atheists, could not take an oath to support the Constitution without perjuring themselves. Nor is it to be supposed that once the barrier separating Church and State be breached the assault on religious freedoms will end there. It is not at all far-fetched to imagine that whatever religious sect happens to be dominant politically at the moment will try to legislate into the Constitution its own brand of religious belief.[71]

In an 1871 essay entitled "Dark Prospects," Douglass seemed to endorse a view on the relationship between religion and politics that is something like the idea popularized by Rawls. The republican form of government, Douglass wrote, should be defined as "a government that guarantees equal rights and equal protection but does not meddle or try to enforce particular social and religious theories."[72]

Perhaps the strongest evidence of Douglass's religious liberalism is his celebration of religious diversity. This view is nowhere more evident than the position he took in the debate over Chinese immigration to the United States during the second half of the nineteenth century. Between 1848 and 1882, more than 300,000 Chinese immigrants came to the United States. Many Americans reacted harshly to what they perceived to be a "Yellow Peril."[73] Among other things, anti-immigrant politicians argued that "the Chinese is a heathen, and that he will introduce his heathen rights and superstitions here."[74] In an 1869 speech in Boston called "Our Composite Nationality," Douglass responded to this charge. In his response, we can see his embrace of pluralism.

Even the matter of religious liberty, which has cost the world more tears, more blood and more agony, than any other interest, will be helped by [the Chinese] presence. I know of no church, however tolerant; of no priesthood, however enlightened, which could be safely trusted with the tremendous power which universal conformity would confer. *We should welcome all men of every shade of religious opinion, as among the best means of checking the arrogance and intolerance which are the almost inevitable concomitants of general conformity.* Religious liberty always flourishes best amid the clash and competition of rival religious creeds.[75]

Douglass welcomed the diversification of American religious life as a greater safeguard for religious liberty. In language reminiscent of John Stuart Mill's celebration of diversity in *On Liberty*, Douglass welcomed the "clash and competition" of religious ideas as an essential part of a flourishing free society.

Douglass's embrace of religious pluralism extended to another group that was often the target of discrimination during the nineteenth century: Mormons. In a review he published in his newspaper, *The North Star*, in 1850, Douglass recommended that a recently published pamphlet "on the persecution visited on the industrious Mormons" be "read avidly by all freedom-lovers." The pamphlet, written by a Philadelphia lawyer named Thomas L. Kane who spent 1846 studying the Mormons in the American west, was applauded by Douglass for its willingness to challenge widespread prejudice against Mormons. The pamphlet, he wrote, "explodes all our cherished myths" about Mormons and "brings the case of this commendable people finally before the public."[76]

It is worth noting that Douglass did believe the virtue of toleration can become a vice when taken to excess. In an 1871 essay entitled "Toleration and Indifference," he made this point clear in response to accusations that he was intolerant toward Democrats: "Toleration is one of the country's greatest virtues and helps keep this heterogeneous nation united. But it ceases to be a virtue when it becomes an excessive leniency toward wrongdoing, either because of indifference, weak convictions or mistaken notions of kindness." The theme of this essay is clear: Douglass was worried that principled tolerance might slide into flaccid indifference. His commitment to tolerance existed alongside his belief in universal human rights. Believers in human rights, he insisted, should not stand by and passively accept as equally legitimate points of view those perspectives that promote injustice. Since Democrats "supported slavery" and "encouraged treason" prior to and during the Civil War and since many Democrats continued to support the murder and persecution of African Americans in the war's aftermath, Douglass argued that it was permissible to maintain that supporters of the Democratic Party were guilty of aiding and abetting "great criminality."[77]

In this section, I have argued that Douglass's attitude toward moral and religious pluralism provides further evidence of his membership in the liberal family. He defended moral and religious freedom on both deontological and consequentialist grounds. As a matter of principle, he adopted the liberal view that the right to liberty includes the right to adopt moral and religious views according to the dictates of one's own conscience, not the heavy hand of the magistrate. As a matter of utility, Douglass held that the clash and competition of rival moral and religious creeds ought to be defended because it is among "the best means" to protect personal freedom. In sum, Douglass's embrace of toleration is an important indication that he is best understood as a member of the liberal family.

Up from Anarchism: Douglass's Defense of Limited Government

Earlier in this chapter, I noted that because of their devotion to personal freedom it is typical of liberals to be drawn toward anarchism. What ultimately makes a thinker liberal, however, is the fact that he ends up rejecting anarchism as the best way to secure individual freedom. Douglass was confronted with the anarchist possibility and rejected it in favor of limited government. This rejection of anarchism is yet another indication that Douglass ought to be grouped with the liberal family.

Douglass began his public career as an associate of William Lloyd Garrison, the most prominent abolitionist in the United States. Garrison was committed to natural rights, but took this commitment to a radical level by embracing a utopian anarchist view of human nature and social relations. Garrison's case for anarchism was remarkably simple.

Premise A: All use of force is unjust.
Premise B: All governments rely on the use of force.
Conclusion: All government is unjust.

Although there is no strong evidence to suggest Douglass ever embraced the anarchist part of the Garrisonian program, he made his rejection of anarchism explicit in an 1851 essay, "Is Civil Government Right?" In this essay, he responded to the Garrisonian anarchist Henry C. Wright, who criticized Douglass and other abolitionists who were joining the Liberty Party, an antislavery political party formed in the 1840s. Association with the Liberty Party was unacceptable, Wright said, because political power was prima facie illegitimate. According to his argument, all government is immoral: "To speak of a righteous human ruler is the same as to speak of a righteous thief, a righteous robber, a righteous murderer, a righteous pirate or a righteous slaveholder."[78] Douglass and Wright agreed that the basic starting point for all questions of political morality should be the natural rights of individuals, but they parted company on the question of how best to secure those rights. The anarchist Wright believed natural rights would be best served by the elimination of all government. The liberal Douglass believed the dark side of human nature makes limited government necessary to secure natural rights.

Wright was one of the most important anarchist thinkers in the abolitionist movement.[79] He disputed the idea "that man can have the right to dictate law to his equal brother" and believed that government rules by force alone: "[T]he government is but an embodiment of death."[80] Wright contended that all government violates divine and natural law: "The history of all attempts of man to rule over man, to dictate to him a rule of life, and to punish him if he disobeys, demonstrates that an assumption of [government] power is opposed to nature and to nature's God. They have made earth a scene of blood and carnage."[81] According to historian Lewis Perry, abolitionist anarchists "insisted that they were striving for, and placing themselves under, the only true and effective government: the government of God." Abolitionist anarchists believed they were the only ones offering a complete and consistent philosophy of liberty: "Slavery, government and violence were considered identical in principle: all were sinful invasions of God's prerogatives; all tried to set one man between another man and his rightful ruler."[82]

Douglass's rejection of the anarchism of his Garrisonian associates was rooted in a fundamental disagreement about human nature. He believed human beings to be naturally social and endowed with rational and moral capacities, but he also thought that each of us is "constantly liable to do evil" and, perhaps of greater concern, there are "hardened villains" among us who are willing to trample upon the natural rights of others.[83] The liability within each of us to do evil is rooted in the selfish, passionate, and willful side of human nature. As I demonstrated in the last chapter, Douglass thought individuals are willing to disregard the rights of others when their moral judgment has been clouded by selfishness. In addition to this natural tendency within human beings to disregard their moral obligations to others, there are those who habitually disregard these obligations. Douglass called individuals who continually or habitually violate the fundamental law of nature "hardened villains." Because hardened villains ignore or disregard their distinctively human capacities of reason and moral judgment, Douglass called them "outcasts of humanity," "monsters," and "bloodhounds."[84] The presence of these hardened villains and the potential for villainy within all of us caused Douglass to reject as unrealistic the anarchist vision of a harmonious life without government. The anarchists may have been right to say that government is nothing more than institutionalized violence, but, as Douglass argued in an 1856 essay on "Bleeding Kansas," sometimes "force is the only effective instrumentality for combating evil."[85]

Douglass's primary concern was to see to it that the natural rights of all individuals were respected. The existence of villainy in human nature made it necessary to establish government to protect these rights. Douglass believed that *civil* government was the solution to the problem of villainy in human nature. The civility of government, he argued, is determined by its respect for and protection of the natural rights of all individuals. According to Douglass, the flaw in the anarchist argument was its failure to distinguish between righteous and unrighteous force. He agreed with the anarchist contention that force wielded in violation of natural rights is unjust. Force wielded in defense of natural rights, he thought, is morally legitimate. This fundamental distinction allows us to distinguish between arbitrary and righteous government. A government that violates or fails to protect natural rights is "arbitrary, despotic, tyrannical, corrupt, unjust, [and] capricious."[86] A civil government, Douglass claimed, committed to "liberty, justice, and humanity" would refrain from violating natural rights and would act to protect innocents from villains.

> The fallacy and fatal error which form the basis of [anarchist] reasoning, are the assumptions that human government is necessarily arbitrary and absolute; and that there is no difference between a righteous and a wicked government. Human government, from its very nature, is an organization, like every other human institution, limited in its powers, and subject to the very wants of human nature which call it into existence.[87]

Only civil government, he argued, is entitled to be called government at all: "Human government is for the protection of human rights; and when human government destroys human rights, it ceases to be a government, and becomes a foul and blasting conspiracy; and is entitled to no respect whatever."[88] Douglass argued that this view was shared by the "Fathers of this Republic," who "told us, and told a then listening world, that, according to their sense of civil Government, fit for the name and fit to exist at all, should secure [the] fundamental rights [to life, liberty, and the pursuit of happiness]."[89]

The use of force by the government, according to Douglass, is legitimate if it is used to protect the natural rights of innocent people. Individuals have obligations to respect the rights of others and if they do not, the government has an obligation to protect innocents. Douglass believed individuals and the government were morally permitted to use force to defend rights.[90]

> This, then, is our reasoning: that when every avenue to the understanding and heart of the oppressor is closed, when he is deaf to every moral appeal, and rushes upon his fellow-man to gratify his own selfish propensities at the expense of the rights and liberties of his brother-man, the exercise of physical force, sufficient to repel the aggression, is alike the right and duty.[91]

"Common sense," Douglass wrote, teaches "that physical resistance is the antidote for physical violence."[92] When "government fails to protect the just rights of an individual man, either he or his friends may be held in the sight of God and man, innocent, in exercising any right for his preservation which society may exercise for its preservation."[93] Douglass's view of this matter was in direct opposition to Garrison, who taught the doctrine of "nonresistance." In a review of *Selections from the Writings of William Lloyd Garrison*, Douglass made this opposition clear: "But as to the doctrine of non-physical resistance to evil, we reject it. The only peace principle we comprehend is justice. The blood of a few tyrants must be spilled in order to warn would-be oppressors in the future."[94] Like his liberal predecessor Locke, though, Douglass believed effective civil government was preferable to the use of private violence in defense of natural rights: "The true object for which governments are ordained among men is to protect the weak against the encroachments of the strong, to hold its strong arm of justice over all the civil relations of its citizens and to see that all have an equal chance in the race of life."[95] In typical liberal fashion, then, Douglass viewed government as a necessary evil.

> Because there are hardened villains, enemies to themselves and to the well-being of society, who will cheat, steal, rob, burn and murder their fellow creatures, and because these are the exceptions to the mass of humanity,

society has the right to protect itself against their depredations and aggressions upon the common weal. Society without law, is society with a curse, driving men into isolation and depriving them of one of the greatest blessings of which man is susceptible. It is no answer to this to say that if all men would obey the laws of God, lead virtuous lives, do by others as they would be done unto, human government would be unnecessary; for it is enough to know, as Mr. Wright declares, that "there are no crimes which man may not and will not perpetrate against his fellowman," to justify society in resorting to force, as a means of protecting itself from crime and its consequences.[96]

It is important to note that just as Douglass's partial distrust of human nature led him to be suspicious of anarchism it led him also to be suspicious of government power. The Liberty Party program, he reminded his anarchist critics, rejected the absolutist idea that governmental power ought to be "unlimited and unrestricted," in favor of the liberal idea that government ought to be granted "limited and restricted power."[97] The power of government, Douglass argued, ought to be limited to the ends for which it was created: "[T]he Liberty Party concedes no governmental authority to pass laws, nor to compel obedience to any laws against the natural rights and happiness of man."[98]

Douglass's attitude toward government, then, is best described as one of qualified or conditional acceptance. *If* the Constitution is against the natural rights of man, *then* its subversion is justified. This is the view that animated Douglass during his time as a Garrisonian abolitionist when he rejected the Constitution as proslavery and called for its overthrow. In the early 1850s, when Douglass changed his view of the Constitution, he said, "My position is now one of reform, not of revolution."[99] Once he viewed the Constitution as fundamentally antislavery, he still held that obedience to individual laws was contingent on their respect for natural rights. In 1854, for example, after Douglass argued that the Fugitive Slave Law ought to be actively resisted by Northerners, the *Rochester American* newspaper criticized him for advocating "revolution." In response, Douglass wrote: "So, however, we do not regard it. Revolution implies a subversion of the Government; this is a simple resistance to the enforcement of one enactment, standing alone."[100] Douglass's changing attitude toward the Constitution and his contention that unjust laws should not be obeyed (and that they should be actively opposed) are indications that he viewed all matters of political morality through the lens of natural rights philosophy. It was for this reason that he endorsed limited government against the anarchists but qualified that support against conservatives who believed even unjust laws ought to be obeyed.

Douglass shared the anarchist love of freedom but doubted the anarchist faith in human nature. If men were always moved by the conscientious side of human nature, no government would be necessary. Alas, Douglass believed, nature has "two voices" and the voice of evil in human nature makes anarchism an untenable option.[101] He recognized that all human beings have the capacity for evil and, as such, limited government is necessary to secure natural rights. "With all the drawbacks upon government which fancy can depict, or imagination conjure up, society possessing it, is a paradise to pandemonium, compared with society without it."[102] Douglass's belief that limited government is preferable to anarchy is yet another indication that he is best understood as a liberal political thinker. While his distrust of human nature committed him to the view that civil government was necessary, his faith in human nature led him to believe that the form of that government ought to be democratic. It is to Douglass's embrace of democracy that we now turn.

Douglass's Embrace of Democracy

Douglass was a liberal democrat. As noted above, the relationship between liberalism and democracy is a close one, but it is not without its quarrels. Although liberalism and democracy are in many ways mutually supportive, Wolin is right to say that there is a fundamental divide between liberals, who prize individual liberty above all else, and democrats, who prize collective self-government above all else. It is possible to be a democrat without being a liberal or to be a liberal without being a democrat. It is necessary, therefore, to examine the nature of Douglass's commitment to democracy. In this section, I argue that he tried to reconcile his commitments to liberty and democracy but his priorities are revealed by the fact that he put his strongest emphasis on defending liberal values. In short, Douglass's attitude toward democracy is consistent with the liberal attitude described above and is therefore another indication that he should be identified as a member of the liberal family.

In the last section, I described how Douglass's *distrust* of the selfish side of human nature led him to believe government was necessary. Interestingly, it was Douglass's *faith* in the goodness of human nature that led him to endorse democracy as the best form of government. In the essay on civil government, Douglass wrote:

Why is this respect to be shown to the majority? Simply because a majority of human hearts and intellects may be presumed, as a general rule, to take a wiser and more comprehensive view of the matters upon which they act than the minority. It is in accordance with the doctrine that good is the rule, and evil the exception in the character and constitution of man. If the fact were otherwise, (that is, if men were more disposed to evil than to good), it would, indeed, be dangerous for men to enter into a compact, by which power should be wielded by the mass, for then evil being predominant in man, would predominate in the mass, and innumerable hardships would be inflicted upon the good.[103]

One might wonder whether or not the suspicious side of Douglass highlighted in the last section can be squared with his trusting side being explored here. It is important to note that he did not lose sight of the fact that the dark side of human nature would be entering the democratic arena, but he did believe hardened villains were the "exceptions to the mass of humanity" and, in an 1873 address on women's suffrage, he declared himself to be "such a believer in the preponderating good in human nature that I believe that all the bad can be trusted with all of the good."[104]

Douglass embraced democracy as a better form of government than monarchy or oligarchy. These other forms of government rely on dark views of human nature to make the case for despotic rule.

The old assertion of the wickedness of the masses, and their consequent unfitness to govern themselves, is the falsehood and corruption out of which have sprung despotic and tyrannical conspiracies, calling themselves governments, in the old world. They are founded not in the aggregate morality and intelligence of the people, but in a fancied divine authority, resulting from the inherent incompetency [sic] of the people to direct their own temporal concerns.[105]

Douglass rejected the premise relied upon by the despots and tyrants of the old world. He acknowledged that "if human nature is totally depraved, if men and women are incapable of thinking or doing anything but evil and that continually," then we "should abandon our Republican government, cease to elect men to office, and place ourselves squarely under the Czar of Russia, the Pope of Rome, or some other potentate who governs by divine right."[106] Douglass did not accept this view. Instead, he believed "human nature is more virtuous than vicious" and "governments are best supported by the largest measure of virtue within reach."[107] Therefore, he concluded, it is safer to place the power of government in the hands of the people than in the hands of one man.

Douglass also rejected the notion that aristocracy is the best form of government. In an 1871 essay, "Is Politics an Evil to the Negro?" he rejected the view that all benefit from the rule of an elite group.

> The standing objection to American institutions, and to free institutions generally, is that they tend to retard industry and endanger public order and safety by drawing the laboring classes away from quiet and useful occupations to mingle in the whirl and excitement of political agitations, where their passions are enflamed and their respect for the majesty of law is undermined. For ourselves, it is scarcely necessary to say that we are opposed to all aristocracy, whether of wealth, power, or learning. The beauty and perfection of government in our eyes will be attained when all the people under it, men and women, black and white, shall be conceded the right of equal participation in wielding its power and enjoying its benefits. Equality is even a more important word with us than liberty.[108]

This last line is especially striking. Prior to the Civil War, Douglass's priority was securing liberty for the millions of enslaved men and women in the United States. After the Civil War, Douglass believed the only way to secure that liberty was by securing equal rights, including the right to participate in self-government. It is clear from Douglass's language in this passage just how inextricably intertwined individual freedom and the right to political participation were in his mind.

Douglass grounded his argument for the right of the people to govern themselves in his theory of human nature. Human beings, he argued, are endowed with the capacities necessary for self-government. In the "Who and What Is Woman?" speech he delivered at the annual meeting of the New England Woman Suffrage Association in 1886, Douglass relied on a natural law argument to make the case that the right of suffrage should be extended to women. We can say Douglass's argument is rooted in natural law because he relies on what he believes to be universal characteristics of human nature in order to draw moral and political conclusions.

> The question which should be put to every man and which every man should put to himself is, Who and what is woman? Is there really anything in her nature and constitution which necessarily unfits her for the exercise of suffrage? Is she a rational being? Has she knowledge of right and wrong? Can she discern good and evil? Is she a legitimate subject of government?

Is she capable of forming an intelligent opinion of public men and public measures? Has she a *will* as well as a mind? Is she able to express her thought and opinions by words and acts? As a member of society and a citizen of the State, has she interests like those of men, which may be promoted or hindered, created or destroyed, by the legislative and judicial action of the Government?[109]

Douglass believed the right to govern ourselves collectively is grounded in the same characteristics of human nature that make us fit to govern ourselves individually: rationality, moral judgment, free will, intelligence, the ability to communicate with others, and the possession of individual interests.

Douglass's understanding of the right to participate in self-government, like his view of natural rights, was universal; no one was excluded. He distinguished between "bastard republicanism," which is republicanism that excludes individuals on the basis of arbitrary characteristics such as gender, race, or religion, and "genuine republicanism," which promises equal rights and imposes equal responsibilities upon all people.[110] In an 1867 address called "Sources of Danger to the Republic," Douglass laid out his vision of genuine democratic republicanism. This speech is worth quoting at length.

I am here tonight as a democrat, a genuine democrat dyed in the wool. I am here to advocate a genuine democratic republic; to make this a republican form of government, purely a republic, a genuine republic; free it from everything that looks toward monarchy; eliminate all foreign elements, all alien elements from it; blot out from it everything antagonistic of republicanism declared by the fathers—that idea was that all governments derived their first powers from the consent of the governed; make it a government of the people, by the people, and for all the people, each for all and all for each; blot out all discriminations against any person, theoretically or practically, and make it conform to the great truths laid down by the fathers; keep no man from the ballot box or jury box or the cartridge box because of his color—exclude no woman from the ballot because of her sex. Let the government of the country rest securely down upon the shoulders of the whole nation; let there be no shoulder that does not bear up its proportion of the burdens of government. Let there [be] no conscience, no intellect in the land not directly responsible for the moral character of the government—for the honor of the government. Let it be a genuine Republic, in which every man subject to it is represented in it, and I see no reason why a Republic may not stand while the world stands.[111]

Just as Douglass believed only a government that protected human rights was worthy of being called a government, he argued that only a republic that recognizes the equality before the law of all people is worthy of being called republican. The use of the terms "bastard" and "genuine" was no mistake. Douglass believed republicanism that included everyone was genuine in the sense that it is grounded in the *true* foundation of universal human equality. Nonegalitarian republicanism, on the other hand, is bastardized in the sense that it is disconnected from its roots in universal human equality.

Douglass's enthusiasm for democracy was heightened after the Fifteenth Amendment provided black men with the right to vote. During the late 1860s and early 1870s he believed it was crucial that black men (and conscientious white men for that matter) use the franchise to secure their rights. Douglass even went so far as to embrace a proposal offered in the Massachusetts legislature to make voting compulsory. In an 1871 editorial on the law published in *The New National Era*, Douglass wrote that failure to exercise one's right to vote "is as great a crime as an open violation of the law itself. If honest men had eschewed political apathy," Americans would have been spared the malfeasance of corrupt political machines in Boston and New York. "All men," he concluded, "should be compelled to vote."[112] Douglass's defense of compulsory voting is, like his support for prohibition, an instance of him deviating from the core tenets of liberalism, which is a doctrine that seems uncomfortable with compulsory anything. Again, though, it should be noted that Douglass's argument in favor of compulsory voting emerged out of his commitment to individual liberty and his sense that political engagement was vital to the protection of that liberty. When we keep in mind the precariousness of the rights of freedmen in the aftermath of the Civil War and the fact that there was such a clear partisan divide on the issue of black civil rights during this period, it is not surprising that Douglass was so adamant about the moral obligation to vote.

While Douglass's embrace of this proposal reveals that his enthusiasm for democracy was heightened by the extension of the franchise to black men, further reflection on his attitude toward democracy reveals that his thinking was closer to that of a liberal than to a radical democrat. His views of human nature, the right to liberty, and the right to vote were intimately connected to one another. In an 1870 essay on "Woman and the Ballot," Douglass explained this connection.

> The grand idea of American liberty is coupled with that of universal suffrage; and universal suffrage is suggested and asserted by universal intelligence. Without the latter the former falls to the ground; and unless

suffrage is made co-extensive with intelligence something of the natural power of society essential to its guidance and well-being is lost. To deny that woman is capable of forming an intelligent judgment concerning public men and public measures, equally with men, does not meet the case; for, even if it were granted, the fact remains the same that woman, equally with men, possesses such intelligence; and that such as it is, and because it is such as it is, woman, in her own proper person, has a right for herself to make it effective. To deprive her of this right is to deprive her of a part of her natural dignity, and the State of a part of its mental power of direction, prosperity, and safety; and thus a double wrong is perpetrated.[113]

Douglass grounded the right to vote, then, in both deontological and consequentialist reasons. First, as a matter of principle, he claimed it is a violation of the natural dignity of women to exclude them from equal citizenship. This exclusion does "positive injury" to women because it is a denial of their humanity.[114] Second, the exclusion of women is harmful to society as a whole because they are unable to include their wisdom and virtue in the process of self-government and hence unable to contribute to the common good.

Although Douglass was a fervent advocate of universal suffrage and genuine republicanism, he was not a thinker who embraced romantic conceptions of political participation associated with the radical democratic tradition. Unlike the thinkers within that tradition who are drawn to the idea that civic engagement is an essential part of human flourishing, Douglass emphasized the idea that political participation is necessary as a means of self-protection. After the Civil War, when giving a speech on black suffrage Douglass said: "To the race to which I belong the ballot means something more than a mere abstract idea. It means the right to live and protect itself by honest industry."[115] In a speech on women's suffrage, he made a similar point, but added a nod to the classical republican notion of civic virtue: "She needs the ballot for her own protection, and men as well as women need its concession to her for the protection of the whole."[116] Douglass's reference to the "protection of the whole" is related to his belief that the infusion of the wisdom and virtue of women into the political sphere would be beneficial to all. His argument for the ballot as a means of self-protection is a manifestation of his persistent fear of the potential for villainy in human nature. He believed universal suffrage was a necessary and important step toward making democracy safe for minorities: "I believe majorities can be despotic and have been arbitrary, but arbitrary to whom? Arbitrary when arbitrary at all, always to unrepresented classes. What is the remedy? A consistent republic in which there shall be no unrepresented classes. For when all classes are represented the rights of all classes will be respected."[117]

Like so many other aspects of his political thought, Douglass's chastened view of democracy was grounded in personal experience. He described his chastened view of the body politic in a speech he delivered in Brooklyn in 1863 entitled "The Present and Future of the Colored Race in America." In the speech, he set out to refute various answers to the question of "what shall be done with the negro?" and to offer one of his own. Douglass countered those who responded to this question by saying that blacks ought to enslaved, sent back to Africa, killed, or freed and denied political rights. As an alternative to these proposals, he declared: "[T]here is but one way of wisely disposing of the colored race, and that is to do them right and justice. It is not only to break the chains of their bondage and to accord them personal liberty, but it is to admit them to the full and complete enjoyment of civil and political equality."[118] One response often offered by those opposed to black political equality was to say that the office of American citizen is too sacred and pure to allow for black suffrage. Those offering this argument contended that "the body politic is a rather fastidious body, from which everything offensive must be excluded." Douglass responded to this argument by drawing attention to the ways in which the reality of American politics often falls short of this ideal.

I, myself, once had some high notions about this body politic and its high requirements, and the kind of men fit to enter it and share its privileges. But a day's experience at the polls convinced me that the "body politic" is not more immaculate than many other bodies. That in fact it is a very mixed affair. I saw ignorance enter, unable to read the vote cast. I saw the convicted swindler enter and deposit his vote. I saw the gambler, the horse jockey, the pugilist, the miserable drunkard just lifted from the gutter, covered with filth, enter and deposit his vote. I saw Pat, fresh from the Emerald Isle, requiring two sober men to keep him on his legs, enter and deposit his vote for the Democratic candidate amid the loud hurrahs of his fellow-citizens. The sight of these things went far to moderate my ideas about the character of what is called the body politic, and convinced me that it could not suffer in its composition even should it admit a few sober, industrious and intelligent colored voters.[119]

In an 1852 essay entitled "The Opening Campaign for the Presidency," Douglass's language was even harsher: "Presidential elections," he wrote, "bring out the worst in us as people." Political parties, he continued, design their campaigns in ways that appeal to the "vices" of selfishness, vanity, ambition, and hypocrisy. Indeed, the "emotional excess" and "the saturnalia of corruption" that dominate political campaigns invite the intelligent observer to flirt with the ideas of "having as few elections as possible" and "limiting the suffrage."[120] Douglass's "sober" assessments of the body politic combined with his view of voting as a means of self-protection undermine characterizations of his thought as civic humanist or classical republican.[121] Douglass's view of the political realm was much closer to liberalism. He believed individuals engage in political conduct with enough reason, sociality, conscience, and moral judgment to make them worthy of governing their own affairs, but that they also enter the political sphere with passion, selfishness, and potential for villainy. For this reason we should not expect the process of self-governance to be particularly virtuous.

In the end, Douglass relied on the language of power, not virtue, to ground the right to participate in collective self-government. In an 1870 essay on "The Woman and the Ballot," he wrote:

> Power is the highest object of human respect. Wisdom, virtue, and all great moral qualities command respect only as powers. Knowledge and wealth are nought [sic] but powers. Take from money its purchasing powers, and it ceases to be the same object of respect. We pity the impotent and respect the powerful everywhere. To deny woman her vote is to abridge her natural and social power, and deprive her of a certain measure of respect. . . . We despise the weak and respect the strong. Such is human nature. Woman herself loses in her own estimation by her enforced exclusion from the elective franchise just as slaves doubted their own fitness for freedom, from the fact of being looked upon as only fit for slaves. While, of course, woman has not fallen so low as the slave in the scale of being, (her education and her natural relation to the ruling power rendering such degradation impossible,) it is plain that, with the ballot in her hand, she will ascend a higher elevation in her own thoughts, and even in the thoughts of men, than without that symbol of power. She has power now—mental and moral power—but they are fettered. Nobody is afraid of a chained lion or an empty gun.[122]

In Judith Shklar's words, Douglass viewed the right to vote as being essential to the individual's "standing" as an American citizen.[123] To deny an individual the basic rights of citizenship is to deny her a modicum of power and, as such, to deny her a fundamental pillar of respect.

Douglass's embrace of the "protective" conception of democracy is best understood through the lens of his natural rights philosophy.[124] Just as he did not adopt romantic views of the democratic process, he was careful to point out that he believed the scope of that process was limited by the natural rights of individuals. The meaning of democracy was an extraordinarily important and controversial topic during the politics of the antebellum period. During the 1850s, Douglass differentiated his view from advocates of "popular sovereignty" like Illinois Senator Stephen A. Douglas. The issue of slavery in the territories, Senator Douglas argued, ought to be resolved by popular vote in those territories. Douglass refused to accept that individuals can be deprived of their natural rights "by a simple vote."[125] In October 1854, Douglass traveled to Illinois to offer his critique of the Kansas-Nebraska Act, a bill sponsored by Senator Douglas that created the Kansas and Nebraska territories and permitted the settlers in those territories to determine whether or not they would permit slavery within their borders. In a speech delivered in Chicago entitled "Slavery, Freedom and the Kansas-Nebraska Act," Douglass focused on the question, "What is meant by Popular Sovereignty?" According to Douglass's understanding, popular sovereignty is defined as "the right of the people to establish a government for themselves, as against all others. Such was its meaning in the days of the revolution. It is the independent right of the people to make their own laws, without dictation or interference from any quarter."[126] Senator Douglas's theory of popular sovereignty, Douglass argued, takes this idea in another direction: "The only shadow of popular sovereignty is the power to give people of the territories by this bill to have, hold, buy and sell human beings. The sovereign right to make slaves of their fellow-men if they choose is the only sovereignty that the bill secures."[127] Douglass wondered how the senator from Illinois could justify this view philosophically: "Whence does popular sovereignty take rise? What and where is its basis? I should really like to hear from the author of the Nebraska bill, a philosophical theory, of the nature and origin of popular sovereignty. I wonder where he would begin, how he would proceed and where he would end."[128]

Douglass argued that the theory of popular sovereignty endorsed by Senator Douglas was unintelligible because it violated the moral foundation of democratic self-governance: the principle of universal human equality.

The only intelligible principle on which popular sovereignty is founded, is found in the Declaration of Independence, there and in these words: We hold these truths to be self-evident, that all men are created equal and are endowed by their Creator with the right to life, liberty, and the pursuit of happiness. . . . The right of each man to life, liberty and the pursuit of happiness, is the basis of all social and political right, and, therefore, how brass-fronted and shameless is that impudence, which while it aims to rob men of their liberty, and to deprive them of the right of the pursuit of happiness—screams itself hoarse to the words of popular sovereignty.[129]

For Douglass, popular sovereignty was justified as the best way to secure natural rights. Like human government itself, popular sovereignty was only legitimate insofar as it served this supreme end. Senator Douglas's theory, then, turned popular sovereignty against its own foundation; it empowered some of the people to trample on the rights of others, if they so chose.

By a peculiar use of words, he confounds *power* with *right* in such a manner as to make the *power* to do wrong the *right* to do wrong. By his notion of human rights, everything depends upon the majority. It is not a bit more absurd and monstrous to say that the first settlers in a Territory have the right to protect murder, than that they have the right to protect slavery. The right to do the one is just as good as the right to do the other. The right of the slaveholder is precisely the right of the highway robber. The one says your money or your life, and the other says your liberty or your life, and both depend on superior force for their existence.[130]

According to Douglass's way of thinking, all human institutions are to be judged according to their impact on the natural rights of individuals. Democracy is the best form of government, he thought, because it is the most consistent with the rights and capacities of human beings. Senator Douglas's understanding of democracy lacks this moral foundation in universal human equality and natural rights. As a result, it amounts to little more than a democratic version of might makes right.

A brief word must be said on *how* Douglass thought a balance should be struck between the will of the democratic majority and the rights of minorities. As a general matter, he believed that constitutions should be established "defining the powers of government" and specifying the rights of individuals. Without a constitution, Douglass argued, "government is nothing better than a lawless mob."[131] Constitutions ought to be crafted in a way that appreciates that both good and bad human beings will have access to political power: "[W]e ought to have our government so shaped that even when in the hands of a bad man we shall be safe."[132] The constitution, he thought, should only empower government to pass laws consistent with the natural rights of individuals: it should concede "no governmental authority to pass laws, nor to compel obedience to any laws, against the natural rights and happiness of man."[133] Once rights are articulated in a constitution or subordinate laws, Douglass contended, they must be backed up by civil government. In an 1869 address called "Our Composite Nationality," he said: "Pen, ink, and paper liberty are excellent when there is a party behind it to respect and secure its enjoyment. Human laws are not self executing. To be of any service they must be made vital, active, and certain."[134]

Douglass's marriage to democracy, to borrow Judith Shklar's felicitous description of the liberal devotion to democracy, was monogamous, faithful, and permanent, but it was not entirely romantic. He viewed democracy as the best form of government for the security of individual freedom, but his fear of majority tyranny led him to view democratic governance as a complement to, rather than a replacement of, his devotion to individual rights. Like others within the liberal family, Douglass offered "two cheers for democracy." He viewed democracy as freedom's best hope and a potential threat at the same time. This half-hearted embrace has all the markings of a *liberal* democrat.

Conclusion

It is not altogether remarkable that Douglass's basic political commitments amount to an embrace of liberal democracy. What is more interesting is how he confronted the fact that in the same country where so many people claimed to accept the principles of liberal democracy there was widespread acceptance of practices and beliefs that were thoroughly illiberal and patently undemocratic. His challenge was to close the gap between the ideal of liberty for all and the reality of the racist, sexist, and xenophobic practices of nineteenth-century America. It is to how he confronted this challenge that we now turn.

"Each for All and All for Each"

Douglass's Case for Mutual Responsibility

Introduction

So far, I have demonstrated that Douglass responded to the experience of slavery by embracing universal self-ownership and that this basic commitment led him to accept a liberal democratic political framework. In this chapter, I consider how he infused his liberalism with a robust philosophy of mutual responsibility. Throughout his career as a progressive reformer, Douglass had to confront the fact that Americans claimed to accept these liberal democratic principles while at the same time engaging in illiberal and undemocratic practices. His challenge as a reformer was to convince his fellow Americans to close the gap between the principles of liberal democratic political morality and their unjust practices of exclusion and subordination. But how does one convince free men that they ought to care about the plight of slaves? In what follows, I examine the rhetoric Douglass used to urge his listeners to behave in socially responsible ways. My hope is that by exploring the series of arguments he made in favor of the claim that each individual should feel obligated to do all that he or she can to ensure that the promises of liberal democracy are extended to all people, we can learn something about the foundations of community in his thought. His case for a robust sense of mutual obligation has implications beyond his own abolitionist project. Consideration of his reflections on this matter is worthwhile because it invites us to reflect on a perennial problem of political life, something I am calling the challenge of liberal community: how do we convince freedom-loving individuals to feel a strong sense of responsibility to others? In this chapter, I discuss the responses Douglass gave to this question. In so doing, my focus is on Douglass as a statesman. Philosophically, Douglass was convinced that the natural equality of human beings was reason enough to care about the well-being of others. Politically, though, he knew that this natural equality argument was not sufficient for many people. As such, he developed a series of other arguments in order to convince these skeptics. In sum, my aim in this chapter is not to convince you that Douglass solved the problem of liberal community, but rather to engage in sustained reflection on his strategies to deal with this problem in order to convince his fellow Americans to abolish slavery.

In the next section, I show how the issue of slavery brought the challenge of liberal community front and center. As a political abolitionist, Douglass's most urgent goal was to convince free people that they should feel a sense of responsibility to bring about the end of slavery. I contend that because the liberal language of rights offered only a limited explanation of why individuals ought to feel responsible for one another's well-being, Douglass infused it with a strong case for interconnection and mutual responsibility. Then, I turn to *how* Douglass made the case for a more robust sense of responsibility to others. He offered a variety of reasons for a deeper sense of connection and responsibility to others. First, I examine his reliance on the idea of human brotherhood. Douglass appealed to the natural bond between human beings and expressed the hope that universal freedom could be achieved through moral suasion. Second, I explore his arguments rooted in a commitment to natural rights. As an alternative to appeals to natural sympathy, Douglass turned to political action and attempted to move his fellows to behave in responsible ways by emphasizing the moral commitments expressed in the Declaration of Independence and Constitution. He argued that a principled commitment to freedom should lead us to care about the rights of others. Third, I explore his appeal to self-interest as a basis for responsibility to others. I show that he appealed to self-interest by arguing that failure to behave in responsible ways weakens "the sheet anchor of a common safety" that protects all of us.[1] Fourth, I discuss Douglass's hope that a stronger sense of sympathy might emerge as a result of respect for virtuous action. He expressed his hope that individuals excluded from the promise of freedom could *earn* the concern of their fellow citizens by exhibiting virtues such as courage and independence. In the concluding section, I take this examination of the foundations of community in Douglass's thought to the next step by exploring how individuals could be molded into more responsible human beings. The answer to this question leads to a discussion of Douglass's attentiveness to "moral ecology"—the idea that there is a moral atmosphere surrounding us that can have an impact on our behavior. I contend that the experience of slavery led him to appreciate that just as the "peculiar institution" begot a whole way of thinking that supported its existence, so too might free institutions. I conclude this chapter with some reflections on the implications of Douglass's response to the problem of slavery for how we think about the problem of liberal community.

No Freedom from Responsibility: What Free Men Owe to Slaves

Douglass's concern with the nature and extent of the individual's obligation to others was rooted in the problem of slavery. His experiences as a slave and abolitionist led him to ask several questions. What responsibilities do free individuals have toward slaves? Have I fulfilled my obligations to others if I do not own slaves? If I have duties beyond forbearance, what are the reasons for these duties? The problem of slavery made these questions urgent in his mind.

Douglass often compared the situation of the slave to that of an innocent person being held captive on a pirate ship. He used the pirate ship analogy to compare his own conception of moral responsibility with the notion of moral responsibility offered by William Lloyd Garrison and his followers who favored disunion. Consideration of the pirate ship analogy is a useful way of explaining Douglass's view that there "is no freedom from responsibility for slavery, but in the Abolition of slavery."[2] In May 1857, Douglass traveled to New York City to deliver a speech to the American Abolition Society on the Supreme Court's decision in *Dred Scott v. Sandford*, the case in which the Court concluded that no person descended from an African slave could be a citizen of the United States. In this speech, Douglass discussed many things, but most important for my purposes here is his use of the pirate ship analogy.

> To leave the slave in his chains, in the hands of cruel masters, who are too strong for him, is not to free ourselves from responsibility. Again: If I were on board of a pirate ship, with a company of men and women whose lives and liberties I had put in jeopardy, I would not clear my soul of their blood by jumping in the long boat, and singing out no union with pirates. My business would be to remain on board, and while I never would perform a single act of piracy again, I should exhaust every means given me by my position, to save the lives and liberties of those against whom I had committed piracy. In like manner, I hold it is our duty to remain inside this Union, and use all the power to restore [to the] enslaved millions their precious and God-given rights. The more we have done by our voice and our votes, in times past, to rivet their galling fetters, the more clearly and

solemnly comes the sense of duty to remain, to undo what we have done. Where, I ask, could the slave look for release from slavery if the Union were dissolved?[3]

The central moral question presented by the pirate ship scenario is this: what is my obligation to the men and women whose lives and liberties are in jeopardy on the pirate ship? It is worth noting that Douglass frames this question in a way that assumes all Americans shared some culpability for the plight of the slaves. This is an indication that he believed each of us shares some responsibility for the social conditions that allow some to be exploited by others and that our obligations to the oppressed are, at least in part, rooted in this fact. Douglass's reference to jumping ship and singing out "no union with pirates" is an attack on the Garrisonian position of nonunionism. In Douglass's reading of Garrison's reasoning, if I remove myself from association with sin, I am no longer complicit in it. Hence, leaving the ship would absolve me of responsibility.[4] If we attempt to translate the Garrisonian view into a conception of what obligations an individual has to a human being in peril, the results are curious. If Douglass's reading of Garrison is correct, then the individual's moral responsibility is more negative than it is positive: do *not* participate in the institutions which have made it possible for the individual to be placed in perilous circumstances. Douglass rejected this view in favor of a more robust and urgent conception of moral responsibility. My "business," Douglass contended, would be to stay on board and do all that I can to save the lives and liberties of the innocent people. This view represents the political abolitionist perspective: our obligation is to use any and all means to combat violations of natural rights. From Douglass's point of view, it was not enough to denounce slavery as immoral or to promise to not allow slavery to extend into new territories. Instead, it was the obligation of everyone to stay in the Union and work to bring about the abolition of slavery.

The problem of slavery presented Douglass with a concrete case of what I am calling the challenge of liberal community. While it is certainly true that slavery violates the essential liberal commitment to personal freedom, it is less clear how one can appeal to the vocabulary of liberalism to make the case that a free person has an obligation to combat slavery. Douglass's task, then, was to convince his contemporaries to adopt a sense of moral responsibility strong enough that they would feel moved to act on behalf of those who had been excluded from the liberal promise of freedom.

"Am I My Brother's Keeper?"
Douglass's Case for Mutual Responsibility

In order to convince people to take action to abolish slavery and to pursue other progressive reforms, Douglass had to argue that individuals ought to feel a sense of responsibility to one another beyond mutual forbearance. In what follows, I contend that Douglass offered four major arguments for a stronger sense of responsibility to others: human brotherhood, commitment to natural rights, self-interest properly understood, and respect for virtuous action. I argue that the arguments from human brotherhood, natural rights, self-interest, and respect can be thought of as foundations for community in Douglass's thought: fraternal, creedal, self-interested, and meritocratic. Douglass imagined a fraternal community as a collection of individuals bound together by a sense of brotherly affection rooted either in a belief in Divine Fatherhood or simply their common humanity, a creedal community as a collection of individuals bound together by commitment to a common doctrine of political morality, a self-interested community as a collection of individuals bound together by their own interests, and a meritocratic community as a collection of individuals bound together by a sense of mutual respect developed as a result of virtuous behavior.

"Nature Makes Us Friends":
Human Brotherhood as the Basis for Community

The first set of arguments Douglass offered as the basis for a strong sense of responsibility to others was rooted in universal human brotherhood.[5] According to this line of thinking, if all human beings are brothers and sisters, then each of us ought to feel a strong sense of obligation to every other human being. This conception of community is what I am calling fraternal. He believed that "nature makes us friends." His autobiographical writings provide several examples of what he interpreted as the exhibition of the feeling of "natural love in our fellow creatures."[6] In Douglass's second autobiography, *My Bondage and My Freedom*, for example, he pointed to evidence for natural human goodness by drawing on his experiences with children. When he was a young boy, he refined his reading skills by bribing his white playmates with bread. During these sessions, he liked to discuss slavery with the white children. "I wish I could be free, as you will be when you get to be men," Douglass would say. He described the scenes that followed.

Words like these, I observed, always troubled them; and I had no small satisfaction in wringing from the boys, occasionally, that fresh and bitter condemnation of slavery, that springs from nature, unseared [sic] and unperverted [sic]. Of all consciences, let me have those to deal with which have not been bewildered by the cares of life. I do not remember ever to have met with a *boy*, while I was in slavery, who defended the slave system; but I have often had boys to console me, with the hope that something would yet occur, by which I might be made free.[7]

Children provided Douglass with an image of human nature uncorrupted. The fact that the children he encountered had a natural abhorrence of slavery was evidence to him that human beings are endowed with a natural affection for others. Douglass's arguments from human brotherhood can be seen as an attempt to remind people of the innocence of their youth, before they began accepting the arbitrary distinctions that provide the basis for unjust social hierarchies.

Although children are the most likely to embody natural affection, adults are able to exhibit this tendency as well. When Douglass was about ten years old, he was sent to live with Thomas and Sophia Auld in Baltimore. Sophia Auld, who had not been a slaveholder prior to Douglass's arrival, seemed to him to be the embodiment of innate human goodness: "She was, naturally, of an excellent disposition, kind, gentle, and cheerful."[8] Although Mrs. Auld was eventually corrupted by "the natural influence of slavery customs," her initial reaction to Douglass's arrival was one of "natural sweetness." "At first," Douglass wrote, "Mrs. Auld regarded me simply as a child, like any other child; she had not come to regard me as *property*."[9] Auld's natural affection for Douglass led her to treat him much like one of her own children. She fed him well, treated him with respect, and even began teaching him to read before her husband forbade her from doing so. Although Douglass claims Sophia Auld ended up *becoming* cold and bitter toward him, his initial experience with her contributed to his view that human beings have a natural tendency toward goodness.

Douglass also thought natural human goodness was shown by our tendency to shudder at the sight or thought of physical violence. He described this view in a speech entitled "Did John Brown Fail?" that he delivered at Harper's Ferry, West Virginia. In the speech, which was delivered in 1881, Douglass offered his reflections on what lessons could be drawn from Brown's raid on Harper's Ferry. In this passage, we see him discuss the idea of natural human sympathy.

Every feeling of the human heart was naturally outraged at [the raid on Harper's Ferry], and hence at the moment the air was full of denunciation and execration. So intense was this feeling that few ventured to whisper a word of apology. . . . Let no word be said against this holy feeling; more than to law and government are we indebted to this tender sentiment of regard for human life for the safety with which we walk the streets by day and sleep secure in our beds at night. It is nature's grand police, vigilant and faithful, *sentineled* [sic] in the soul, guarding against violence to peace and life.[10]

Douglass made a similar argument in 1854 in an essay entitled "The Right to Kill a Kidnapper," written after a mob killed a man who was attempting to capture a runaway slave:

The shedding of human blood at first sight, and without explanation is, and must ever be, regarded with horror; and he who takes pleasure in human slaughter is very properly looked upon as a moral monster. . . . These tender feelings so susceptible to pain, are most wisely designed by the Creator, for the preservation of life. They are, especially, the affirmation of God, speaking through nature, and asserting man's right to live.[11]

Rather than offering a dark picture of human beings as naturally depraved, wolflike creatures that enjoy doing violence to one another, Douglass argued that affection for human life is a part of our nature.

Douglass offered both divine and secular versions of the argument from human brotherhood. Sometimes, he emphasized the idea of Divine Fatherhood. Emancipation, he argued in an 1857 commemoration of emancipation in the West Indies, ought to be motivated by "the pure, single-eyed spirit of benevolence" rooted in "the heavenly teachings of Christianity, which everywhere teaches that God is our Father, and man, however degraded, is our brother."[12] At other times, his arguments were more secular in character. In 1894, as he reflected on his career as a humanitarian reformer, he described his motivation in this way: "In the essential dignity of man as man, I find all necessary incentives and aspirations to a useful and noble life. Manhood is broad enough, and high enough as a platform for you and me and all of us."[13] Human brotherhood was, for Douglass, a powerful moral idea. Whether one believes that all human beings are children of God or that all men are dignified by virtue of their humanity, the appeal to human brotherhood is one possible basis for a strong notion of responsibility to others.

Douglass usually discussed the idea of human brotherhood in connection with the abolitionist movement. Abolitionists were moved by two fundamental beliefs: the inviolability of the right to self-ownership and the universal brotherhood of humanity. He believed the idea of human brotherhood was enough to move morally good men to feel a sense of responsibility to others. "Every well-formed man," Douglass said, "finds no rest to his soul while any portion of his species suffers from a recognized evil."[14] True humanity, he argued, consists "in a disposition of the heart" to remedy such evils "as they unfold." True virtue, he continued, "should prompt men to charitable exertions in correcting abuses."[15] If only the rest of the nation would follow their hearts, Douglass thought, slavery would fall.

Our Civic Catechism: The Creedal Case for Mutual Responsibility

Douglass called the Declaration of Independence our "civic catechism."[16] The fundamental commitment of the Declaration, as he read it, was to universal natural rights. Douglass appealed to this foundational commitment of natural rights as a basis for a stronger sense of obligation to others. According to this argument, one's feeling of obligation is rooted less in a sense of connection with others than it is in a devotion to principles of political morality. Political scientist Samuel Huntington calls this rationale for community "creedal" in the sense that it is rooted in devotion to a common set of ideas.[17] In making the case for abolition and equal citizenship, Douglass often appealed to the creed expressed in the Declaration of Independence as the basis for linking individuals together. Even if you do not love your neighbor, he argued, your belief in the American Creed expressed in the Declaration should move you to care if his rights are violated.

Douglass's understanding of the power of the creedal basis for community was rooted in his reflections on the impact the creed of "slaveocracy" had on Southern life. He argued that slavery was able to persist in the South because it begot "a character in the whole network of society surrounding it, favorable to its continuance." The "friends of slavery," he said, "are bound by the necessity of their system to do just what the history of the country shows they have done—that is, to seek to subvert all liberty, and to pervert all the safeguards of human rights."[18] The friends of freedom, Douglass argued, ought to learn a lesson from the friends of slavery. In order to achieve and maintain a political ideal, a moral ecology supportive of its existence must be developed. This moral ecology "shapes" individuals in a way that promotes the ideal of universal freedom.

Just as the friends of slavery acted in ways consistent with their devotion to the idea of slavery, the friends of freedom, Douglass contended, should draw on their devotion to freedom as the basis for political action. One of the best examples of Douglass utilizing this line of argument can be found in a speech he delivered in the midst of the Civil War. In the speech "Fighting the Rebels with One Hand," which he delivered in Philadelphia in 1862, he described the power and importance of devotion to common principles:

> In order to have union, either in the family, in the church, or in the State, there must be unity of idea and sentiment in all essential interests. Find a man's treasure, and you have found his heart. Now, in the North, freedom is the grand and all-comprehensive condition of comfort, prosperity, and happiness. All our ideas and sentiments grow out of this free element. Free speech, free soil, free men, free schools, free inquiry, free suffrage, equality before the law, are the natural outgrowths of freedom. Freedom is the center of our Northern social system. It warms life into every other interest, and makes it beautiful in our eyes. Liberty is our treasure, and our hearts dwell with it, and receive its actuating motives from it.[19]

Douglass's hope was that men could be so devoted to freedom—the value he identified as the center of the Northern social system—that they would be moved to action on behalf of their neighbors.

To a liberal mind, this may seem like a decidedly more promising rationale for mutual responsibility than human brotherhood. Whereas language like fraternity and community often seems to be rooted in irrational or emotional interpersonal affection, connection based on commitment to a creed appeals to our reason.[20] According to this argument, I express concern when my neighbor is deprived of his liberty not because I love him as a brother, but because I am deeply committed to personal freedom as an ideal of political morality. This may seem like a more reasonable foundation for community and it seems better suited to a pluralistic society, where inclusive bases for interpersonal affection are hard to find.

But is the conversion of minds to the idea of freedom possible? Douglass thought so. He argued that the rational faculty enabled human beings to understand the truth of the natural rights philosophy at the foundation of liberalism. According to his view, these truths are "easily rendered appreciable to the faculty of reason in man."[21] He contended that the "human mind is so constructed . . . that, when left free from the blinding and hardening power of selfishness, it bows reverently to the mandates of truth and justice."[22] This belief provided Douglass with some hope that a just social order could be achieved *if* "free discussion" was allowed. He expressed this view in a speech on the Emancipation Proclamation, delivered in New York City in February 1863:

> [L]ittle hope would there be for this world covered with error as with a cloud of thick darkness, and studded with all abounding injustice, wrong, oppression, intemperance, and monopolies, bigotry, superstition, King-craft, priest-craft, pride of race, prejudice of color, chattel-slavery—the grand sum of all human woes and villainies—if there were not in man, deep down, and it may be very deep down, in his soul or in the truth itself, an elective power, or an attractive force, call it by what name you will, which makes truth in her simple beauty and excellence, ever preferred to the grim and ghastly powers of error.[23]

Douglass seemed to think there is something mysterious about the human attraction to truth. Whatever the source of this attraction, he believed that something in the human constitution was drawn to it. If human beings realize the moral rightness of universal freedom, Douglass hoped, they might feel a sense of connection with and responsibility to those deprived of it.

Particularly in the 1850s, Douglass expressed some hope that appeals to principles of political morality might move American citizens to challenge slavery. His emphasis on the creedal line of argument manifested itself politically in his shift from the Garrisonian focus on moral suasion to the political abolitionist case for state action to abolish slavery. In the late 1840s, Douglass rejected the Garrisonian reading of the Constitution as proslavery and in 1851 he announced his conversion to the antislavery reading developed by Lysander Spooner, Gerrit Smith, and William Goodell.[24] The question of whether Douglass converted to antislavery constitutionalism on the basis of principle or pragmatism is beyond my scope here.[25] What is important for my purposes is the way in which the conversion impacted his case for a robust sense of responsibility to others. When he announced his conversion in *The North Star*, Douglass wrote that he now believed it was "the first duty of every American citizen, whose conscience permits him to do so, to use his political as well as his moral power for [slavery's] overthrow."[26] The basis of this "first duty," Douglass could now argue, was devotion to the Declaration of Independence and the Constitution—the two basic expressions of American political morality.

"The Sheet Anchor of Common Safety":
Self-Interest as a Basis for Community

Douglass's third argument for a strong sense of community appeals to an essential part of human nature, "the spirit of selfishness." Individuals might be moved to feel a greater sense of responsibility to one another, he thought, by appealing to their self-interest. Douglass argued that a stronger sense of mutual obligation would *benefit* everyone. The prevalence of a more robust sense of obligation to others, he reasoned, makes all our rights more secure and makes our communities more hospitable to economic, intellectual, and moral progress. In this section, I examine Douglass's appeal to what Alexis de Tocqueville called "self-interest well understood."[27]

Negative and positive dimensions of self-interest were appealed to in order to motivate free people to feel a stronger sense of responsibility to slaves. Abolitionists appealed to the fear of Northerners by warning of a "slavehold-ers' conspiracy"—a plot by Southerners to extend slavery over as much of the nation as possible.[28] This conspiracy was a threat to free Northerners not because they were likely to be enslaved but because these conspirators would be willing to trample on the rights of all Americans in order to accomplish their nefarious aims. In an essay entitled "The Ballot and the Bullet," published in 1859, Douglass warned that "white men's liberties" would not survive unless slavery was abolished.[29] The slave power, he argued, wanted to extend the institution into the territories so it could dominate the federal government. Once the slave power dominated the federal government it would subordinate Northern values and interests. Douglass's warnings about the "slaveholders' conspiracy" and "the slave power" are examples of appealing to the self-interest of his Northern audience in order to get them to feel a stronger sense of obligation to abolish slavery.

In addition to appealing to Northern fears about the secret machinations of the slave power, Douglass appealed to self-interest by making arguments that everyone *benefits* from stronger bonds of community. This is a sort of "we are all in the same boat" argument for stronger bonds of community. Douglass often defended the principle "each for all and all for each" by appealing to self-interest: "The principle involved [in the struggle for equal rights] is one for which every man ought to contest. It involves the right to life, liberty, and the pursuit of happiness, and it is the business of every American citizen, white and black, to stand for this principle, each for all, and all for each, as the sheet anchor of common safety."[30] It is *my* business to stand up for the rights of others, Douglass argued, because *my* willingness to do so would strengthen the "sheet anchor" that protects *my* rights.

In addition to the debate over slavery, Douglass extended the self-interest argument to the issue of universal suffrage. "Public opinion," he wrote in 1856, "is changing on this issue." Americans are "starting to see that to deprive one class of citizens of their rights jeopardizes the rights of all citizens, and that if acquiesced in will lead to political domination by a small oligarchy."[31] Douglass's argument abandons appeals to universal human rights or to devotion to the Founding idea of legitimate government being rooted in the consent of the people and goes directly to the self-interest of his reader. If I fail to stand up for universal suffrage, my rights will eventually be threatened by oligarchs.

Douglass extended the self-interest argument to economic matters. In 1889, as former slaves were still being systematically discriminated against in the South, he delivered a speech on the so-called "Negro Problem." He hoped that Northerners would intervene once again on behalf of Southern blacks: "There is yet good reason to believe in the virtue of the loyal American people. They hate fraud, loathe rapine, and despise meanness."[32] He expressed less faith in the virtue of Southerners, but there was still some basis for hope that they would begin to behave in responsible ways. A great moral revolution would not take place overnight but perhaps, Douglass thought, the selfish side of human nature might move them to alter their treatment of blacks.

> There is still another ground of hope for the freemen of the southern states. It is that the good citizens of these states cannot afford, and will not consent, to lag far behind the old free states in all the elements of civilization. They want population, capital, invention, and enterprise. They have rich resources to be developed, and they want both men and money to develop them and enhance their prosperity. The wise and loyal people in these states know very well that they can never be prosperous; that they can never have their share of immigration at home or abroad, while they are known and distinguished for intolerance, fraud, violence, and lynch law. . . . Thus the self-interest of the people of these states will yet teach them justice, humanity, and civilization.[33]

Twenty years after the conclusion of the Civil War, Douglass had little hope that Southern culture would be reformed on the basis of humanitarianism or a rediscovery of the principles of the Declaration of Independence. Instead, he thought, the best hope for former slaves was an appeal to the self-interest of their white oppressors.

In this section, I have suggested that, perhaps paradoxically, Douglass thought self-interest might be appealed to in making a case for a stronger sense of responsibility to others. One dimension was to appeal to the self-interest of Northerners by warning about the rise of the "slave power," which sought to extend its dominion throughout the Union. The second dimension of the self-interest argument was more positive: stronger bonds of community will benefit all of us in both political and economic terms. Politically, the prevalence of a strong sense of mutual responsibility will benefit all of us because it will strengthen "the sheet anchor of common safety," which protects all our rights. Economically, responsible behavior will establish conditions that are more hospitable to development and prosperity. In his role as a reformer-statesman, Douglass attempted to convince his fellow Americans that it was in their interest to concern themselves with the well-being of slaves and other marginalized individuals. Prevalence of a strong sense of duty to others, he insisted, was in each individual's interest.

A critic may worry that Douglass's appeal to self-interest suffers from serious shortcomings. Although it is difficult to gauge the effectiveness of Douglass's appeal to self-interest, difficulties arise when we consider this strategy in hindsight. Most importantly, the reliance on white self-interest seems to be a rather precarious foundation for black elevation. The appeal to self-interest is essentially contingent. If you believe that your interests are served by feeling a stronger sense of concern for your neighbor, then you ought to behave in a morally responsible way. If not, your neighbor is out of luck. Furthermore, the idea of appealing to white interests, one might argue, perpetuates the existence of a hierarchical and unjust social structure.

Although this is a potent critique of Douglass's appeal to self-interest, I think it would be a mistake to conclude that such appeals were unwise. It is important to remember the context within which Douglass offered these arguments. Before and after the Civil War, he lamented the fact that the vast majority of Americans were unmoved by appeals to reason and morality. As a statesman with concrete and urgent political goals, Douglass could not afford to stand by and wish that he was operating in a more humanitarian political culture. We may look back at the appeal to self-interest and see it as an inherently problematic strategy, but it is certainly an understandable one, given the context in which Douglass operated.

Earned Sympathy: Proving Oneself Worthy of Concern and Respect

So far, I have described three of Douglass's arguments for a stronger sense of community: sympathy based on human brotherhood, commitment to the idea of natural rights, and self-interest properly understood. The final category of argument is what I am calling earned, or merit-based, sympathy— sympathy that arises in response to the virtuous action of others. Even if I do not believe you are entitled to concern and respect as my brother or because of my devotion to a creed, I may come to believe you have *earned* my concern and respect.

It may seem strange to include Douglass's discussion of how individuals can earn the respect of others in the context of an exploration of the arguments he offered to build up the bonds of community. What, a critic may ask, does Douglass's encouragement of virtuous behavior have to do with the problem of cultivating a robust sense of duty to others? It is my contention that this discussion is appropriate here because Douglass thought that what marginalized groups do for themselves was crucial to the quest for inclusion. Douglass always had two audiences. First, he was speaking to those in positions of power—the white population and their elected representatives. His hope was that he could convince them to feel a sense of moral duty to slaves and other marginalized groups that was strong enough to move them to take action. As I demonstrated above, he did this by appealing to feelings of human brotherhood, commitment to the idea of natural rights, and to self-interest properly understood. Douglass's second audience was composed of those at the margins of, or excluded from, American citizenship: the free black population, women and, to the extent he could reach them, the enslaved population. Understanding his message to these outsiders is crucial to my task here because Douglass believed their behavior was essential to the cultivation of stronger bonds of community. By demonstrating himself to be virtuous, Douglass hoped, the outsider could enhance his self-respect and earn the sympathy of those in power and inspire them to take action to include him in the political community.

Douglass's belief that individual behavior could impact self-respect and shape the attitudes and proclivities of others was rooted deep in his own experience. His famous fight with Edward Covey, a man "who enjoyed the execrated reputation, of being a first rate hand at breaking young negroes," served as the foundation for this view.[34] As a young slave, Douglass began to exhibit "character" and "conduct" that was troubling to his master, Thomas Auld. In order to correct this, Auld sent Douglass to live with Covey, a man who was charged with the task of breaking the wills of "difficult" slaves. Douglass endured several beatings at the hands of Covey before he famously "resolved to fight" back. Douglass claimed that the next time Covey attacked him, they engaged in an epic battle, Douglass prevailed, and Covey never set a finger on him again.

In Douglass's first autobiography, *Narrative of the Life of Frederick Douglass, An American Slave*, published in 1845, he concluded his description of the fight with Covey with these words:

> This battle with Mr. Covey was the turning-point in my career as a slave. It rekindled the few expiring embers of freedom, and revived within me a sense of my own manhood. It recalled the departed self-confidence, and inspired me again with a determination to be free. The gratification afforded by the triumph was a full compensation for whatever else might follow, even death itself. He only can understand the deep satisfaction which I experienced, who has himself repelled by force the bloody arm of slavery. I felt as I never felt before. It was a glorious resurrection, from the tomb of slavery, to the heaven of freedom. My long-crushed spirit rose, cowardice departed, bold defiance took its place; and I now resolved that, however long I might remain a slave in form, the day had passed forever when I could be a slave in fact. I did not hesitate to let it be known of me, that the white man who expected to succeed in whipping me, must also succeed in killing me.[35]

Ten years later, in his second autobiography *My Bondage and My Freedom*, Douglass added to his account of the fight with Covey in ways that are significant for the argument I am making here: "I was *nothing* before; I WAS A MAN NOW. . . . A man, without force, is without the essential dignity of humanity. Human nature is so constituted, that it cannot *honor* a helpless man, although it can *pity* him; and even this it cannot do long, if the signs of power do not arise."[36]

Although it would not be fair to say that Douglass's courageous behavior earned him the *respect* of Covey (or any identifiable third party), he drew some important lessons from the episode. After a particularly savage beating at the hands of the slave-breaker, Douglass went to his master, Thomas Auld, "humbly to invoke the interposition of his power and authority, to protect me from further abuse and violence." Douglass hoped that Auld might be moved to intervene by "motives of humanity" or even "selfish" concerns about abuse to his property. According to Douglass, Auld responded by "finding excuses for Covey, and ending with a full justification of him, and a passionate condemnation of me."[37] The appeal to Auld's humanity and reason failed to liberate Douglass from Covey's lash, so he was moved to action. Douglass's heroic fight with Covey enlivened in him a sense of self-respect that he described as a "resurrection." Through courageous action, he proved to himself that he was worthy of respect. It is clear that the lines added to Douglass's account in *My Bondage and My Freedom* are intended to endow his existential transformation with broader moral and political significance. Although he had once expressed hope that slavery could be abolished by appealing to reason and humanitarian sentiments, he was now prepared to say that the recognition of human dignity may require something more. The fight with Covey taught Douglass that when reason and morality fail to bring about change, action may be necessary. Although it is probably too much to say that Douglass's action earned him the respect of Covey, it is clear that his respect for himself grew and Covey's changed attitude led Douglass to reach important conclusions about human nature.[38]

In the important 1860 essay, "The Prospect in the Future," Douglass's strategy of encouraging individuals to *earn* concern and respect is evident. He began the essay by acknowledging that abolitionists had "reached a point of weary hopelessness." Douglass had once believed that enlightenment would bring about emancipation, but he now recognized that this was not to be. The American people acknowledge the "horrid truths" of slavery, "but they are not moved to action."

> An able advocate of human rights gratifies their intellectual tastes, pleases their imaginations, titillates their sensibilities into a momentary sensation, but does not move them from the downy seat of inaction. They are familiar with every note in the scale of abstract rights, from the Declaration of Independence to the orations of Charles Sumner, but seem to regard the whole as a grand operatic performance, of which they are mere spectators. You cannot relate a new fact, or frame an unfamiliar argument on this subject. —Reason and morality have emptied their casket of richest jewels into the lap of this cause, in vain.[39]

Douglass's loss of faith in reason and morality is striking, but not surprising. The 1850s were difficult for abolitionists. The congressional compromises, the *Dred Scott* decision, and the execution of John Brown were, for abolitionists like Douglass, indications that most Americans were not sufficiently moved by appeals to human brotherhood or the "civic catechism of the Declaration of Independence" to do the right thing. The big question was why: "What is the explanation for this terrible paradox of passing history?"[40]

Douglass said the problem was not that the American people "fail to appreciate the value of liberty." History, he wrote, demonstrates that they "have shown great courage and patriotism in defending *their own freedom*, but have utterly failed in the magnanimity and philanthropy necessary to prompt respect for the rights of another and a weaker race." It is not, he continued, "because we fail to appreciate or lack the courage to defend our own rights that we permit the existence of slavery among us, but it is because our patriotism is intensely selfish, our courage lacks generosity, and our love of liberty is circumscribed by our narrow and wicked selfhood, that we quietly permit a few tyrants to crush a weak people in our midst."[41] Douglass declared that our national character was based on the selfish philosophy of Cain. We, as a nation, look at the plight of the slave and ask, "Am I my brother's keeper?"[42]

Where in the midst of such a moral abyss could the slave turn? "The motive power which shall liberate the slave," Douglass wrote, "must be looked for in slavery itself—must be generated in the bosom of the bondman. Outside philanthropy never disenthralled any people."[43] He said that while "our" philanthropy, sense of justice, religion, and politics have all failed to motivate action, "there is a latent element in our national character which, if fairly called into action, will sweep anything down in its course. The American people admire courage displayed in defense of liberty, and will catch the flame of sympathy from the sparks of its heroic fire."[44] Unlike sympathy rooted in the simple fact of shared humanity, sympathy based on merit depends upon action.[45] Throughout the 1850s Douglass had doubted the practical wisdom of slave revolts, but by late 1860 his state of "weary hopelessness" led him to conclude that "the mere animal instincts and sympathies of [the American] people will do more for [American slaves] than has been accomplished by a quarter of a century of oratorical philanthropy."[46] Douglass concluded the essay by expressing regret that we had reached this point, but he offered some hope that once slavery was abolished and the moral ecology of American society was changed, a more humane politics might emerge.

> We can never cease to regret that an appeal to the higher and better elements of human nature is, in this case, so barren of fitting response. But so it is, and until this people have passed through several generations of humanitarian culture, so it will be. In the meantime the slave must con-

tinue to suffer or rebel, and did they know their strength they would not await the tardy growth of our American sense of justice.[47]

Douglass's essay on "The Prospect in the Future" demonstrates that he believed an exhibition of courage might foster self-respect and the respect of others. Through action, those excluded from the promise of freedom could undermine the notion that they were content with their condition and hence gain the respect of others. We must, Douglass declared, "struggle and make sacrifices for our rights," because "next to the dignity of being a freeman, is the dignity of striving to be free."[48] If one's dignity is not acknowledged on the basis of human brotherhood or a commitment to freedom or self-interest, perhaps it might be acknowledged in response to courageous action in pursuit of liberty.

During the Civil War, Douglass relied on a similar argument as one of reasons for black enlistment.[49] In the March 1863 issue of the *Douglass Monthly*, he penned an essay entitled "Men of Color to Arms" in which he made the case that free blacks ought to enlist in the Union army. During this time period, Douglass also joined several other black leaders in a journey to upstate New York where they attempted to persuade young black men to enlist.[50] Your enlistment, he told his audiences, may give others reason to respect you as a human being and fellow citizen.[51] For one thing, Douglass told the young men, enlistment would serve to combat the notion that the enslaved condition of blacks was due to a "lack of manly courage." By enlisting and "nobly defending" their liberties, he hoped, black men could "disprove the slander."[52] In addition to challenging the notion that they are naturally a "servile class," Douglass believed black enlistment could encourage whites to accept the idea of equal citizenship: "By enlisting in the service of your country at this trial hour . . . you stop the mouths of traducers and win applause from the iron lips of ingratitude. Enlist and you make this your country in common with all other men born in the country or out of it." Finally, in a spirit reminiscent of his reflections on the fight with Covey, Douglass encouraged his listeners to enlist in order to enhance their own self-respect.

Enlist for your own sake. Decried and derided as you have been and still are, you need an act of this kind by which to recover your own self-respect. You have to some extent rated your value by the estimate of your enemies and hence have counted yourself less than you are. You owe it to yourself and your race to rise from your social debasement and take your place among the soldiers of your country, a man among men. Depend upon it, the subjective effect of this one act of enlisting will be immense and highly beneficial. You will stand more erect, walk more assured, feel more at ease, and be less liable to insult than you ever were before. He who fights the battles of America may claim America as his country—and have that claim respected. Thus in defending your country now against rebels and traitors you are defending your own liberty, honor, manhood and self-respect.[53]

Douglass's rhetoric on black enlistment provides ample evidence that he believed in what I am calling earned, or merit-based, sympathy. First, Douglass connected "manly courage" with "fitness" for freedom. By taking action in defense of the Union, black men could demonstrate themselves to be worthy of the respect of others. Second, Douglass made the related point that service to the country would entitle black men to "all the rights of citizenship" enjoyed by other Americans. Just as the display of manly courage should demonstrate that black men are not fit for slavery, so it should demonstrate that they are fit for equal citizenship. Third, Douglass connected enlistment with self-respect. Just as he identified his fight with Covey as a moment of existential transformation that made him worthy of honor and respect, Douglass hoped that the black man could become "a man among men" by fighting for his rights.

Courage is not the only virtue Douglass thought could lead to a greater sense of concern and respect. Throughout his writings, he emphasized the importance of striving to be self-reliant for self-respect and the respect of others. Before and after the Civil War, he traveled widely and lectured black audiences on the importance of behaving virtuously in order to demonstrate that slavery and other forms of subordination were unjust. In an 1854 speech to free blacks who had settled in Canada, Douglass said:

The world says the black man is unfit to live in a mixed society—to enjoy, and rightly appreciate the blessings of independence—that he must have a master, to govern him, and the lash to stimulate him to labor. Let us be prepared to afford, in our lives and conversation, an example of how grievously we are wronged by such a prevailing opinion of our race. Let us prove, by facts, not by theory, that independence belongs to our nature, in common with all mankind, that we have intelligence to use it rightly, when acquired, and capabilities to ascend to the loftiest elevations of the human mind. Let such examples be given in the mental cultivation, and moral regeneration of our children, as they increase in knowledge, in virtue and in every ennobling principle in man's nature.[54]

In an 1853 editorial entitled "Learn Trades or Starve!" Douglass put this point in even starker terms: "Men are not valued in this country, or any country, for what they *are*; they are valued for what they can *do*. It is in vain that we talk about being men, if we do not the work of men. We must show that we can *do* as well as *be*. . . . Society is a hard-hearted affair."[55] Statements like these are further indications that Douglass believed the concern and respect of one's fellows does not always follow from the dictates of reason or morality. Sometimes this concern and respect must be earned through virtuous action. Douglass believed this to be an essential part of the quest for full citizenship and assimilation into American society. In 1854, he said the American people "can pity us as they can sympathize with us. But we need something more than sympathy—something more than pity. *We must be respected*. And we cannot be respected unless we are either independent or aiming to be."[56]

The importance of what we *do*, as opposed to what we are, as a part of Douglass's understanding of community is also evident in his decidedly unsentimental understanding of friendship. In 1854, Douglass delivered an address to the Odd Fellows Festival in Rochester, New York. The Odd Fellows are a fraternal organization and the Festival was held to collect funds for indigent blacks.[57] The Odd Fellows called themselves "United Friends," so Douglass took the occasion to speak to the group about the subject of friendship. "The central idea of friendship," Douglass said, "and the main pillar of it is '*trust*.' Where there is no *trust*, there is no friendship. We cannot love those whom we cannot trust. The basis of all *trust* is truth. There can be no trust—lasting trust—where truth is not. Men must be true to each other, or they cannot trust each other."[58] An alternative explanation, he said, is that love forms the basis of friendship. Douglass rejected this idea and says that love "simply crowns and glorifies a friendship already established on the basis of 'TRUTH and TRUST.'" Furthermore, love is not the basis for the "perpetuation" of a friendship already established. A friendship is perpetuated, Douglass said, when men are "true to each other." "Do all that you promise to do," he instructed, "and as much more as you can." This is "of vital importance," because no society "can hang together without" friendship.[59]

Douglass's trust-based account of friendship is relevant to the idea of earned sympathy being explored in this section. His claim that no society can hang together without friendship is an indication that he believed in the importance of "civic friendship." Civic friendship, which was introduced into the Western tradition by Aristotle and is part of many contemporary communitarian theories, is said to exist when individuals within a polity feel a sense of mutual affection, concern, respect, and trust with their fellow citizens. Rather than relying on mutual affection as the basis of friendship, Douglass relied on mutual trust, which is developed on the basis of action: *Do all you promise to do and as much more as you can.* Rather than appealing to common humanity or mutual love, Douglass urged us to prove ourselves worthy of friendship, civic or otherwise, by *acting* in ways that will earn the respect and trust of others.

Douglass's strategy of appealing to blacks to behave virtuously and appealing to whites to feel a greater sense of sympathy in response to this virtuous behavior is not without its difficulties. As Douglass himself would come to acknowledge later, virtuous behavior and individual success often intensified racism in the South. Blacks who were considered too bold and enterprising were often targets of white anger and violence. These blacks, the oppressors claimed, did not "know their place" and had to be taught to respect traditional hierarchies. Given this atmosphere, Douglass's insistence that blacks act courageously and attempt to achieve independence may have been an invitation to further alienation and subordination, not greater concern and respect.

Once again, we may be tempted to use our hindsight to condemn Douglass's strategy. Given what Douglass knew about the evil in human nature, a critic might say, he should not have been so naïve. But we must keep in mind what options were available to him. Douglass's earned sympathy arguments were aimed at those moderates who were not completely determined in their opposition to equal rights. His hope was that those who were unable to reason or moralize their way out of a selfish understanding of justice might be moved by "mere animal instincts" to feel sympathy for victims of injustice who behaved in virtuous ways.

Conclusion: The Moral Ecology of Liberal Community

Douglass's experiences as a slave and as a reformer taught him that freedom is not a given; it is an ideal that must be fought for and defended. We are better off if we do not have to engage in this fight alone. It is for this reason that Douglass confronted the challenge of liberal community in the ways I have described in this chapter. One may wonder if Douglass's appeal to fraternal, creedal, self-interested, and respect-based reasons for caring about others constitutes a coherent response to this challenge. After all, can it be the case that all of these are legitimate reasons for feeling a strong sense of obligation to other human beings? In short, I think Douglass's answer to this question is yes. As noted in the Introduction, he believed natural equality *should be* a sufficient reason to care about the well-being of others, but alas, for many people it is not. It is therefore the task of conscientious statesmen and citizens to appeal to the plurality of reasons that might move human beings to act in more responsible ways.

Douglass's concern with the challenge of liberal community led him to reflect extensively on what contemporary scholars call moral ecology—the idea that human beings can be influenced by the moral atmosphere that prevails around them. The task of achieving and securing liberty, he believed, requires the creation and maintenance of a moral ecology that promotes respect for rights and motivates virtue. In this conclusion, I offer some thoughts about the meaning and importance of moral ecology in Douglass's thought and in the next two chapters I explore how Douglass believed a moral ecology supportive of liberty could be cultivated from the bottom up by individuals and from the top down by principled statesmen.

Douglass's concern for moral ecology was rooted in his belief that there is a constant struggle within human nature between humanity and selfishness. In order to achieve and maintain liberty, he argued, men must act in responsible ways.

> Men have their choice in this world. They can be angels, or they can be demons. In the apocalyptic vision, John describes a war in heaven. You have only to strip that vision of its gorgeous Oriental drapery, divest it of its shining and celestial ornaments, clothe it in the simple and familiar language of common sense, and you will have before you the eternal conflict between right and wrong, good and evil, liberty and slavery, truth and falsehood, the glorious light of love, and the appalling darkness of human selfishness and sin. The human heart is a constant seat of war. . . . Just what takes place in individual human hearts, often takes place between nations, and between individuals of the same nation. Such is the struggle now going on in the United States.[60]

Douglass's appreciation for the importance of moral ecology was rooted in observations of the institution of slavery, which shaped the individuals around it in the direction of selfishness. The moral ecology of the antebellum South, he observed, moved individuals in the direction of selfishness.

> Slavery in the United States was but a small thing seventy years ago, but going onward it has gained strength, till now it threatens wholesale destruction to everything connected with it. It may be seen corrod-

ing their vitals, their morals, and their politics, and linking itself with the very best institutions of America. It destroys all the finer feelings of our nature—it renders people less humane—leads them to regard cruelty with indifference, as the boy born and bred within the sound of the thundering roar of Niagara, feels nothing strange because he is used to the noise; while a stranger trembles with awe, and feels he is in the presence of God—in the midst of his mighty works. People reared in the midst of slavery become indifferent to human wrongs, indifferent to the entreaties, the tears, the agonies of the slave under the lash; all of which appear to be music to the ears of slaveholders. Slavery has weakened the love of freedom in the United States—they have lost much of that regard for liberty which once characterized them. It has eaten out the vitals from the hearts of Americans.[61]

Douglass contended that the moral ecology of slavery molded individuals in ways that were adverse to freedom and in direct opposition to strong feelings of mutual responsibility. Slavery teaches people that the rights of some individuals need not be respected, that those who stand up for the rights of others are to be regarded as enemies of the community, and only some individuals ought to be treated fairly. Douglass's assessment of the impact of slavery on individuals who lived in its presence led him to believe that institutions "educated" people to "look upon" and treat their fellows in particular ways. Just as the moral ecology of slavery had "taught" people to behave in vicious ways that undermined liberal ideals, so too might a moral ecology of freedom teach people to behave in ways supportive of these aims.[62]

Before the Civil War, Douglass focused on altering the moral ecology in a way that was conducive to reform because his first task was to close the gap between the ideals of the Declaration of Independence and the realities of American life. After the war, Douglass turned his attention to the problem of securing newly attained liberty and offering arguments about what was necessary for the freedmen to flourish. He viewed the task of achieving and maintaining freedom as an ongoing and difficult *moral* project. In the midst of the Civil War, he wrote:

> The arduous task of the future will be to make the Southern people see and appreciate Republican Government, as a blessing of inestimable value, and to be maintained at any and every cost. They have got to be taught that slavery which they have valued as a blessing has ever been their direct calamity and curse. The work before us is nothing less than a radical revo-

lution in the modes of thought which have flourished under the blighting slave system. The idea that labor is an evil, that work is degrading and that idleness is respectable, must be dispelled and the idea that work is honorable must take its place. Above all they must be taught that the liberty of a part is never to be secured by the enslavement or oppression of any. . . . Time, experience, and culture must gradually bring society back to the normal condition from which long years of slavery have carried away under its iron sway.[63]

Douglass believed that the achievement and security of freedom has an important moral dimension. He thought the transformation of moral ecology was necessary not only for the oppressors but also for the oppressed. When Martin Delany, a black abolitionist, Union soldier, and trial justice in postwar South Carolina wrote to Douglass to complain of "the changed manners of the colored people of South Carolina," Douglass responded by urging Delany to be patient. Moral transformation takes time: "If there be this offensive insolence in the manners of the colored people of South Carolina of which you complain—the result of sudden elevation—time and enlightenment will surely correct the evil. Liberty has its manners as well as slavery, and with those manners true self-respect goes hand in hand with a just respect for the rights and feelings of others. Have patience, my old friend."[64]

Douglass thought that each of the foundations for a stronger sense of community described above was affected by moral ecology. First, although a sense of human brotherhood and mutual affection is natural, it can be destroyed by a "moral atmosphere" that "renders people less humane."[65] Just as the sense of human brotherhood can be eroded by a corrupt moral atmosphere, it is also possible that "humanitarian culture" can make individuals more responsive to "the higher and better elements of human nature."[66] Second, our devotion to freedom is affected by moral ecology. Because human beings are, at least in part, responsive to truth, he expressed the hope that men could be educated to love freedom: "The more men know of the essential nature of things, and of the true relation to mankind, the freer they are from prejudice of every kind. . . . [I]gnorance is full of prejudice, but it will disappear with enlightenment."[67] This education, Douglass thought, should take place not just through formal educational institutions, but from the day-to-day moral education that takes place through the interaction of individuals. Third, the moral atmosphere of the community affects the way individuals conceive of their self-interest. One of the difficult tasks for liberals is to establish an atmosphere in which most individuals believe it is in their interest to care about the well-being of their neighbors. Finally, Douglass believed that moral ecology impacts how we define and respond to virtuous behavior. The moral atmosphere of the community determines what virtues we admire and what sorts of character we honor.

In sum, the problem of slavery led Douglass to believe that the achievement and maintenance of liberty is a difficult and never-ending task. In order to shape responsible citizens willing to take on this task, Douglass believed it was important to be attentive to moral ecology. Throughout his writings, we see him go beyond a formalistic concern with rights and institutions to emphasize the importance of "the soul," "the moral sense," "the moral atmosphere," and the "conscience" of the American polity.[68] What remains to be seen is *how* a moral ecology supportive of liberty can be developed. It is to this matter that we now turn.

"Friends of Freedom"

*Reformers, Self-Made Men, and
the Moral Ecology of Freedom*

Introduction

Frederick Douglass's philosophy of virtue is captured in two of his most famous exhortations. First, it has been reported that in 1895, when a young man asked the seventy-seven-year-old Douglass for advice on what he ought to do with his life, he responded: "Agitate! Agitate! Agitate!"[1] Second, in a speech entitled "Self-Made Men," which he delivered more often than any other speech in his repertoire, Douglass contended: "[W]e may explain success mainly by one word and that word is WORK! WORK!! WORK!!! WORK!!!!"[2] The call to agitate captures the essence of Douglass's view that each of us has extensive obligations to take action in order to combat injustice. The call to work captures the essence of his view that although extraneous factors can be limiting or empowering, each individual has it within his power to shape his own destiny. In this chapter, we turn our attention to Douglass's philosophy of agitation and work in order to gain a better sense of how he believed individuals could act in ways that promote a moral ecology supportive of liberal aims *and* the sense of community necessary to secure those aims.

At the center of Douglass's view of how individuals ought to behave is an emphasis on personal responsibility. The morally responsible actions of individuals are of the utmost importance because of the tangible impact they have on others and the impact they have on the moral ecology of the community. The idea of moral ecology, according to sociologist Robert Bellah, entails the belief that individuals "are deeply interrelated, and the actions we take have enormous ramifications for the lives of others."[3] The link between the ideal types explored in this chapter and the idea of moral ecology was expressed by the philosopher Michael Novak when he described moral ecology as "the ethos that must be cultivated and preserved if liberal democratic societies are to survive."[4] Virtuous behavior develops this ecology from the bottom up in the sense that the beliefs and behavior of individuals helps to create and maintain the "humanitarian culture" Douglass viewed as essential to a healthy liberal polity.[5]

In order to gain a better appreciation of what virtues and behavior, in Douglass's view, are supportive of liberal aims, I focus on two "ideal types" he developed in the course of his public life: the Reformer and the Self-Made Man. Douglass's discussions of the Reformer and the Self-Made Man are expressions of his belief that there is a certain ethos that contributes to the moral health of a free society. I start with the Reformer because he engages in the crucial first task of *achieving* liberalism. The Reformer goes above and beyond the call of duty by dedicating his life to closing the gap between moral ideals and political realities. He is the model of principled engagement in the political sphere. I conclude the discussion of the Reformer with a discussion of what "ordinary" people can learn from this ideal type about principled and responsible engagement in the political sphere.

After discussing the Reformer, I turn my attention to Douglass's views of virtuous behavior in the private sphere by examining his exaltation of hard work, self-reliance, and other bourgeois virtues through the ideal type of the Self-Made Man. If the model of the Reformer provides a guide for how to achieve and maintain the political conditions supportive of freedom, one could say that the matters dealt with in the second part of the chapter deal with the sorts of behavior Douglass believed would lead to individual and communal flourishing in a free society. In short, the ideal of the Self-Made Man served as Douglass's model of personal responsibility and development. He contended that the Self-Made Man is the "best representative" of the "powers and possibilities" of human nature.[6] The Self-Made Man, in Douglass's mind, exemplified the good life that could be pursued if "simple justice" was secured for all individuals.[7] He dignifies his freedom by using it in a virtuous way in order to achieve individual, familial, and community flourishing. Using one's liberty virtuously is crucial, Douglass believed, because it demonstrates the dignity of human freedom and, at least in theory, strengthens the community's commitment to its protection.

Achieving Liberty: The Reformer as an Ideal Type

Douglass's writings are replete with references to "the Reformer." A discussion of the Reformer is an appropriate starting point for an inquiry into his understanding of how individuals ought to behave, because the Reformer engages in the crucial *first* task of "achieving liberty." In other words, the Reformer's project is to achieve liberalism: to secure the conditions necessary for all people to exercise personal freedom. Once freedom is achieved, then one can focus upon what is necessary to maintain it and for individuals to flourish under these conditions. The Reformer is the embodiment of what Douglass called "true virtue." "Every well-formed man," Douglass said, "finds no rest to his soul while any portion of his species suffers from a recognized evil."[8] True humanity, he argued, consists "in a disposition of the heart" to remedy such evils "as they unfold." True virtue, he continued, "should prompt men to charitable exertions in correcting abuses."[9] The Reformer is a model of virtuous behavior in two senses. First, his actions are valuable because they help bring about a state of affairs in which all human beings are free. Second, the Reformer's actions are valuable because he serves as an example for others, and hence has a positive impact on the moral ecology. Although he goes above and beyond what most individuals will contribute to the common good, he can teach others about the spirit that ought to animate their engagement in the political sphere. In Douglass's words, the Reformer does his work by the "power of precept and example."[10] In what follows, I provide a detailed account of Douglass's idea of the Reformer by addressing several questions. First, who is the Reformer? Second, what does the Reformer do? Third, why is the Reformer so important?

First, who is the Reformer? Douglass began his response to this question with a basic dictionary definition of reform: "to put in a new and improved condition; to bring from bad to good; to change from worse to better."[11] A reformer, then, is an individual who engages in the work of bringing society into a new and improved condition; he attempts to change it from worse to better. For Douglass, bad and good were determined by natural rights theory. He believed the fundamental requirement of natural law is that the rights of all individuals ought to be respected and protected. So Douglass's Reformer is an individual who attempts to bring society into a state of affairs in which the natural rights of all individuals are respected.

Second, what does the Reformer do? Throughout his career, Douglass offered a consistent description of the "mission" or "work" of the Reformer. He developed his most extensive analysis of the Reformer in a speech he delivered a number of times in 1855 entitled "The Antislavery Movement." Douglass wrote and delivered this speech at a crucial time in his career as a progressive agitator. Among other things, he used the speech to further distance himself from the Garrisonian sect within the antislavery movement. Of crucial importance to my argument here is the fact that central to Douglass's critique of Garrison and his followers was their rejection of political engagement as a means to bring about social change. Douglass's Reformer is not just in the business of moral sermonizing; he is a man of action. In the speech, he described the Reformer's "work" in the following way:

> The moral life of human society—it cannot die, while conscience, honor and humanity remain. If but one man be filled with it—the cause lives. Its incarnation in any one individual man leaves the whole world a priest-hood—occupying the highest moral eminence—even that of disinterested benevolence. Whoso ascended this height, and has the grace to stand there, has the world at his feet, and is the world's teacher, as of divine right. He may sit in judgment on the age, upon the civilization of the age, and upon the religion of the age; for he has a test, a sure and certain test, by which to try all institutions, and measure all men.[12]

The Reformer's "sure and certain test" is the philosophy of natural rights. Institutions and men are measured by the impact they have on the natural rights of individuals. Does the institution or individual violate natural rights? Does the institution or individual promote the security of natural rights? In other words, natural rights philosophy provides the Reformer with the critical lens through which to view his society. Social criticism is not, though, the sum of the Reformer's task. "The great work," Douglass continued, "to which he is called is not that of judgment."

> His great work on earth is to exemplify, and to illustrate and to engraft those principles upon the living and practical understandings of all men within the reach of his influence. This is his work; long or short his years, many or few his adherents, powerful or weak his instrumentalities, through good report, or through bad report, this is his work. It is to snatch from the bosom of nature the latent facts of each man's individual experi-ence, and with steady hand to hold them up fresh and glowing, enforcing, with all his power, their acknowledgement and practical adoption.[13]

The Reformer's task is to remind citizens of the moral requirements of natural law, to shed light on the gaps between those requirements and political reality, and to take action to close those gaps. Each component of this task is important.

First, the Reformer engages in the task of reminding others of the fun-damental moral truths of natural law. In the case of the United States, those commitments are most clearly stated in the Declaration of Independence.

The Reformer is a high priest of our civil religion in the sense that he is animated, first and foremost, by an orthodox devotion to the fundamental moral principles expressed in that sacred civic text.

Second, the Reformer engages in the important task of calling attention to the gaps that exist between our civic catechism and political reality. With the civic catechism of the Declaration of Independence as his basis, the Reformer points out all the ways in which the society has fallen short of its ideals. In Douglass's words, the Reformer commits himself to "blistering" the public "conscience."[14] The Reformer passes judgment on his fellows for failing to live up to their creed and scolds them for their moral and civic hypocrisy.

Third, the Reformer engages in the difficult task of *acting* to close the gap between moral ideals and political realities. The ideal type Douglass has in mind transcends the confines of social criticism into the practical world of political action. Engaging in the arduous task of acting to close the gap is, he said, the true "work" of the Reformer. Douglass's emphasis on political engagement is what he believed separated his view from Garrison's.

The uncompromising commitment to moral principle and the strong sense of responsibility exhibited by the Reformer are what separate him from others. Because of John Brown's unwavering moral conviction that every man ought to be free and his willingness to take on the responsibility of pursuing this ideal, Douglass described him as "our noblest American hero."[15] In the decades after Brown's execution, Douglass devoted a significant amount of energy to defending Brown's legacy against those who believed he was a lunatic or a fanatic. A characteristic document of Douglass's defense of Brown is a speech he delivered in Harper's Ferry, West Virginia, in 1883 entitled, "Did John Brown Fail?" In the speech, Douglass argued that like Socrates and Jesus, Brown was a man "born in advance" of his times who set out to "disturb the moral sense" of those around him by practically illustrating his undying devotion to "the sacredness and value of liberty." Douglass even reflected on the ways in which he believed Brown was morally superior to himself.

> I could live for the slave, but he could die for him. The crown of martyrdom is high, far beyond the reach of ordinary mortals, and yet happily no special greatness or superior moral excellence is necessary to discern and in some measure appreciate a truly great soul. Cold, calculating and unspiritual as most of us are, we are not wholly insensible to real greatness; and when we are brought in contact with a man of commanding mold, towering high and alone above the millions, free from all conventional fet-

ters, true to his own moral convictions, a "law unto himself," ready to suffer misconstruction, ignoring torture and death for what he believes to be right, we are compelled to do him homage.[16]

In this passage, we see that for Douglass, part of Brown's greatness was his ability to transcend the cold, calculating rationalism that animates "most of us." Brown's passionate commitment to the cause of justice allowed him to see through what Douglass called "the cobwebs" of conventional morality to the light of a higher truth. The idea of Brown as a moral trailblazer was crucial to Douglass's defense. In the midst of the Civil War, Douglass declared that in many ways the course of history had already vindicated Brown: "Good old John Brown was a madman at Harper's Ferry. Two years pass away, and the nation is as mad as he."[17] Douglass invites critics of Brown's violent means to ask themselves this question: was the Civil War a just war? If our answer to that question is yes, as Douglass believes it should be, then we might be less ready to condemn Brown's tactics. For Brown (and for Douglass), "slavery was a state of war" and the Civil War was properly thought of as the antislavery side fighting back against those who had started the conflict. Conceived in this way, Brown is best thought of, in Douglass's words, as the man who began "the war that ended slavery."[18]

Douglass was also attracted to the substance of Brown's views. He compared Brown's creed of "liberty for *others*" to Patrick Henry's exhortation, "Give *me* liberty or give me death."[19] When we compare the two figures, Douglass thought, it is hard not to admire Brown's altruism. Although Brown's means seemed repugnant to most of his contemporaries, Douglass believed he would be judged positively by history because of his deep commitment to moral principle and unwavering willingness to speak truth to power. In this sense, Brown was an embodiment of Douglass's ideal of the Reformer.

Douglass's endorsement of John Brown is not without its problems. First, one might question whether or not it is acceptable to endorse Brown given the means he used in pursuit of abolition. Douglass's extensive reflections on Brown reveal that he was fully cognizant of Brown's shortcomings. In the "Did John Brown Fail?" speech cited above, Douglass even compares Brown to a wolf, saying he crept upon his foes "stealthily" and "dealt his blow in the dark while his enemy slept."[20] These normally condemnable actions, Douglass said, are excusable in this context because of Brown's aim in undertaking them: "to disturb the moral sense" of his fellow Americans. Discerning men, Douglass concluded, should be able to appreciate that Brown's morally questionable tactics can be excused in light of this noble aim.

Second, a critic might say that although the strength of Brown's moral commitment was remarkable, his major shortcoming was his lack of prudence. Holding up Brown as an ideal type, a critic might say, is troubling because it invites the vision of a political community populated by individuals with little appreciation for the complexities of social life. Douglass was willing to hold Brown up as an exemplar, though, because he believed there was an important role to be played by impractical idealists like Brown. Prudence is certainly an important virtue, but so is justice. In a well-formed political community, Douglass thought, it is important to have prudent statesmen and citizens, but it is also vital to have individuals animated by the virtue of justice. This latter group plays the crucial role of shining a light on the shortcomings of the society and urging those in power to take action to address those shortcomings. We need our Lincolns, Douglass seemed to be suggesting, but we also need our Browns.[21]

I have now said something in response to the third question raised above: why is the Reformer so important? There are two additional reasons why the Reformer is such an important figure in Douglass's political thought. The first has to do with the direct impact of the Reformer's actions on the ongoing struggle between good and evil. Second, the Reformer is important because of the example he provides for others. At this point, I will address each of these contributions in turn.

First, it is necessary to discuss Douglass's view of the direct impact of the Reformer on social progress. It is important to remember, as noted in chapter 3, that he held a decidedly humanistic view of social change. By this, I mean that he believed the fate of the world is largely (if not entirely) in human hands. Just before the outbreak of the Civil War he delivered a Sunday afternoon lecture entitled "The American Apocalypse" at Spring Street A.M.E. Zion Church in Rochester. In it he said, "All the progress towards perfection ever made by mankind, and all the blessings which are now enjoyed, are ascribable to some brave and good man, who, catching the illumination of a heaven-born truth, has counted it a joy, precious and unspeakable, to toil, suffer, and often to die for the glorious realization of that heaven-born truth."[22] In 1883, Douglass affirmed this strongly humanistic theory of social progress in an important speech entitled "It Moves, or the Philosophy of Reform."

It may not be useless speculation to inquire whence the disposition or suggestion of reform; whence that irresistible power that impels men to brave all the hardships and dangers involved in pioneering an unpopular cause? Has it a natural or a celestial origin? Is it human or divine or both? I have no hesitation in stating where I stand in respect to these questions. It seems to me that a true philosophy of reform is not found in the clouds, or in the stars, or anywhere else outside humanity itself. So far as the laws of the universe have been discovered and understood, they seem to teach that the mission of man's improvement and perfection has been wholly committed to man himself. So he is to be his own savior or his own destroyer. He has neither angels to help him nor devils to hinder him.[23]

Douglass went on to offer explicit criticisms of Christian doctrines that emphasize prayer and worship rather than political action. Instead of praying and hoping that God will bring about social change, he argued that human beings must exercise their free will in order to make progress. It was particularly important, Douglass thought, for reformers to push others to close the gap between their professed moral ideals and concrete political realities.

The importance of human action in Douglass's philosophy of reform was rooted in his belief that there is a constant struggle between the spirit of selfishness and the spirit of humanity within human nature. Although human beings are essentially good, they are "constantly liable to do evil."[24] In order for good to prevail and progress to be made, individuals must choose to act righteously. In the "American Apocalypse" speech cited above, Douglass declared:

> Men have their choice in this world. They can be angels, or they may be demons. In the apocalyptic vision, John describes a war in heaven. You have only to strip that vision of its gorgeous Oriental drapery, divest it of its shining and celestial ornaments, clothe it in the simple and familiar language of common sense, and you will have before you the eternal conflict between right and wrong, good and evil, liberty and slavery, truth and falsehood, the glorious light of love, and the appalling darkness of human selfishness and sin. The human heart is a seat of constant war.[25]

The constant battle that occurs *within* individuals manifests itself *between* individuals. The "dignity of the anti-slavery movement" is revealed, Douglass said, when we think of it as part of the eternal struggle between good and evil:

> It must be looked at as a part of that eternal and universal conflict everywhere in progress between human justice, enlightenment and goodness on the one hand, and human pride, selfishness, injustice and tyrannical power

on the other; a conflict that has gone on from the beginning and must go on forever until, by truth and love, the baser nature of man shall be subdued and refined and become subject to his higher and better nature.[26]

"If there is no struggle," Douglass said, "there is no progress."[27] Reformers are on the frontlines of the eternal struggle between liberty and tyranny.

The actions of reformers can take many forms. While a rare few engage in the sort of radical action we associate with Brown, others take more moderate paths. Douglass, for example, engaged primarily in agitating with his pen and voice. Although his work was focused primarily on persuading people in the "Court of Public Opinion," he also attempted to influence elites through direct lobbying. Perhaps the most prominent example of this is his attempts to persuade President Lincoln to declare first, that the Civil War was a war for abolition and second, to allow black men to enlist in the Union army on equal terms with whites.[28] Against those who believe that when "the President has avowed a policy, sanctioned a measure, or commended a general" his "action must be treated as final," Douglass declared: "Our rulers are agents of the people. They are fallible men. They need instruction from the people, and it is no evidence of a factious disposition that any man presumes to condemn a public measure if in his judgment that measure is opposed to the public good."[29] Douglass utilized his pen, his voice, and direct contact with the president to persuade him to change his rhetoric and policies during the Civil War.

It is worth noting that critics have called Douglass's humanistic view of social change, which had the ideal-type of the Reformer at its core, "egocentric." In his thoughtful study of Douglass and other African American thinkers, *Creative Conflict in African American Thought*, Wilson Jeremiah Moses argues that Douglass's "major flaw" was his "egocentric interpretation of history."[30] According to Moses, the power Douglass imagined the Reformer to have may have led him to overemphasize what individuals can accomplish absent dramatic structural change in their societies. While this criticism is worth keeping in mind, it is not particularly problematic for my purposes here. What matters at this point is that Douglass held a tremendous amount of faith in the power of the Reformer to actually bring about change in the world. Moses is right to say that sometimes this faith was overblown, but there is little question that it was a central part of Douglass's thought.

The second major contribution of Reformers is through the example they set for others. The Reformer offers an alternative to the classical republican conception of civic virtue, which emphasizes the willingness of the individual to sacrifice his interests for the good of the community. The conception of civic virtue offered by the Reformer is not completely removed from this classical republican formulation, but it differs in important ways. Reformers are often alienated from others in the political community in a moral sense because they are devoted to principles that have not been realized in the world. The moral alienation of the Reformer does not, though, lead to political quietism. Instead, the Reformer engages in the difficult task of closing the gap between his moral ideals and political reality. The critical disposition of the Reformer can serve as a model for other individuals. Douglass recognized that most citizens would not attain the moral heights of the Reformer, but he hoped that the average person would incorporate at least some of the Reformer's commitment to principle into their own attitude toward political engagement.

According to Douglass, the American Founders embodied classical republican virtue. In his famous 1852 oration "What to the Slave Is the Fourth of July?" he said,

> [The American Founders] loved their country more than their own private interests; and, though this is not the highest form of human excellence, all will concede that it is a rare virtue, and that when it is exhibited, it ought to command respect. He who will, intelligently, lay down his life for his country, is a man whom it is not in human nature to despise. Your fathers staked their lives, their fortunes, and their sacred honor, on the cause of their country.[31]

It is clear Douglass admired classical republican virtue, but it is important to note that he did not believe it is the "highest form of human excellence." In his mind, the doctrine of "true virtue" embodied by the Reformer was higher. In an 1866 essay, Douglass described this doctrine.

> I have now spoken plainly, but not more than the case requires. If any have been shocked at my plainness of speech, I beg them to remember that *true* delicacy does not consist in a squeamish ear. In the language of the eloquent Fox, I would remind them "that true humanity does not consist in shrinking and starting at such recitals, but in a disposition of the heart to remedy evils they unfold. True virtue belongs to the mind rather than to the nerves, and should prompt men to charitable exertions in correcting abuses. To shudder at enormities, and do nothing to remove them, is little better than to stamp ourselves with the most pitiful and contemptible hypocrisy."[32]

Douglass believed *true* virtue is animated by principled devotion to the universal moral truths of natural law, not simple devotion to one's country. The Reformer's devotion to these truths and his commitment to bringing the world closer to their realization make him the embodiment of true virtue. As a conception of civic virtue, this view requires individuals to adopt a critical attitude within the political sphere and to devote themselves to using all means available to them to close the gap between moral ideals and political realities.

What does the doctrine of true virtue embodied by the Reformer offer in terms of guidance for other citizens? Douglass's discussions of "true patriotism" and "true citizenship" demonstrate that he believed the critical edge of the Reformer was essential to the proper disposition of individuals in the political sphere. In a speech entitled "An Antislavery Tocsin," delivered at Corinthian Hall in Rochester, New York, in 1850, Douglass touched on these themes:

> We have heard much of late of the virtue of patriotism, the love of country, and this sentiment, so natural and so strong, has been impiously appealed to, by all the powers of human selfishness, to cherish the viper which is stinging our national life away. . . . I, too, would invoke the spirit of patriotism; *not* in a narrow and restricted sense, but I trust, with a broad and manly signification; *not* to cover up our national sins, but to inspire us with sincere repentance; *not* to hide our shame from the world's gaze, but utterly to abolish the cause of that shame; *not* to explain away our gross inconsistencies as a nation, but to remove the hateful, jarring, and incongruous elements from the land; *not* to sustain an egregious wrong, but to unite all our energies in the grand effort to remedy that wrong.[33]

Douglass's "broad and manly" patriotism does not emphasize the subordination of one's interests to the interests of the state but an uncompromising devotion to moral principle. This devotion, he argued, may lead to harsh criticism. While traveling throughout Great Britain in the late 1840s, Douglass delivered a speech entitled "American Slavery Is America's Disgrace." In the speech, he pointed out that many of his critics were appalled at his willingness to criticize his country from abroad. In response, Douglass reminded his critics that "Love for America . . . is not inconsistent with the strongest rebuke of its crimes."[34] Only days after his return to the United States, Douglass delivered a speech in New York City entitled "Country, Conscience, and the Anti-Slavery Cause," in which he argued that true patriotism sometimes requires a good citizen to annoy his neighbors:

I admit that we have irritated [our fellow Americans]. They deserve to be irritated. I am anxious to irritate the American people on [the slavery] question. As it is in physics, so in morals, there are cases which demand irritation and counter-irritation. The conscience of the American public needs this irritation, and I would *blister it all over from center to circumference,* until it gives signs of a purer and a better life than it is not manifesting to the world.[35]

The true patriot, Douglass believed, does not always strive for popularity. At the beginning of the Civil War, he began a speech entitled "Fighting the Rebels with One Hand," by saying: "My purpose to-night is not to win applause. I have no high-sounding professions of patriotism to make. He is the best friend of this country, who, at this tremendous crisis, dares tell his countrymen the truth, however disagreeable that truth may be; and such a friend I will aim to be to-night."[36]

In 1867, as Douglass was becoming more and more concerned with President Andrew Johnson's resistance to Reconstruction, he authored a speech entitled "Sources of Danger to the Republic," in which he offered an important account of what he called "true" citizenship. Rather than focusing on dangers posed from outside the country, he discussed the dangers posed by what he called "bastard" (or incomplete) republicanism. Douglass argued that a crucial part of good citizenship is a willingness to criticize one's own government; we should take "a little less extravagant view of the excellences of our institutions" and offer honest criticism when it is appropriate. He said such criticism could be offered in the "spirit" of a "true citizen" who has a genuine interest in "the welfare, the stability, the permanence and the prosperity of our free institutions."[37] Over the next few months, Douglass would deliver this speech to audiences in New York, Massachusetts, Pennsylvania, Ohio, Missouri, Iowa, and Minnesota—thus embodying his ideal of active, critical citizenship.

After his break with the Garrisonians in the late 1840s, Douglass's understanding of good citizenship came to include a strong sense of obligation to participate in politics. In the early 1850s, when he was confronted with a constant barrage of criticism for abandoning the antipolitical philosophy of the Garrisonians in favor of the political abolitionism of the Liberty Party, Douglass repeatedly made the case for morally infused political action. In an article entitled "R. D. Webb—George Thompson and the Liberty Party," he responded to criticisms from Garrison's American Antislavery Society in this way: "We, too, believe that moral reform must precede political reform, and we believe we can infuse a correct moral sentiment into the government by voting for good men, and against bad men."[38] Good citizenship, Douglass argued, included direct involvement in conventional politics. This was required, he believed, even though the political realm is fraught with moral compromise. Indeed, Douglass was forced to grapple with the complexities of "voting for good men" when he had to weigh whether or not to vote for the politically weak radical abolitionist parties or for the more politically viable, but less morally pure, Republican Party. In 1852, Douglass was staunchly committed to the idea that abolitionists were morally bound to vote for candidates who were uncompromising in their devotion to the antislavery cause. In early 1856, he continued to believe that antislavery voters should support the Radical Abolitionist Party instead of the moderate Republican Party. In an essay entitled "What Is My Duty as an Antislavery Voter?" Douglass encouraged his readers to support the Radical Abolitionist Party even though "such a policy of principle would throw the election to the Democrats," because antislavery voters had an obligation to put "first things first" and the first thing in their hearts and minds should be the abolition of slavery.[39] By late 1856, however, he began to back away from this purist view, perhaps realizing that he was committing a Garrisonian-like error of allowing moral purity to blind him to the importance of pragmatism in politics. In an essay entitled "Can an Abolitionist Vote for Fremont?" we begin to see Douglass become more open to the idea of supporting the somewhat wishy-washy Republican Party. In previous essays, he seems to lump the Republicans with Whig compromisers he disdained like Henry Clay. In the essay on Fremont, he acknowledges that "a vote does not signify the sweeping significance" attributed to it by the Garrisonians. A vote, he argued, is not an absolute endorsement of everything a candidate stands for, but rather something much more modest: "Our rule in this matter is to 'vote for the best man you can reasonably hope to elect.' If the choice, however, is between evils, then one should abandon this rule and select the candidate of the highest virtue, regardless of his election chances." He went on to say that the Republicans are not evil because "a Republican victory will not postpone or defeat the aim which we seek. The issue, in short, is not personal consistency, but the question, what is the present duty of abolitionists?"[40]

Douglass believed the Reformer's devotion to principle, critical attitude, and commitment to political engagement could serve as a model for others. Although few individuals could live up to the high moral standards of the Reformer, Douglass hoped average citizens would adopt some of his critical edge. By viewing political realities through the moral lens of natural law, the

Reformer has the critical distance necessary to point out the shortcomings of his society. Social criticism was only half of the Reformer's task. His true "mission," Douglass said, was to do the responsible thing and encourage others to do the same: take action to close the gap between shared moral ideals and political realities. Douglass's application of his view of good citizenship to the obligation to vote reveals how his philosophy became more pragmatic over time. Although one should always be guided by first principles in the political sphere, it is vital that one also use prudence to determine the best course of action in a particular political context.

Douglass's Dream of Soulful Self-Reliance: Self-Made Men and the Manners of Liberty

A complete consideration of Douglass's view of morally responsible behavior requires some reflection on his commitment to the ideal of the Self-Made Man and his defense of the bourgeois virtues. The Self-Made Man exemplifies the "good life" born of liberty: he labors faithfully so that he can secure a home for his family and acquire the material foundation necessary for moral and intellectual development. Furthermore, he contributes to a healthy moral ecology by exemplifying the virtues of personal responsibility, industriousness, and perseverance. Douglass was a firm believer in the free labor ideology that animated nineteenth-century Republicanism: the system of ideas that held that free individuals who work hard and behave virtuously should be able, in most circumstances, to attain middle-class respectability.[41] Douglass's "dream of soulful self-reliance" was that free and virtuous individuals who labored faithfully would be able to "secure a home" to serve as a foundation from which they could pursue various forms of flourishing. What he wanted for himself and all Americans were those things that slavery denied: the stability of home and family, the opportunity to enjoy the fruits of one's labor, the pleasure of friendship, and the satisfaction of intellectual and moral development. Securing this dream was an immense challenge, but Douglass believed two things would go a long way toward making it a reality. First, he thought "fair play" was essential. Under unfair conditions, hard work, virtue, and perseverance would be of little consequence. Without fair play, Douglass believed, the promise of freedom must be branded a lie. Second, he thought individuals needed to behave virtuously in order to secure the material foundation instrumental to intellectual and moral development.

Before proceeding to a consideration of Douglass's ideal of the Self-Made Man, a word must be said about how this discussion fits with my aims in this chapter. The virtues embodied in the Self-Made Man contribute to a moral ecology supportive of liberty in at least three ways. First, the Self-Made Man serves as a model of honest, well-directed labor, self-reliance, and perseverance. Second, the Self-Made Man contributes to the well-being of society by "doing his part" to secure individual, familial, and communal well-being. With material well-being as the foundation, individuals are able to pursue intellectual and moral cultivation. Third, emulation of the virtues embodied in the Self-Made Man can strengthen the bonds of community by enhancing the sense of mutual respect between individuals. As I demonstrated in chapter 4, Douglass believed those who behaved virtuously were more likely to be accepted as equal members of the community. Taken together, these three contributions are crucial to Douglass's political project because they affirm the centrality of personal responsibility for the moral health of the liberal order.

According to historian John Blassingame, Douglass delivered his lecture "Self-Made Men" more than fifty times between 1859 and 1893.[42] In this oft-delivered speech, he aimed to "awaken" in his audiences "a sense of the dignity of labor" and "the value of manhood."[43] The virtues exhibited by the Self-Made Man, he claimed, contribute to the development of a healthy moral atmosphere and are worthy of respect and emulation. In Douglass's words, self-made men "are entitled to a certain measure of respect for their success and for proving to the world the grandest possibilities of human nature" and every instance of their "success is an example and help to humanity."[44]

Douglass began his discussion of the Self-Made Man with a significant caveat. This caveat is particularly important because it gets to the core of one of the central arguments of this book. It concerns the relationship between the idea of "individual independence" and the ideas of "brotherhood and inter-dependence."[45] Douglass's lecture on the Self-Made Man is a decidedly liberal text, but his discussion of interdependence at the beginning of the speech is an indication that he did not see individualism and a strong sense of connection as mutually exclusive.

> It must in truth be said though it may not accord well with self-conscious individuality and self-conceit, that no possible native force of character, and no depth or wealth of originality, can lift a man into absolute independence of his fellow-men, and no generation of men can be independent of the preceding generation. The brotherhood and inter-dependence of mankind are guarded and defended at all points. I believe in individuality, but individuals are, to the mass, like waves to the ocean. The highest order

of genius is as dependent as is the lowest. It, like the loftiest waves of the sea, derives its power and greatness from the grandeur and vastness of the ocean of which it forms a part. We differ as the waves, but are one as the sea.[46]

Douglass's speech focuses on a class of human beings that seem to embody the virtues of liberal individualism, but he thought exaltation of the Self-Made Man was consistent with beliefs in brotherhood and interdependence. Rather than seeing self-reliance and interconnection as antagonistic, he saw them as closely related.[47]

With this caveat on the table, Douglass offered his definition of self-made men: "Self-made men are the men who, under peculiar difficulties and without the ordinary helps of favoring circumstances, have attained knowledge, usefulness, power and position and have learned from themselves the best uses to which life can be put in this world, and in the exercises of these uses to build up worthy character."[48] Self-made men are individuals who have succeeded, in one way or another, without the benefits of being well-born or socially privileged. "They are in a peculiar sense," Douglass said, "indebted to themselves for themselves."[49]

After offering this definition, Douglass explored various theories of the success of self-made men. First, Douglass rejected the idea that human greatness could be explained by "superior mental endowment." This theory, he said, "has truth in it, but it is not the whole truth."[50] Some great men are blessed with superior mental endowments, but some are not. Furthermore, some individuals endowed with superior mental endowments fail to achieve greatness. Douglass thought it mattered less what men began with than what they did with it.

Next, Douglass offered a strong rejection of both the "good luck" and the "supernatural intervention" theories of self-made men. No theories were more foreign to Douglass's worldview than these. The good luck theory, he said, "divorces a man from his own achievements, contemplates him as a being of chance and leaves him without will, motive, ambition, or aspiration." Similarly, the divine hand theory makes man "a very insignificant agent in his own affairs."[51] As noted in the discussion of the Reformer, Douglass rejected the "celestial" explanation of human progress because he believed God gave human beings free will to shape events in the world. The good luck and divine hand theories of self-made men are simply individualized versions of the celestial theory of human progress. "Faith, in the absence of work, seems to be worth little, if anything."[52] Douglass was a strong believer in voluntarism: human beings have free will and although luck plays a role in the world, it should not be "made to explain too much."[53] He concluded that both the good luck and divine hand theories ought to be rejected as explanations of self-made men.

Instead of good luck and divine intervention, Douglass contended that the success of self-made men can be explained "mainly by one word and that word is WORK! WORK!! WORK!!! WORK!!!! Not transient and fitful effort, but patient, enduring, honest, unremitting and indefatigable work, into which the whole heart is put, and which, in both temporal and spiritual affairs, is the true miracle worker."[54] The Self-Made Man is the embodiment of hard work, perseverance, determination, and self-reliance. As noted above, Douglass did not believe human beings could be completely independent of one another. He did, though, think that individuals are more likely to be assisted by others if they demonstrate themselves to be worthy of assistance: "He who does not think himself worth saving from poverty and ignorance, by his own efforts, will hardly be thought worth the efforts of anybody else."[55] Douglass did not shy away from the individualistic implications of this view: "Personal independence is a virtue and it is the soul out of which comes the sturdiest manhood. But there can be no independence without a large share of self-dependence, and this virtue cannot be bestowed. It must be developed from within."[56]

In his response to the "superior mental endowments" theory of self-made men, Douglass offered the core of his view. The key thing self-made men possess is not superior brain power or physical prowess, but "soul":

> Sound bodily health and mental faculties unimpaired are very desirable, if not absolutely indispensable. But a man need not be a physical giant or an intellectual prodigy, in order to make a tolerable way in the world. The health and strength of the soul is of far more importance than that of the body, even when viewed as a means of mundane results. The soul is the main thing. Man can do a great many things; some easily and some with difficulty, but he cannot build a sound ship with rotten timber.[57]

Douglass's belief that the strength of the soul is the most important thing is a reflection of his focus on the moral dimension of human life. Like his contention that the health of the political community depends upon its moral life, he believed flourishing was, first and foremost, a matter of soul.

Douglass summarized his theory of self-made men in this way: "My theory of self-made men is, then, simply this; that they are men of work. Whether or not such men have acquired material, moral or intellectual excellence, honest labor faithfully, steadily and persistently pursued, is the best, if not the only, explanation of their success."[58] Because the idea of self-made men is often associated with material wealth, it is worth noting that Douglass held a broader view. Self-made men, he said, are moved by a variety of "commanding objects." Rather than saying that material wealth is *the* commanding object of self-made men, Douglass included this end as one among many and said it is *not* what moves most men:

> All are not moved by the same objects. Happiness is the object of some. Wealth and fame are the objects of others. But wealth and fame are beyond the reach of the majority of men, and thus, to them, these are not motive-impelling objects. Happily, however, personal, family and neighborhood well-being stand near to us all and are full of lofty inspirations to earnest endeavor, if we would but respond to their influence.[59]

This is the essence of Douglass's dream of soulful self-reliance: he envisioned a society of free, industrious individuals who seek personal, family, and neighborhood well-being and respect the right of others to do the same.

Two additional points about the lecture on self-made men are worth making. First, in the middle of the lecture, Douglass discussed how this idea applies to former slaves. His reflections on this question are significant because they demonstrate his belief that the ideal of the Self-Made Man only makes sense under conditions of fair play. In response to the question of how the theory of self-made men affects freedmen, Douglass said: "Give the negro fair play and let him alone." It is important to understand, he said, that by this "I mean a good deal more than some understand by fair play." We must remember, Douglass said, that the freedman did not begin the race of life from the same starting line as his fellow citizens. So while he advised the freedman to practice the virtues of the Self-Made Man, he also demanded that the rest of society observe the requirements of "simple justice" (do not violate the rights of others) and "fair play" (do not rig the game to the advantage of some and/or to disadvantage others). Douglass believed a society in which the rights of individuals were respected, the rules were not rigged to advantage or disadvantage a particular group, and individuals worked hard and behaved virtuously would be ideal.

Second, it is worth noting that Douglass offered a brief discussion of the ideas and institutions that are supportive of self-made men. He argued that America is the "home and patron of self-made men" because "labor is so respected and so honored," there is not much class strife, there is a broad commitment to "the principle of measuring and valuing men according to their respective merits," there is a rough "equality of rights," there is not an excessive amount of respect for elders or family names, and there is a relatively large amount of social mobility.[60] This argument provides a useful example of Douglass's attentiveness to moral ecology. The relatively high level of respect for labor in American culture and the perception that individual merit matters, he believed, has an important impact on the formation of individual souls. In a culture where labor is respected, individuals will be more likely to labor faithfully. Although Douglass does not say so here, it is worth pointing out that the work of the Reformer is crucial to the achievement of the state of affairs in which we can declare that the United States is indeed a home and patron of self-made men. Douglass's discussion of the institutional conditions supportive of self-made men is further evidence of his belief that justice and fair play are essential for the ideal of the Self-Made Man to be realistic.

Douglass's devotion to the ideal of the Self-Made Man is a manifestation of his belief in the bourgeois virtues.[61] In chapter 4, I referred to a letter Douglass wrote to Martin Delany in which he said, "Liberty has its manners as well as slavery, and with those manners true self-respect goes hand in hand with a just respect for the rights and feelings of others."[62] The manners of liberty include not only the obligations to respect the rights of others and to treat others fairly, but also the bourgeois virtues of self-reliance, industriousness, sobriety, integrity, orderliness, and a desire for self-improvement.[63] Douglass's "free man" is not an amoral libertine but the embodiment of personal responsibility. Indeed, contemporary readers may find Douglass's rhetoric on these matters surprisingly moralistic in nature. As I have been arguing throughout this book, his political thought was rooted in the idea that the promise of liberty could only be realized if individuals behaved in responsible ways.

Douglass believed the practice of the bourgeois virtues essential to the achievement of independence and to gaining the respect and concern of others. This view is evident in his speeches to freedmen after the Civil War. His frustration with Reconstruction had three major elements. First, he was angered by the lack of energetic action by the state.[64] Second, he was infuriated by the lack of fairness in the relationships between freedmen and their former masters. Although Douglass often seemed to embrace a negative conception of liberty—liberty as freedom from—he recognized that under unfair conditions, individuals may have "only the freedom to starve."[65] Third, and most relevant to my theme here, he was disappointed with the lack of moral progress of the freedmen. Just after the war, he told Martin Delany to "have patience" because the manners of liberty would take time to develop. Toward the end of his life, though, Douglass began to offer sharp criticisms of freedmen for failing to behave virtuously. His frustration with freedmen is evident in a speech he delivered in 1891 to the black congregation at Centennial Methodist Episcopal Church in Baltimore, Maryland. In this speech, Douglass was critical of unfair public policies and discriminatory practices by employers and labor unions, but he also took aim at the freedmen themselves. He was particularly concerned with what he believed to be their irresponsible financial habits. Among other things, he expressed frustration at the lack of progress of freedmen compared to Chinese and German immigrants:

> When I walk the streets and see Lung Wung hard at work at his wash tub, and see our Teutonic friends stropping their razors and plying the barber's trade, I can't help but think that they are taking away the occupations that belong to us. Do you know why they can do it? It is because our people, instead of attending to their business, will buy a banjo and spend most of their time thumping it.[66]

In the speech on self-made men, Douglass repeated this message when he said, "I do not desire my lecture to become a sermon; but, were this allowable, I would rebuke the growing tendency to sport and pleasure. The time, money and strength devoted to these phantoms, would banish darkness and hunger from every hearthstone in our land."[67]

Douglass's stern moral rhetoric was rooted in his belief that the practice of bourgeois virtues was a necessary part of the path to independence. He wanted individuals to behave virtuously so they could acquire property, which he hoped would serve as the material foundation for intellectual and moral progress.

> Accumulate property. Yes, accumulate property. This may sound to you like a new gospel. You have been accustomed to hear that money is the root of all evil; that it is hard for the rich to enter the kingdom of Heaven; that this world is of no account; that we should take no thought for tomorrow, and much more of the same sort. In answer to all which I say: that no people can ever make any social or mental improvement whose exertions are thus limited. Poverty is our greatest calamity. . . . [P]roperty, money, if you please, will purchase of us the only condition upon which any people can rise to the dignity of genuine manhood; for, without prop-

erty, there can be no leisure. Without leisure, there can be no thought. Without thought, there can be no invention. Without invention, there can be no progress.[68]

In order to develop self-respect and the respect of others, Douglass believed it was necessary for individuals to acquire property and guard it by the "Puritan ethic of deferred gratification."[69] Self-improvement, he argued, is largely the work of individuals themselves.

> We must improve our condition. And here the work is ours. It cannot be done by our friends. They can pity as they can sympathize with us. But we need something more than sympathy—something more than pity. *We must be respected.* And we cannot be respected unless we are either independent or aiming to be. We must be as independent of society as society is of us, and lay society under as many obligations to us as we are under to society. We cannot be paupers and be respected, though we may be paupers and be pitied. The fact is, my friends, we must not only work, but we must make money—not only make money, but save it; and when we use it, we must use it wisely.[70]

Confronted with the question of what individuals must do to realize the promise of freedom, Douglass's response was the same as his theory of self-made men: WORK! WORK!! WORK!!! WORK!!!! The toil of individuals should be directed toward the acquisition of property, which could serve as the basis for intellectual and moral improvement.

This last point is an important one because it indicates that Douglass did not embrace the bourgeois virtues as ends in themselves, but rather as means to the higher end of personal cultivation. For Douglass, in the words of contemporary political philosopher Gayle McKeen, "work, and the economic progress that was its intended consequence, was but the foundation for the cultivation of moral and mental faculties; it is only with wealth that one can enjoy leisure and education and that one has the opportunity to pursue the most important thing: the cultivation of the human soul."[71] This aspect of Douglass's thought is most evident in an 1894 address entitled "The Blessings of Liberty and Education," which he delivered at the dedication of the Colored Industrial School in Manassas, Virginia. In that address, Douglass said:

> [Man's] true dignity is not to be sought in his arms or his legs, but in his head. Here is the seat and source of all that is of especially great or practical

importance to him. . . . There is power in the human mind, but education is needed for its development. As man is the highest on earth it follows that the vocation of the scholar is among the highest known to man. It is to teach and induce man's potential and latent greatness. It is to discover and develop the noblest, highest and best that is in him. In view of this fact that no man whose business it is to teach should ever allow himself to feel that his mission is mean, inferior or circumscribed. In my estimation neither politics nor religion present to us a calling higher than this primary business of unfolding and strengthening of the human soul. It is a permanent vocation.[72]

This passage provides us with evidence that it would be a mistake to interpret Douglass's embrace of bourgeois virtue as an endorsement of shallow materialism. Douglass did not offer a recipe for a life that was, as Leo Strauss put it in his famous critique of liberalism, a "joyless quest for joy."[73] Instead, Douglass hoped that individuals would transcend possessive individualism to the "true dignity" of intellectual, moral, and spiritual development. Furthermore, as historian John Stauffer has pointed out, Douglass's philosophy of self-making was not about self-improvement for the sake of self, but rather for the sake of others. According to Stauffer, "the *goal* of self-making" for Douglass "was to improve society rather than to get rich. . . . In remaking the self, you reformed society and worked tirelessly to realize a heaven on earth."[74]

Confronted with this prescription for self-development in the private realm, one may ask what Douglass identified as the "seedbeds of virtue."[75] How do individuals learn the bourgeois virtues? First, Douglass believed we learn from one another—individuals who act in responsible ways serve as models for others to emulate. If I see my neighbor behaving virtuously and it leads to positive results, it may influence me to model my behavior after his. Second, Douglass thought economic relationships have an important impact on moral ecology and character development. The slave system, for example, produced an unhealthy moral ecology because it degraded labor, dignified idleness, and encouraged vicious behavior by both masters and slaves. Slavery, he argued, "is adverse to freedom" because it "sets a premium on idleness, and degrades both labor and laborers."[76] Under the Southern system, it was considered desirable to own slaves so that one did not have to degrade oneself by working. Under such a system, idleness was a sign of distinction. The idle masters were free to indulge their vicious appetites. On a trip to Washington, D.C. after the Civil War, Douglass described the moral atmosphere of the city when it had slavery: "Like most slaveholding communities, Washington was tolerant of drinking, gambling, sensuality, indolence, and many other forms of vice, common to an idle and lounging people. It was the home of the bully and the duelist."[77] On another occasion, Douglass pointed out that the deleterious moral effects of slavery extended to the slave. Because the slave was denied self-ownership, he argued, he was unable to feel a strong sense of personal responsibility and he was also denied "every safeguard to virtue," including the institution of marriage.[78]

Douglass was hopeful that the free labor system would have a positive impact on the morality of former masters and slaves. He recognized, though, that nothing short of a cultural revolution would transform attitudes in the South. A passage cited above captures this point:

> The work before us is nothing less than a radical revolution in the modes of thought which have flourished under the blighting slave system. The idea that labor is an evil, that work is degrading and that idleness is respectable, must be dispelled and the idea that work is honorable made to take its place. Above all they must be taught that the liberty of a part is never to be secured by the enslavement or oppression of any. . . . Time, experience, and culture must gradually bring society back to the normal condition from which long years of slavery have carried away all under its iron sway.[79]

Douglass expressed a similar view of the need for moral transformation among the freedmen. In an 1883 address entitled "Freedom Has Brought Duties," he said:

> Freedom has brought duties, responsibilities and created expectations which must be fulfilled. There is no disguising the fact that the price of liberty is eternal vigilance, and if we maintain our high estate in this republic, we must be something more than driftwood in a stream. We must keep pace with the nation in all that goes to make a nation great, glorious and free.[80]

The ideal of the Self-Made Man is important, in part, because it dignifies labor. Given the "values" of the slave system, the exaltation of labor was crucial to the development of a liberal moral ecology. Douglass hoped that the arena of free labor would be a seedbed that could teach individuals the bourgeois virtues.

Another seedbed of virtue is the home. As noted above, Douglass did not believe most self-made men are motivated by grand illusions of wealth or fame. Instead, most self-made men are motivated by a modest desire to achieve a secure home for themselves, their families, and their neighborhoods. In this sense, the home represents a "commanding object" that can motivate men to practice the bourgeois virtues. In an 1894 address delivered at the Metropolitan A.M.E. Church in Washington, D.C., Douglass put this point strongly and succinctly in response to those who argued that blacks should go back to Africa:

> Every man who thinks at all must know that the home is the fountain head, the inspiration, the foundation and main support not only for all social virtue, but of all motives to human progress and that no people can prosper or amount to much without a home. To have a home, the negro must have a country, and he is an enemy to the moral progress of the negro, when he knows it or not, who calls upon him to break up his home in this country for an uncertain home in Africa.[81]

In addition to serving as the primary motivation for social virtue and progress, Douglass believed the home plays a crucial role as a moral restraint on the tendency to indulge in vice. In 1877, just before he was to assume his new post as marshal for the District of Columbia, he argued that the nation's capitol was a city with a low "moral tone" because members of Congress did not have their families present to keep them in check: "In the absence of good women and the family, man sinks rapidly to barbarism. In the olden times Members of Congress came here and left behind them all the restraints and endearments of home. Their manners and morals were shaped by those of the restaurant, the hotel and the gambling hall, and other resorts of men of the world."[82]

Last, Douglass believed educational institutions could be a seedbed of moral virtue. I will discuss the importance of education in Douglass's thought in some detail in the next chapter, but it is worth noting here that he believed vital political and social virtues could be developed through educational institutions. Indeed, he believed there was a direct connection between intellectual and moral development: "With increased intelligence and a wider dissemination of earnest thought and sound reasoning will come also the moral advancement. Ignorance and immorality usually go hand in hand. So intelligence and self-respect are almost synonymous."[83] Although Douglass vacillated on the question of whether former slaves should receive a primarily practical or liberal education, he believed either would contribute to their moral development.

In sum, Douglass believed the virtues embodied in the Self-Made Man were essential to the flourishing of a free society. Like the Reformer, the ideal type of the Self-Made Man is a model of moral responsibility. One might say that the Reformer embodies an ideal of moral responsibility to others while the Self-Made Man embodies an ideal of personal responsibility. Douglass believed responsible behavior in the private realm entailed working hard and behaving virtuously in order to achieve personal, familial, and community well-being. Individuals should strive to be as self-reliant as possible; this, he thought, was crucial for self-respect and the respect of others. In order to become self-reliant, individuals must labor with focus, intensity, and perseverance. In addition, achieving and sustaining self-reliance requires individuals to be virtuous. Without prudence, honesty, thrift, and temperance, the gains of individuals are insecure. Douglass exalted the Self-Made Man and the bourgeois virtues because he hoped American society would reach a point when individuals who worked hard and played by the rules would have a good chance of achieving material security. With secure homes as their physical and spiritual foundations, he hoped individuals would pursue intellectual and moral development.

Conclusion: Douglass's Measure of Men

Douglass believed the conditions necessary for the exercise of personal freedom could only be achieved and maintained if individuals behaved in responsible ways. He identified Reformers and Self-Made Men as models of morally responsible behavior and, as such, as worthy of admiration and emulation. Who a society identifies as "great" is a telling commentary on its moral health. In a speech entitled "Of Men and Morals," delivered at the annual meeting of the American Anti-Slavery Society in 1849, Douglass said, "No nation has yet produced a higher standard of morality than that embodied in the character of its great men." The greatness of men, he continued, is determined by what the community truly holds dear. "In a community where men love freedom," Douglass said in 1849, "that man only will be popular who is sacredly and continually engaged in shedding the blessings of freedom upon mankind around him."[84] A community that truly loved freedom, in other words, would exalt individuals with the character of reformers and self-made men.

The Reformer's greatness is to be found in the fact that he is animated to action by his deep devotion to the moral principles at the core of the liberal project: universal freedom and equality. In a speech delivered in Salem,

Ohio, in 1852 to the Garrisonian Western Anti-Slavery Society, Douglass said that abolitionism had made him a "great man" in the sense that it "delivered" him from the "bondage" of self-interest and "race pride" to a belief in the equal dignity of "every man under the wide canopy of heaven."[85] As noted above, from Douglass's perspective, the greatness of John Brown was not to be found in his actions but in the fact that he "loved liberty for all men . . . for those most despised and scorned, as well as those most esteemed and honored."[86] The Reformer embodies the devotion to moral ideals and willingness to work to realize those ideals in the world that is essential to the health of a free society. Although not all citizens can emulate the moral devotion and altruism of the Reformer, Douglass hoped the average citizen would adopt some of his critical edge, commitment to principle, and vigilance.

The virtues embodied in the Reformer and the Self-Made Man are essential to the achievement of basic liberal rights and to securing the conditions necessary for individuals to flourish in a free society. Douglass believed that once rights are protected and the conditions of fair play are ensured, individuals who work hard and behave virtuously have a good chance of achieving material security that can serve as a foundation for intellectual and moral development. The Self-Made Man is a model of self-reliance, moral uprightness, and perseverance. He serves as an inspiration for others because he is able to achieve greatness against all odds. The Self-Made Man serves as evidence that hard work animated by a healthy soul can lead to success. He dignifies freedom by demonstrating the heights that can be achieved by exercising liberty virtuously. For individuals to flourish in a free society, Douglass thought, it is necessary for them to practice the virtues exhibited by the Self-Made Man.

It may be worthwhile to pause before concluding to consider whether or not the sorts of virtues embodied in the Reformer can be squared with the sorts of virtues embodied in the Self-Made Man. The Reformer presents us with an ideal to which we can aspire in our feelings of responsibility to others and the Self-Made Man presents us with an ideal to which we can aspire in personal development. But can one be the sort of person who is devoted to others while at the same time striving to perfect oneself? There is little question that Douglass believed that the answer to this question was yes. Indeed, although humility prevented him from saying so explicitly, Douglass himself embodied both of the ideal types he championed. It is difficult to imagine a more inspiring story of "self-making" than Douglass's and few Americans devoted more time and energy to the well-being of others. For Douglass, then, the highest form of life would be one animated by the virtues of the

Self-Made Man in pursuit of the sorts of "commanding objects" that move the Reformer. There can be little question that the goal of personal development will sometimes conflict with the goal of helping others, but Douglass's hope is that the former will better enable us to achieve the latter.

During the several decades of his public life, Douglass was preoccupied with the moral health of the American republic. Late in life, far removed from the optimism of his early days as a Garrisonian abolitionist, he said that he had come to realize that it "is hard for men to be just."[87] In order to help men find and stay on the path of virtue, it is crucial to cultivate a healthy moral atmosphere. The development of a moral ecology supportive of freedom is not, Douglass thought, a task that should be left entirely to the state. Instead, the project of achieving and flourishing under conditions of freedom is one that is primarily the responsibility of individuals who live within the political community. Individuals can be "friends of freedom" by acting in responsible ways. If individuals were perfect, no government would be necessary. Because human beings fall short of perfection, the state has some role to play in creating and maintaining a moral ecology that is supportive of freedom. It is to Douglass's thoughts on the top-down cultivation of moral ecology that we now turn.

6

"Man Is Neither Wood Nor Stone"

Top-Down Moral Education in
Douglass's Liberalism

Introduction

Frederick Douglass was not a systematic political thinker. He did not offer a detailed account of the role institutions play in the moral development of citizens. He was not, though, completely silent on top-down forms of moral education. By top-down, I mean those forms of moral education that originate with state institutions and officials or that have a more formal character than the matters discussed in the last chapter. In this chapter, my aim is to show that Douglass recognized the importance of top-down mechanisms for securing the conditions necessary for the exercise of personal freedom. More specifically, he thought individuals could be "taught" to behave in responsible ways by the threat of force, the promulgation of positive law, the rhetoric of statesmen, the celebration of political ideals in civic ceremonies, and through a robust system of elementary, secondary, and higher education.

As I said at the end of the last chapter, if human beings were perfect, no top-down mechanisms would be needed to achieve a political culture that promotes freedom and responsibility. Douglass recognized that individuals sometimes behave in less than virtuous ways. Whether or not individuals are disposed to act in responsible ways in support of liberal ideals is not a matter of chance. Instead, Douglass believed individuals could be encouraged to behave in responsible ways through various mechanisms of moral education. Implicit in this view was a belief in the malleability of human nature. In an important 1869 speech entitled "Our Composite Nationality," Douglass contended that "men are improvable," an idea he called "the grand distinguishing attribute of humanity."[1] Responsible behavior, he held, can and must be encouraged by state action.

In what follows, I discuss several top-down mechanisms of moral education that are part of Douglass's political thought. I begin with an exploration of his defense of the use of physical force as an educative measure. He defended the use of force by the state and by private parties in defense of rights not only as a matter of justice but also as a way to "teach" others about the requirements of liberal political morality. Then, I examine various "public messages" sent by state officials through positive law, the rhetoric of statesmen, and civic ceremonies before proceeding to discuss Douglass's hope that a robust system of public and private education would make individuals better citizens. Realizing the promises of liberalism is largely up to citizens but, Douglass believed, the state has some role to play in teaching individuals about what it means to be a responsible member of a free society.

"We Are Writing the Statutes of Eternal Justice": The Educative Potential of Force

Liberals are suspicious of moral education because they value autonomy and usually doubt the legitimacy of state attempts to make men moral. According to contemporary political theorist Thomas Spragens, liberal suspicions of moral education are rooted in "epistemic humility," "respect for individual autonomy," and "insistence on the equal moral worth and political standing of all liberal citizens."[2] As a result of these suspicions, liberals believe "character development" should occur, if at all, through "education and habituation rather than through coercion or indoctrination."[3] Although the liberal discomfort with state-directed moral education is evident, it would be a mistake to say that liberals completely reject the use of coercion to educate individuals. This is because liberals believe coercion is justified in defense of individual rights and such coercion is often imbued with educative potential. When Douglass defended the use of force, he often appealed to the educative value of violence in defense of natural rights.

Douglass's belief in the educative value of force was rooted in his fundamental assumptions about human nature. Before, during, and after the Civil War, Douglass had to confront the arguments of racists who questioned whether or not black people were fit for self-government. In a speech delivered in Brooklyn in 1863, Douglass responded to these skeptics by declaring: "The foundation of all governments and all codes of laws is the fact that man is a rational creature, and is capable of guiding his conduct by ideas of right and wrong, of good and evil, by hope of reward and fear of punishment."[4] It is precisely because human beings are capable of altering their behavior in response to hope of reward and fear of punishment that civil government is a possibility. In the 1851 essay "Is Civil Government Right?" Douglass reiterated this idea: "[R]ewards and punishments are natural agents for restraining evil and promoting good, man being endowed with faculties keenly alive to both."[5] According to this view, human reason enables men to understand what is right and wrong, and when this is not enough to move them to act justly their reason also enables them to understand that acting unjustly may lead to punishment. The promulgation and enforcement of positive law, Douglass believed, is justified because human beings are endowed with rationality, which allows them to understand the potential consequences of disobeying the law.

For Douglass, the "governmental authority to pass laws" and "compel obedience to any laws" is limited by the "natural rights and happiness of man."[6] "Human government," he said, "is for the protection of human rights" and it is sometimes necessary for the state to "repel aggression by force."[7] As I demonstrated in chapter 3, Douglass's commitment to natural rights led him to reject anarchism and endorse limited government: "Society without law is society with a curse, driving men into isolation and depriving them of one of the greatest blessings of which man is susceptible."[8] The use of force is necessary and justified, in Douglass's view, because there are "hardened villains" who "will cheat, steal, rob, burn, and murder their fellow creatures, and because there are these exceptions to the mass of humanity, society has a right to protect itself against their depredations and aggressions upon the common weal."[9] The creation of laws to combat hardened villains is only effectual, he said, when there is a state strong enough to enforce them: "Pen, ink, and paper liberty are excellent when there is a party behind it to respect and secure its enjoyment. Human laws are not self executing. To be of any service they must be made vital, active, and certain."[10]

What does Douglass's embrace of the use of state force in defense of natural rights have to do with moral education? His discussions of just force almost always include some reference to what "lessons" are "taught" by the enforcement of law. In the essay on civil government cited above, Douglass wrote:

Men need to be taught, not only the happy consequences arising from dealing justly, but the dreadful consequences which result from injustice; their fears, therefore, may be as legitimately appealed to as their hopes, and he who repudiates such appeals, throws away an important instrumentality for establishing justice among men, and promoting peace and happiness of society. All tyrants, all oppressors should be taught, by precept and by example, that, in trampling wantonly and ruthlessly upon the lives and liberties of their unoffending brother-men, they forfeit their own right to liberty.[11]

In response to William Lloyd Garrison's pacifism, Douglass repeated his case for the educative value of force: "There are lessons needful to mankind, which will be learned only when written in blood; and however it may be deplored, it is which can secure 'peace,' to the sons of man."[12] The use of force in defense of natural rights, Douglass hoped, could teach individuals to behave justly.

Douglass's belief that government action in defense of natural rights could contribute to a healthy moral ecology was rooted in his reflections on the "education" of slavery, which had the opposite effect. In an 1846 speech in Paisley, Scotland, cited above, he discussed the process by which the moral ecology of slavery shapes individuals in the wrong direction:

[Slavery] destroys all the finer feelings of our nature—it renders the people less humane—leads them to regard cruelty with indifference, as the boy born and bred within the sound of the thundering roar of Niagara, feels nothing strange because he is used to the noise; while a stranger trembles with awe, and feels he is in the presence of God—in the midst of his mighty works. People reared in the midst of slavery become indifferent to human wrongs, indifferent to the entreaties, the tears, the agonies of the slave under the lash; all of which appear to be music to the ears of slaveholders. Slavery has weakened the love of freedom in the US—they have lost much of that regard for liberty which once characterized them. It has eaten out the vitals from the hearts of the Americans.[13]

Just as slavery lessened respect for the dignity of man by allowing the rights of individuals to be violated, the use of force in defense of natural rights can deepen the community's respect of human dignity. In 1894, Douglass spoke to a large audience in the Metropolitan A.M.E. Church in Washington, D.C., on the topic of "The Lessons of the Hour." Among other things, he discussed the problem of lynching in the South, which occurred in a moral atmosphere that was shaped by "the education" of slavery. Many Northerners, he said, doubted the veracity of lynching stories from the South because they had a hard time understanding how individuals could "shoot and hang their fellowmen without just cause." The mistake of Northern skeptics, Douglass said, was "in their assumption that the lynchers are like other men." Northerners "overlook the natural effect and influence of the life, education and habits of the lynchers. Their institutions have taught them no respect for human life and especially the life of the negro. It has in fact taught them absolute contempt for his life. The sacredness of life which ordinary men feel does not touch them anywhere."[14] The culture of slavery excluded some individuals from the protection of the law and in so doing taught the rest of the population to disregard their dignity as human beings. The inclusion of all human beings under the shield of the law, Douglass hoped, would strengthen the community's respect for individual rights.

Douglass's hope was that the creation of a just society in which the natural rights of *all* individuals were protected under law would contribute to the development of a "humanitarian culture" in which the dignity of all human beings is respected.[15] Perhaps paradoxically, he thought the use of force could contribute to a greater appreciation for the dignity of human life. When the state uses force in defense of natural rights, Douglass argued, it teaches its citizens that there are "dreadful consequences" for acting unjustly. He hoped these dreadful consequences would have a deterrent effect on would-be villains and he thought the use of force in these circumstances would have a beneficial effect on the moral atmosphere.

Interestingly, Douglass did not extend this view to support for the death penalty. In a speech entitled "Capital Punishment Is a Mockery of Justice" delivered in Rochester, New York, in 1858, he laid out his case against this practice. A local man by the name of Ira Stout was scheduled to be executed and Douglass rose to speak "to save Rochester from being disgraced," and "to save a human being from being slain in cool blood."[16] If Ira Stout dies "by the hand of the executioner," Douglass warned, then "the responsibility falls heavily upon the whole community." In language that seems to be a departure from the words cited above in defense of educative violence, he argued that life should "not be deliberately or voluntarily destroyed, either by individuals separately or combined in what is called Government."[17] Douglass again relied on the idea of moral ecology in defense of this position.

[A]ny settled custom, precept, example or law, the observance of which necessarily tends to cheapen human life, or in any measure serves to diminish and weaken man's respect for it, is a custom, precept, example and law utterly inconsistent with the law of eternal goodness written on the constitution of man by his Maker, and is diametrically opposed to the safety, welfare and happiness of mankind.[18]

It seems that Douglass accepted the use of educative violence in self-defense and in a state of war (which he believed slavery to be), but he did not think that the execution of a murderer could be justified if the "criminal is firmly secured in the iron grasp of the government."[19]

In sum, Douglass believed the use of force to protect natural rights was the first "office of government."[20] When the state acts to defend the natural rights of individuals, it sends a message about the dignity of human beings. Failure to respect human dignity, the liberal state instructs us, will lead to "dreadful consequences" for the perpetrator. The failure of Southern governments to protect the natural rights of some individuals had a deep impact on the moral atmosphere of the South for decades after the Civil War. By declaring that some individuals were outside the protection of the law, Southern governments cultivated an inhumane culture. The moral education provided by the use of force in defense of natural rights, Douglass thought, would take time to sink in. In 1860, he predicted that it would take "several generations of humanitarian culture" to alter the moral ecology of the United States.[21] In 1878, he commented on the slow rate of moral progress of many Southerners: "Men are not changed from lambs into tigers instantaneously, nor from tigers into lambs instantaneously," but a strong state commitment to the protection of natural rights is a necessary first step in the moral education of a liberal citizenry.[22]

Laws, Statesmen, and Ceremonies: Moral Education by Statute, Rhetoric, and Ritual

Douglass believed the use of force by the state could serve as a blunt instrumentality to teach men the dreadful consequences that follow from violating the rights of others. At this point, I would like to explore other means of moral education that he believed the state and its officials could use to communicate messages to individuals about proper behavior in a liberal polity. First, I discuss his belief that positive law could play an important educative role. Second, I explore Douglass's idea of statesmanship and show that he believed it was important for political leaders to utilize the bully pulpit to educate individuals about rights and responsibilities. Third, I examine Douglass's belief that civic ceremonies can play a key role in reminding individuals about the shared moral commitments that should animate their political lives.

"This Law, Though Dead, Did Speak": Moral Education through Positive Law

Douglass believed positive law could play an important role in the moral education of liberal citizens because it can have an impact on the moral atmosphere of a community. He argued that even when a positive law is not enforced it can play an important educative role because it is a formal state-ment of the political morality of the community. From Douglass's perspec-tive, then, laws can serve as moral ideals to which members of the commu-nity ought to aspire. Contemporary scholars call this an "aspirational" view of law. According to legal scholar Philip Harvey, an aspirational law is "a kind of law by means of which human societies 'legislate' goals for themselves. By asserting that everyone has [human] rights, even when we are not prepared to honor them in practice, we challenge ourselves to live up to our own aspi-rations and pre-authorize actions . . . to bring our practice into compliance with our aspirations."[23] Although, Douglass admitted, "a people is sometimes worse than their laws," it is worthwhile to have the laws on the books for aspirational reasons.[24] In this section, I explore several examples Douglass offered of how positive laws can communicate aspirational messages to citi-zens and, as such, serve as important means of moral education.

The first example of Douglass adopting an "aspirational" attitude toward positive law is his antislavery reading of the Constitution.[25] Once he rejected the proslavery reading of the Constitution accepted by the Garrisonians, he began to view the Constitution as an important statement about the aims of the American union. Douglass was particularly fond of pointing to the Pre-amble's call "to secure the blessings of liberty to ourselves and our posterity" as a moral message from the Founders to later generations. Each generation's task, Douglass argued, was to move America closer to the ideal of freedom for all human beings. Citizens and statesmen can appeal to the Constitution as an authoritative text that teaches us about the goals of the American polit-ical project. Douglass believed the text itself could serve as a moral teacher for those who would heed its words.

Similarly, Douglass viewed the Emancipation Proclamation as an impor-tant symbolic gesture in the fight against slavery. Although the Proclamation did little to actually liberate slaves from their masters, it offered a moral mes-sage about the mission of the Civil War. The Proclamation communicated to the nation that the war was about slavery and that Union victory would mean abolition. The Proclamation gave a deeper moral meaning to the vio-lence that was taking place. In the words of historian David Blight, Douglass believed the Proclamation "had invested the war with sanctity" and hence its symbolic significance could not be overstated. After the Proclamation was issued, Blight writes, the "cruel and apocalyptic war had become holy."[26]

After the Civil War, Douglass argued that the Thirteenth, Fourteenth, and Fifteenth Amendments to the Constitution established not only political but moral standards by which citizens ought to abide. Even though the government's ability and willingness to enforce these amendments were called into question almost immediately, these laws played an important aspirational role—by promising the end of slavery, due process, equal protection, and the right to vote to all men, these amendments played an important role in establishing goals for postwar America. Another example is provided by Douglass's attitude toward the Civil Rights Act of 1875. In 1883 the Supreme Court struck down the Act, which guaranteed equal treatment in "public accommodations." Many observers said the Supreme Court's decision was of little consequence because the Civil Rights Act had not been enforced in the South. Douglass disagreed:

> It is said that this decision will make no difference in the treatment of colored people; that the Civil Rights Bill was a dead letter, and could not be enforced. There is some truth in all this, but it is not the whole truth. That bill, like all advance legislation, was a banner on the outer wall of American liberty, a noble moral standard, uplifted for the education of the American people. There are tongues in trees, books, in the running brooks,—sermons in stones. This law, though dead, did speak. It expressed the sentiment of justice and fair play, common to every honest heart. Its voice was against popular prejudice and meanness. It appealed to all the noble and patriotic instincts of the American people. It told the American people that they were all equal before the law; that they belonged to a common country and were equal citizens.[27]

"Advance legislation" is Douglass's term for "aspirational law"—it is law that, even if not enforced, sends a moral message to citizens; it establishes moral ideals to which individuals ought to aspire. In the case of the Civil Rights Bill, Douglass believed that Congress sent an important message about justice and fair play. Even if the law had little immediate practical impact, he thought it might contribute to the cultivation of a humanitarian culture.

Douglass's belief that positive law should promote moral ideals such as justice and fairness is also revealed by his endorsement of legislative action on the "labor question." The "labor question" was a catch-all phrase used during the nineteenth century for matters related to the working conditions, compensation, and advancement opportunities of the laboring class. Douglass worried about the growing gap between rich and poor and endorsed a bill offered by Representative George F. Hoar of Massachusetts that would create a Commission to "investigate the subject of the wages and hours of labor, and of the division of the joint profits of labor and capital between the laborer and the capitalist, and the social, educational, and sanitary conditions of the laboring classes of the United States, and how the same are affected by existing laws regulating commerce, finance, and currency."[28] This Commission would be charged with the task of offering legislative suggestions in response to issues raised by the labor question.

As noted in chapter 3, Douglass's concerns about the compensation and conditions of the working class belie the claim that he was a laissez-faire thinker.[29] His endorsement of legislative action to ensure that "American civilization" was designed "primarily for Man" and not "Property" is evidence that he believed the state had some role to play in promoting fairness that goes beyond the laissez-faire embrace of the night watchman state. In addition to general concerns about the labor question, Douglass believed the state had an important role to play in combating the systematic unfairness of the postwar economy in the South. After lamenting the nefarious impact of the sharecropping and trucking systems, he said, "The true object for which governments are ordained among men is to protect the weak against the encroachments of the strong, to hold its strong arm of justice over all the civil relations of its citizens and to see that all have an equal chance in the race of life."[30] Even a limited liberal state, he argued, must have enough power to secure the basic rights of individuals.

> I know it is said that the general government is a government of limited powers. . . . If the general government had the power to make black men citizens, it has the power to protect them in that citizenship. If it had the right to make them voters it has the right to protect them in the exercise of the elective franchise. . . . If it has not this right, it is destitute of the fundamental quality of a government, and ought to be hissed and hurried out of the sisterhood of governments, for it is then only a pretended government, a usurper, a sham, a delusion, and a snare.[31]

Douglass believed the state had an important role to play in promoting fair play. Like his defense of the use of force to protect natural rights, he endorsed state action in pursuit of fairness because of its direct impact on the lives of individuals as well as its impact on the moral ecology of the community. Legislative action to combat discriminatory and systematically unfair labor practices sends a message about the liberal commitment to equal opportunity and the importance of rewarding merit.

Douglass's discussions of the Constitution, the Emancipation Proclamation, the Civil Rights Bill, and labor legislation provide evidence that he believed positive law can be a useful instrumentality of moral education. According to his reading, the Constitution's preamble sends a moral message about the duty to secure the blessings of liberty to all people, the Emancipation Proclamation sent a message about the meaning of the Civil War, the Civil Rights Bill established a moral ideal for the social sphere, and labor legislation articulated a message to the American people about the importance of fairness in the economic sphere. Taken together, these examples provide evidence that Douglass believed positive law could play an important educative role in a liberal society. Even those laws that are not enforced, he claimed, communicate valuable messages that can have an impact on the moral ecology.

"Teach the People for Once": Statesmen as Moral Educators

Douglass believed political leaders have an important role to play in nurturing a just and virtuous political community. Statesmen are able to impact the attitudes of citizens through legislation and by articulating moral and political messages about the fundamental values of the community.[32] Throughout his public career, Douglass maintained a firm faith in the power of language to move human beings to act. A good statesman, he thought, is an individual whose rhetoric defends the value of freedom and reminds citizens of the responsibilities that are supportive of freedom.

Douglass's belief in the importance of statesmanship was, at least in part, rooted in his faith in the power of speech. "Great is the miracle of human speech," he said, "by it nations are enlightened and reformed; by it the cause of justice and liberty is defended, by it evils are exposed, ignorance dispelled, the path of duty made plain, and by it those that live today are put into the possession of the wisdom of ages gone by."[33] By the end of the 1850s, Douglass had lost some of his faith in the power of speech to move men from "the downy seat of inaction," but he never completely abandoned his belief in the power of preaching.[34] In 1884, as many civil rights advocates were in a state of despair over the abandonment of Reconstruction, Douglass remained hopeful: "[There is] one very strong ground of hope I have for the negro. It is this: the discussion of his claims to consideration still goes on. Happily for him, we live in a country governed by ideas as well as by laws, and these ideas are constantly changed and modified by the light of discussion. . . . While there is one voice heard in behalf of justice and fair play, the negro need not despair."[35]

It is clear that Douglass believed the art of rhetoric is an important tool of statesmen, but what is it that statesmen ought to say? Like so many other aspects of his thought, Douglass assessed statesmen by the presence of "moral feeling" in their rhetoric. After reading President Lincoln's letter to Horace Greeley in which he said he would "save the Union without freeing *any* slave" if he could, Douglass declared, "Our chief danger lies in the absence of all moral feeling in the utterances of our rulers."[36] At the time Lincoln wrote these words, Douglass read them as appalling evidence of his moral shallowness. Rather than denying claims that the point of contention between the North and the South was the issue of slavery, Douglass thought an honorable statesman should admit this to be true and attempt to rally the people to the cause of liberty. During the war, Douglass said, "The lesson for the statesman at this hour is to discover and apply some principle of Government which shall produce unity of sentiment, unity of idea, unity of object. Union without unity is, as we have seen, body without soul, marriage without love, a barrel without hoops, which falls at the first touch."[37] What principle of government should the statesman appeal to as the moral glue of the Union?

> We want a country, and we are fighting for a country, which shall not brand the Declaration of Independence as a lie. We want a country whose fundamental institutions we can proudly defend before the highest intelligence and civilization of the age. . . . We want a country, and are fighting for a country, which shall be free from sectional political parties—free from sectional religious denominations—free from sectional benevolent associations—free from every kind and description of sect, party, and combination of a sectional character. We want a country, and are fighting for a country, where social intercourse and commercial relations shall neither be embarrassed nor embittered by the imperious exactions of an insolent slaveholding Oligarchy, which required Northern merchants to sell their souls as a condition precedent to selling their goods.[38]

These passages are evidence that Douglass believed it was the role of statesmen to nurture a sense of community by talking about the values that unite us. For Douglass, the values at the core of the American polity are the commitments to liberty and equality, which, he believed, should serve as the touchstones of political discourse and action.

Douglass's own speaking and writing is a model of the sort of moralized rhetoric he hoped American statesmen would adopt. His reflections upon and discussions of the "soul of the nation" are models of righteous statesmanship. During the Civil War, Douglass said: "What our rulers at Washington stand in need of, in order to [bring about] a speedy end of this slaveholding rebellion, and to place the nation on a firm foundation of peace and prosperity, is neither men nor money, but a living and all-controlling faith in the principles of freedom avowed in the Declaration of Independence, and which are the foundation of the Government."[39] In 1894, Douglass continued to express his concern about the health of the American soul:

> Could I be heard by this great nation, I would call to mind the sublime and glorious truths with which, at its birth, it saluted a listening world. . . . It announced the advent of a nation, based upon human brotherhood and the self-evident truths of liberty and equality. . . . Apply these sublime and glorious truths to the situation now before you. . . . Recognize the fact that the rights of the humblest citizen are as worthy of protection as those of the highest, and your problem will be solved; and, whatever may be in store for it in the future, whether prosperity or adversity; whether it shall have foes without, or foes within, whether there shall be peace, or war; based upon the eternal principles of truth, justice and humanity, and with no class having any cause of complaint or grievance, your Republic will stand and flourish forever.[40]

Statesmen, like the Reformers discussed in the last chapter, play the important role of reminding their listeners of the "eternal principles" expressed in the Declaration of Independence and encouraging them to observe them in practice. Douglass desired to see more statesmen like Charles Sumner, who did not lose sight of fundamental moral principles when engaged in practical politics. Douglass even went so far as to call one of his mortal enemies, John C. Calhoun, a statesman for offering a principled defense of his views, appalling though they were. In a "Weekly Review of Congress" in 1850, Douglass offered this favorable comparison of Calhoun to Daniel Webster: "Calhoun is at least a statesman, candid and consistent with his principles, though they be abhorrent. . . . Webster, on the other hand, is a miserable, time-serving politician still seeking the Presidency, and willing to do anything to propitiate the slave power."[41] A calculating politician, Douglass believed, is lower in the rank of statesmanship than a public figure who is openly committed to immoral principles.

Douglass's belief in the power of rhetoric to morally educate the people is evident in his reaction to the death of Robert E. Lee. In an 1870 editorial tellingly entitled "Great Public Virtues," Douglass chastised public officials for praising Lee upon his death; contending that praising this "perjured traitor" sends a bad message to the people about the rights and responsibilities they have as citizens of the American republic. "We feel no remorse," Douglass wrote, "at the passing of Robert E. Lee. During the war he did all he could to destroy the government, and since the war he has labored to keep alive the embers of sectional discord. He was also a base traitor who violated his constitutional oath—and he was a cruel slavemaster."[42]

In addition to reminding citizens of these fundamental principles, statesmen have the difficult task of motivating citizens to practice the virtues supportive of these principles. For a statesman in a liberal regime, this task is complicated. Liberals are, by definition, uncomfortable with coercion and indoctrination and the moral vocabulary of solidarity within liberalism is limited. It is necessary, therefore, for liberal statesmen to offer a series of justifications for responsible behavior that are similar to those offered by Douglass. In order to cultivate a sense of community and responsibility, liberal statesmen must appeal to the variety of "actuating motives" that influence human beings.[43] Appeals to human brotherhood, principles of political morality, self-interest, and respect for virtuous action are all potential instruments for liberal statesmen engaged in the important business of crafting the souls of citizens in ways supportive of freedom.

It is worth noting that Douglass believed statesmen had an opportunity to teach these important moral lessons through the bully pulpit of elected office as well as the platforms provided during political campaigns. Soon after the creation of the Republican Party, he wrote: "Teach the people for once in a political campaign the sacredness of human rights, the brotherhood of man, and expose to all the living light of day the soul and terrible abomination of Southern slavery, and your Republican party will deserve success, which is better even than success itself."[44] For Douglass, political campaigns were great opportunities for moral education. Through the debates, pamphlets, and speeches that are part of every campaign, he hoped, righteous statesmen would teach their listeners important lessons about the fundamental commitments of liberal political morality.

Douglass believed good statesmen can serve as moral teachers that remind citizens of the ideals of the polity and the ethos that promotes those ideals. Good statesmen separate themselves from reformers by demonstrating the political skill necessary to navigate the complex waters of democratic politics. Douglass's views on good statesmanship find their fullest expression in his reflections on Abraham Lincoln. Although Douglass expressed frustration with what he perceived to be Lincoln's lack of moral feeling in the early 1860s, he grew to believe that he was "the greatest statesman that ever presided over the destinies of this Republic."[45] As noted above, when Douglass caught wind of the letter to Horace Greeley in which Lincoln declared that his "paramount object" in the struggle with the Confederacy was to "save the Union" and that he did not care about the fate of slavery, he expressed outrage.[46] Although in times like these Lincoln seemed to fall short of the moral righteousness of the Reformer, the passage of time led Douglass to appreciate how "Father Abraham" combined his pragmatic political skills with a devotion to the moral principles of the Declaration of Independence. In 1876, on the eleventh anniversary of Lincoln's assassination, Douglass delivered a speech at the unveiling of the Freedmen's Monument in Washington, D.C. In this speech, which was delivered before an audience of dignitaries that included members of Congress and the U.S. Supreme Court, Douglass offered his most extensive assessment of Lincoln. Douglass's speech is nuanced, but his central conclusion is captured when he said: "Viewed from the genuine abolition ground Mr. Lincoln seemed tardy, cold, dull, and indifferent: but measuring him by the sentiment of his country, a sentiment he was bound as a statesman to consult, he was swift, zealous, radical, and determined."[47] In the words of political theorist Peter C. Myers, Douglass came to accept the extent to which Lincoln was bound by "the imperative of democratic statesmanship to consult the sentiment of a country largely benighted on race and increasingly divided on moral fundamentals."[48] In the end, Douglass ended up believing that Lincoln was a prudent statesman who fell short of the moral righteousness of the Reformer, but played the important role of using his political skills to move the country closer to justice.

For Douglass, then, the role of a good statesman is to use his position of prominence to "teach the people" about the "sacredness of human rights" and the "brotherhood of man."[49] He thought that rhetoric, in the words of Peter C. Myers, was often "meant to serve pedagogical ends."[50] The use of moralized rhetoric is not, though, the sum of good statesmanship. Instead, Douglass's reflections on Abraham Lincoln reveal that the moral purity of a statesman's rhetoric can falter without jeopardizing the value of his contribution. In the end, Douglass expressed a deep appreciation for Lincoln's political acumen, which was often the source of his less than inspiring rhetoric on the issue of slavery. Lincoln's ability to navigate the torrents of mid-nineteenth-century American politics was a necessary foundation for the series of events that led to the accomplishment of what Douglass believed to be the most urgent goal for the republic: the abolition of slavery.

This consideration of Douglass's evolving views of Lincoln draws our attention to the important question of where pragmatism fits within his conception of good statesmanship. Although we associate Douglass's own activism with the moral righteousness of the Reformer, there is ample evidence that he appreciated the duty of the statesman to be sensitive to the demands of the political context. Fidelity to moral principle is important, he thought, but it must always be coupled with an understanding that realizing those principles in the real world requires willingness to adapt to the circumstances of the moment. A couple of examples will bear this out.

First, I mentioned above Douglass's change of mind about the legitimacy of the U.S. Constitution. In his early years as an abolitionist, he accepted William Lloyd Garrison's position that the Constitution condoned slavery and, as such, must be rejected as illegitimate. In the late 1840s, Douglass was confronted with the arguments of several antislavery activists—most notably Lysander Spooner and Gerrit Smith—who contended that the Constitution could be read as an abolitionist document. After years of study and debate, Douglass was "converted" to the antislavery reading of the Constitution. The political significance of this conversion was great. One of the most important consequences of the Garrisonian position was a rejection of conventional political participation because such participation was thought to be a tacit acceptance of constitutional legitimacy. By moving away from the Garrisonian position, Douglass was able to begin endorsing involvement in conventional politics through voting, electioneering, and the like. The true cause of Douglass's conversion has been a subject of great debate since he announced it. Douglass's contemporaries and scholars have offered theories that have ranged from financial and political motivations to philosophical and psychological explanations for the conversion. We will never know for certain why Douglass changed his mind, but I think a fairly strong case can be made that the most likely explanation is that some combination of these factors led him to this new position. Among other things, Douglass argued that the Garrisonian position was problematic because it forced the antislavery movement to fight for abolition with one hand tied behind its back. The unacceptability of the Garrisonian attitude toward the Constitution was compounded by the fact that, in Douglass's eyes, it did not contribute to any compelling end. What, Douglass asked, was the Garrisonian refusal to engage in conventional politics really accomplishing? It may have provided its devotees with a greater sense of moral righteousness, but Douglass said it did not appear to be bringing the country any closer to the real prize: the abolition of slavery. It might be too much to say that history vindicated Douglass's position in this debate. It is not, however, too much to say that developments in conventional politics—most notably the election of radical and even moderate Republicans—helped precipitate the Civil War.

A second example demonstrates the pragmatic dimension of Douglass's statesmanship. During the 1890s, a group of civil rights activists in Louisiana led by Louis A. Martinet formed a Citizens' Committee to challenge the Jim Crow separate railroad car law. The group published an appeal in Martinet's weekly civil rights newspaper, *The Crusader*, in which they "insisted that the character of American citizenship was threatened if the issue of segregation was not pursued in the courts." The Citizens' Committee worked to create a test case—the case that would eventually become *Plessy vs. Ferguson*—to force the courts to address whether or not the separate car law was consistent with the Fourteenth Amendment to the U.S. Constitution. The Committee wrote to the elder statesman Douglass to request his support for their legal challenge. Historian Blair Kelley's description of Douglass's response reveals his sensitivity to political context.

> The *Crusader* published Douglass's response, in which he declined because "he was opposed to making decisions and establishing precedents against his race." Douglass doubted that the courts, which had previously been unsympathetic to the question of Negro rights, would remedy the crisis of Southern segregation.[51]

In response to the request from Martinet and the Citizens' Committee, Douglass did not limit his analysis to the question of whether or not, as a matter of principle, he believed the separate car law could be squared with the letter and spirit of the Constitution; clearly, it could not. Instead, Douglass asked a prudential question: is the Citizens' Committee's strategy likely to bring about an end to the separate car law or is it likely to enshrine in the annals of constitutional law a doctrine that might undermine the cause of civil rights? When Douglass reflected on the make-up of the Supreme Court and the trajectory of constitutional law at that particular moment in history, he concluded that the strategy of the Citizens' Committee was not the right one, so he declined to lend his symbolic support.

"It Is More Than Ribbons, or Stars, or Garters": Moral Education by Ritual

Douglass believed civic ceremonies could serve as valuable moments of moral education for the American people. On certain days of the year, such as the Fourth of July and Memorial Day, he thought it was necessary and appropriate to reflect on the meaning of our civic life. Although civic ceremonies are not necessarily state-sanctioned or -directed, he believed it was legitimate for the state to offer official recognition of such holidays as a way of encouraging citizens to engage in civic reflection. These occasions, he hoped, would provide citizens with opportunities to think about and discuss the meaning of their political lives. Douglass's well-known "What to the Slave Is the Fourth of July?" oration is one example of utilizing a civic ceremony to provoke citizens to think about the gap between the moral ideals of the Declaration of Independence and the realities of American life.[52] After the Civil War, Douglass was a vocal advocate of the rituals associated with "Decoration Day" (now known as Memorial Day), a day featuring a "bevy of flags, floral wreaths on soldiers' graves, and brightly uniformed marchers in a large parade."[53] Although the celebration of civic holidays blurs the line between bottom-up and top-down cultivation of moral ecology, I am discussing it here because it has a more formal character than the sorts of things discussed in the previous chapter. So why did Douglass believe Decoration Day was such an important opportunity for civic education?

In 1882, Douglass delivered a speech entitled "We Must Not Abandon the Observance of Decoration Day." In it, he offered a detailed defense of the civic ritual of memorializing American soldiers. "Annual memorial occasions," he began, "have deep and sacred significance" because they are about "more than ribbons, or stars, or garters." To be invited to participate in such a ceremony, he continued, is an immense honor because it makes an individual "a man among men, a full partaker in the rights, duties, privileges, and immunities of American citizenship—a citizenship of having a grander future than any bestowed by any other country in the world."[54] Douglass's connection of the ceremony with the "rights, duties, privileges, and immunities of American citizenship" is significant. On occasions such as Decoration Day, individuals are able to participate in a ritualized celebration of the idea of American citizenship. This ritual is a celebration of the rights that are promised in American founding documents *and* it is a reminder of the duties of citizenship. Indeed, the day is a microcosm of one of the forms of civic virtue Douglass believed to be vital for the health of the liberal project.

On Decoration Day, citizens are invited to set aside their *private* concerns so they can contribute to the discussion and celebration of *public* ideals. Douglass began his defense of Decoration Day by asking a series of questions:

> Does any man question the right or the propriety of this annual ceremony? Can any man who loves his country advise its discontinuance? Is there anywhere another altar better than this, around which the nation can meet one day in each year to renew its national vows and manifest its loyal devotion to the principles of our free government? Is there any eminence from which we can better survey the past, the present, the future?[55]

Douglass responded, "For my part I know no other such day. There is none other so abundant in suggestions and themes of immediate national interests as this day."[56] The celebration of Decoration Day, he argued, was a crucial part of the ongoing struggle over the soul of the nation; it was an attempt to push the souls of citizens in the direction of freedom. "While good and evil, loyalty and treason, liberty and slavery remain opposites and irreconcilable, while they retain their fighting qualities, and shall contend, as they must contend, for ascendancy in the world, their respective forces will adopt opposite emblems and tokens."[57] For Douglass, the meaning of Decoration Day was clear: it was an opportunity to honor the sacrifice of those who fought and died for the cause of freedom in the Civil War. Some argued that it was time to forgive and forget, but Douglass said he could not accept this suggestion "to the extent of abandoning the observance of Decoration Day. If rebellion was wrong and loyalty right, if slavery was wrong and emancipation right, we are rightfully here today."[58]

Douglass's explanation of the moral meaning of Decoration Day has implications beyond memorializing the Civil War. Indeed, Decoration Day was, for him, a celebration of the civic virtues necessary to secure freedom:

> We come around this national family altar, one day in each year, to pay our grateful homage to the memory of brave men—to express and emphasize by speech and pageantry our reverence for those great qualities of enlightened and exalted human nature, which in every land are the stay and salvation of the race; the qualities without which states would perish, society dissolve, progress become impossible and mankind sink back into a howling wilderness of barbarism. In a word, we are here to reassert and reproclaim [sic] our admiration for the patriotic zeal, the stern fortitude, the noble self-sacrifice, the unflinching determination, the quenchless enthu-

siasm, the high and measureless courage with which loyal men, true to the Republic in the hour of supreme peril, dashed themselves against a wanton, wicked and gigantic rebellion, and suppressed it beyond the power to rise again.[59]

Against those who sought to abandon Decoration Day out of deference to the wounded ego of the South, Douglass argued that the day was less about the sins of the Confederacy than the virtues of the Union. In other words, he wanted to use Decoration Day as a way to vindicate what historian David Blight calls the "emancipationist vision" of the Civil War as a revolutionary moment in the history of freedom. According to Blight, Douglass was the "intellectual godfather" of the emancipationist understanding of the war. Events like Decoration Day were, for Douglass, opportunities to shape "postwar ideological memory" in a way that understood the Civil War as "an American second founding" that transformed the meaning of the Union.[60]

In addition to the celebration of civic ceremonies like Decoration Day, Douglass offered support for monuments that could serve as tangible recognition of the virtue demonstrated by members of the political community. Toward the end of the Decoration Day speech, he said:

> It is fit and proper that [Rochester] should have a monument to the virtues developed in her in the momentous crisis wherein was involved the life and death, the salvation and destruction of the Republic. This monument, symmetrical and beautiful, would be a tribute to the dead, and a noble inspiration to the living. It would stand before your people mute but eloquent—a sacred object around which your children and your children's children could rally, and draw high inspiration of patriotism and self-sacrifice by studying the deeds of their fathers, which saved their country to peace, to union and to liberty.[61]

A monument dedicated to the memory of the Union soldiers who fought in the Civil War, Douglass hoped, could serve as the basis for a moral, even religious, education for future generations. Such an object would, in his view, be "sacred" and could inspire future citizens to study the virtuous deeds of their predecessors. Like a preacher blessing a place of worship, Douglass offered this strong endorsement of a civic holy site where individuals could reflect upon the "price" of freedom.

In "Douglass, Ideological Slavery and Postbellum Racial Politics," Gene Andrew Jarrett draws our attention to the role Douglass imagined monuments might play in influencing moral ecology.[62] According to Jarrett, Douglass recognized that his own "moral philosophy of political egalitarianism" was at war with "the unwritten laws of racial injustice and chauvinism" in nineteenth-century American culture.[63] For this reason, Jarrett writes, Douglass believed that "cultural artifacts and institutions such as monuments" were a crucial part of the egalitarian arsenal in the fight for inclusion. These artifacts, he writes, "further helped to mount the ideological attack on the 'unwritten' laws that oppressed blacks."[64]

Like so many other aspects of his thought, Douglass rooted his defense of civic ceremonies and monuments in his understanding of human nature:

> I base my views of the propriety of this occasion not upon partisan, partial and temporary considerations, but upon the broad foundations of human nature itself. Man is neither wood nor stone. He is described by the great poet, as a being looking before and after. He has a past, present and future. To eliminate either is a violation of his nature and an infringement upon his dignity. He is a progressive being, and memory, reason, and reflection are the resources of his improvement. With these perfections everything in the world, every great event has an alphabet, a picture, a voice to instruct.[65]

As I pointed out at the beginning of this chapter, Douglass believed in the malleability of human nature. There are core characteristics that all human beings share, he thought, but human nature can be altered by the moral atmosphere. Douglass hoped occasions like Decoration Day would promote freedom by contributing to the development of a humanitarian culture in which individuals would be sensitive to the rights of others and aware of the responsibilities upon which freedom depends.

Douglass's faith in the transformative power of civic ritual was not unlimited. After extolling the virtues of Decoration Day, he pointed out that the impact of such ceremonies is necessarily limited:

> But even here in this broad domain of memory, reason, experience and reflection, upon which man moves so grandly and so like a god, he is still a circumscribed and limited being. He can only travel so far. The ocean is large, but it has its bounds beyond which it may not pass. The same is the case with man. The strongest memory gives him at last only a vague, confused, and imperfect impression of the facts and experiences of the past. He at last sees men in that direction only as trees walking.[66]

Civic ceremonies, like moral ecology itself, can have an impact on the behavior of men, but they do not determine human behavior. Memorializing and celebrating the sacrifices of those who fought for freedom, Douglass thought, has only a slight impact on the mind-set of citizens, but it is a practice well worth continuing.

Douglass's case for the celebration of Decoration Day captures the spirit of his political thought because it is replete with arguments that tie freedom and responsibility together. Freedom is not a given, he insisted, it is an ideal that must be fought for and defended. "Eternal laws of rectitude are essential to the preservation, happiness and perfection of the human race," Douglass proclaimed, and they do not enforce themselves. Instead, it is left up to human beings to see to it that they are observed in the world. Civic holidays are worth celebrating, he believed, if they serve to deepen our devotion to the ideal of freedom and to remind us of the vigilance that is needed to maintain that freedom.[67]

"Education Means Emancipation": Educating Citizens for Freedom and Virtue

The last mechanism of "soulcraft" I wish to discuss is universal education. By universal education, I mean the state guarantee that all individuals will receive at least a primary and secondary education. The two major obligations of government, Douglass thought, are to ensure that all citizens are protected from violations of their rights and to see to it that all citizens are educated. He believed intellectual development was a crucial foundation for both freedom and virtue. In *My Bondage and My Freedom*, he explained that his belief in the connection between knowledge and freedom was born the moment his master said "knowledge unfits a child to be a slave."[68] There is something about enlightenment, he thought, that makes human beings fit to be free. Douglass also believed that intellectual development and moral virtue were connected. He often said that "ignorance and immorality" go hand in hand, so the enlightenment of individuals can serve the end of promoting moral virtue.

Universal education, Douglass argued, is required as a matter of justice to individuals and in the interest of the greater good. For individuals, education is a crucial tool for realizing the promise of freedom. "Knowledge," Douglass said in 1873, "is power" because theoretical and practical knowledge empowers individuals to secure and enjoy their freedom.[69] For the political community, the education of every individual should be a concern because educated human beings, he believed, are more likely to contribute to the economic and moral well-being of society: "[T]he whole country is directly interested in the education of every child that lives within its borders. The ignorance of any part of the American people so deeply concerns all the rest that there can be no doubt of the right to pass a law compelling the attendance of every child at school."[70] In this section, I explore three questions. Why was universal education so important to Douglass? Did he believe education was a state responsibility? How do these views fit into his political philosophy?

Douglass's deep commitment to universal education was rooted in his belief that the intellectual and moral capacities of human beings are only potentially great. Human beings are endowed with reason and the capacity for virtue, he thought, but these attributes must be developed through various forms of education:

> In his natural condition . . . man is only potentially great. As a mere physical being, he does not take high rank, even among the beasts of the field. . . . His true dignity is not to be sought in his arms or in his legs, but in his head. Here is the seat and source of all that is of especially great or practical importance in him. . . . There is power in the human mind, but education is needed for its development. As man is the highest on earth it follows that the vocation of the scholar is among the highest known to man. It is to teach and induce man's potential and latent greatness. It is to discover and develop the noblest, highest and best that is in him. In view of this fact no man whose business it is to teach should ever allow himself to feel that his mission is mean, inferior or circumscribed. In my estimation neither politics nor religion presents to us a calling higher than this primary business of unfolding and strengthening the powers of the human soul. It is a permanent vocation.[71]

In the background of Douglass's belief in the power of education to move men toward virtue was his conviction that the culture of slavery had educated individuals toward vice. After Thomas Auld, his former master, released his slaves in 1849 Douglass wrote him a letter in which he discussed the relationship between education and virtue:

> I congratulate you warmly, and I rejoice most sincerely, that you have been able, against all the suggestions of self-interest, of pride, and of love of power, to perform this act of pure justice and humanity. It has greatly increased my faith in man, and in the *latent virtue* of the slaveholders. I

say *latent virtue*, not because I think slaveholders are worse than all other men, but because, such are the power and influences of education and habit even upon the best constituted minds, that they paralyze and disorder, if not destroy their moral energy; and of all persons in the world, slaveholders are in the most unfavorable position for retaining their power. It would be easy for me to give you the reason of this, but you may be presumed to know it already. Born and brought up in the presence and under the influence of a system which at once strikes at the very foundation of morals, by denying—if not the existence of God—the equal brotherhood of mankind, by degrading one part of the human family to the condition of brutes, and by reversing all right ideas of justice and brotherly kindness, it is almost impossible that one so environed can greatly grow in virtuous rectitude.[72]

It was Douglass's belief that the despotic "oligarchy" of the South sapped the moral energy of its citizens.[73] His hope was that a new system of education that inculcated the idea that all human beings are born equal and endowed with natural rights could serve as the basis for a "humanitarian culture" in which freedom would be more secure.

There are three major reasons why Douglass believed education was so important. First, education serves the end of providing individuals with tools that are supportive of the ideal of the Self-Made Man. The intellectual and practical skills acquired through the process of education better equip individuals to achieve the material security necessary to survive and, potentially, flourish. In order to achieve material security, Douglass believed, individuals do well to get educated so they equip themselves to be versatile contributors to the marketplace. "Men are not valued in this country, or in any other country, for what they *are*; they are valued for what they can *do*. . . . Society is a hard-hearted affair."[74]

One may wonder what sort of education Douglass thought was appropriate for cultivating independent and responsible citizens. At times, he emphasized the importance of practical or industrial education. In 1853, when Harriet Beecher Stowe expressed a desire to use her wealth to "do something which should permanently contribute to the improvement and the elevation of the free colored people in the United States," Douglass urged her to help establish "an Industrial College in which shall be taught several important branches of the mechanical arts." He argued that "the colored men must learn the trades" in order to serve "new modes of usefulness to society." By becoming skilled workmen, Douglass contended, black men would be able to offer their communities services that are not easily provided by others. The development of a skilled, black working class would serve that class well in material terms and, perhaps more important, it would contribute to the quest for racial equality. "The most telling, the most killing refutation of slavery," Douglass wrote to Stowe, "is the presentation of an industrious, enterprising, thrifty, and intelligent free black population."[75]

At other times, Douglass emphasized the importance of a more liberal education than industrial colleges had to offer. By the 1890s it was evident that he did not believe an "education of the hands" was sufficient:

> While I have no sympathy with those who affect to despise labor, even the humblest forms of it, and hold that whatever is needed to be done, it is honorable to do; it is nevertheless plain that no people, white or black, can, in any country, continue long respected, who are confined to mere menial service for which but little intelligence or skill are required, and for which but the smallest wages are paid or received, especially if the laborer does not make an effort to rise above that condition. . . . In my opinion there is no useful thing that a man can do that can not be better done by an educated man than by an uneducated man.[76]

With strong hands *and* strong minds, Douglass thought, individuals are best equipped to operate in the world. In addition to equipping men to compete in the marketplace, the development of the mind, he believed, is a crucial part of the task of demonstrating that one is worthy of concern and respect. Douglass thought it was essential that individuals move from the realm of argument to the realm of action in order to assimilate into the American polity:

> The world says the black man is unfit to live in a mixed society—to enjoy, and rightly appreciate the blessings of independence—that he must have a master to govern him, and the lash to stimulate him to labor. Let us be prepared to afford in our lives and conversation, an example of how grievously we are wronged by such a prevailing opinion of our race. Let us prove, by facts, not by theory, that independence belongs to our nature, in common with all mankind,—that we have intelligence to use it rightly, when acquired, and capabilities to ascend to the loftiest elevations of the human mind. Let such examples be given in the mental cultivation, and the moral regeneration of our children, as they increase in knowledge, in virtue and in every ennobling principle of man's nature.[77]

The acquisition of both practical and intellectual skills, Douglass believed, was crucial to the development of self-respect and earning the respect of others. As I demonstrated in chapter 4, he thought individuals could earn the respect of others through virtuous action. By developing one's intellect, an individual may be able to gain the respect and admiration of his fellow citizens.

The second major end served by universal education is the promotion of moral virtue. "With increased intelligence," Douglass said, "and a wider dissemination of earnest thought and sound reasoning will come also the moral advancement. Ignorance and immorality usually go hand in hand."[78] In an 1870 editorial entitled "Curing Symptoms," Douglass's devotion to the power of education to bring about moral improvement is clear:

> In medicine there is no greater mistake than to try to cure symptoms instead of the roots of a disease. Just so it is with social diseases. Our peace friends imagine that their exhortation to pacifism will end war—the greatest social evil in human history. They fail to understand that wars are and have been the pastimes of monarchs and despots, and serve only the interests of the selfish few. Wars are unthinkable in a Republic, except in those instances (such as the Mexican War and the Slaveholders' Rebellion) when despotic cliques are able to prevail. Peace advocates should, therefore, join us in the effort to educate mankind up to a correct understanding of the principles of liberty and equal rights. This is the surest method of pacificating [sic] the World.[79]

Douglass was a natural rights thinker who believed moral facts were discoverable and human beings were capable of catching hold of them and acting accordingly. Education, he hoped, would develop the rational capacity of individuals and make them better able to acquire moral knowledge.

It is not only the substance of education that promotes moral goodness, but also the setting and process. Douglass viewed the schoolhouse as an important site of character formation. Just being present at that site with others, he thought, could serve as the basis to strengthen the bonds of community. It was for that reason that he was so adamant about the need for racial integration. In an 1848 editorial published in *The North Star*, Douglass wrote: "Let the colored children be educated and grow up side by side with white children, come up friends unsophisticated and generous childhood together, and it will require a powerful agent to convert them into enemies, and lead them to prey upon each other's rights and liberties."[80] Once the bonds of humanity between individuals are developed in the innocence of youth, Douglass hoped, they would not be easily broken upon reaching adulthood. The education of young people of all races is crucial to the development of the "humanitarian culture" he believed must be at the foundation of a free society.

The development of the intellectual and moral capacities benefits individuals and, Douglass thought, it has a positive impact on the community. Well-educated individuals are better able to contribute to the economic well-being of society, he argued, because all jobs are better done by individuals who have been trained in "the use of both mind and body."[81] Even physical labor, Douglass believed, was likely to be done better and more efficiently by individuals who have received some "book learning." In addition to having a positive impact on the economic well-being of the community, Douglass believed universal education would be beneficial to the moral atmosphere of the community. As I have been arguing throughout this book, he was acutely concerned with the "moral health" of the American polity and believed a variety of mechanisms were needed to direct individuals toward the path of virtue. The education of all individuals without regard to race or sex was one such mechanism. An educated citizenry, Douglass thought, was more likely to be a morally responsible one.

In sum, universal education was valuable to Douglass for three primary reasons. First, a good education equips individuals with the practical and intellectual skills necessary to have a decent chance to achieve material security. Second, education promotes moral virtue. Third, these effects of education have a positive impact on the economic and moral well-being of the community. A year before he died, Douglass said: "Education . . . means emancipation. It means light and liberty. It means the uplifting of the soul of man into the glorious light of truth, the light by which men can only be made free."[82] In this statement, we see Douglass articulate his belief that knowledge, freedom, and moral truth are closely related to one another. Because education serves both freedom and virtue, it is not surprising that Douglass was so deeply devoted to the idea that all individuals must be educated.

The second question raised above—whether or not universal education is a state responsibility—directs us to the institutional implications of Douglass's devotion. First, in a speech entitled "Parties Were Made for Men, Not Men for Parties," delivered at the National Colored Convention in 1883, he offered clear endorsement of compulsory education laws when he said: "[T]here can be no doubt of the right to pass a law compelling the attendance of every child at school." The context and details of Douglass's endorsement are worth noting. He began his discussion of compulsory education by noting "the widespread and truly alarming illiteracy" revealed by the census of 1880. In response to this crisis, Douglass said, "it will not do to trust the philanthropy of wealthy individuals or benevolent societies to remove it," and the states with the worst literacy rates (Alabama, Florida, Georgia, Louisiana, Mississippi, North Carolina, South Carolina, and Virginia had rates around 40 percent) "either can not or will not provide adequate systems of education for their own youth." In the face of a crisis of this magnitude, Douglass declared, bold *national* action was required. He called on Congress to pass legislation that would "carry the benefits of a sound common-school education to the door of every poor man from Maine to Texas."[83] His endorsement of national action should not be seen as an indication that Douglass neglected to see that an important role should be played by the states. In an 1871 editorial entitled "A Progressive State," Douglass wrote: "By enacting a compulsory education law, Michigan continues in the tradition of progressive pioneering." In addition to being "the first state to abolish capital punishment," he applauded the state for creating "a free education system (from common school to University)" and concluded by declaring that because of these policies, "she has a great future."[84]

Second, Douglass was a "Radical Republican" who supported an activist role for the federal government in promoting the safety and well-being of all citizens. Among the measures he supported in pursuit of these ends was the Blair Education Bill, which proposed a large amount of federal support to build public schools throughout the Union. The Bill called for the money to be allocated according to illiteracy rates, meaning that the former slave states would have received a bulk of the funds. The Blair Bill passed the Republican Senate several times throughout the 1880s but failed to get through the House of Representatives. The failure of the Republicans to get comprehensive education funding passed was a source of great frustration for Douglass, who complained that the party had been "converted" into a "party of money rather than a party of morals, a party of things rather than a party of humanity and justice."[85] Congressional leadership of the 1880s, he contended, abandoned the zealous humanitarian spirit of Thaddeus Stevens and Charles Sumner in favor of an emphasis on economic growth. In 1890, he lamented that "this Congress has preferred protection to commerce and property to protection of personal and political liberty. We had hoped that it would adopt the Federal election bill and the Blair educational bill. It has done neither."[86] In sum, Douglass believed it was essential that the government provide the material support necessary for the education of all citizens.

How does Douglass's strong embrace of state-supported education fit within his political philosophy? It is clear that he believed education was crucial for the development of free and responsible citizens. Education contributes to freedom by equipping individuals with the practical and intellectual skills necessary to achieve material security that can serve as the foundation for the "unfolding and strengthening of the powers of the human soul," which he called "the very end" of man's "being."[87] Also, education encourages the forms of moral responsibility that are essential to civic life. Education promotes responsible behavior because educated people, Douglass believed, are less likely to behave immorally and it can contribute to the development of stronger bonds of civic connection by bringing (or forcing) citizens together into a public space where they must interact with one another. Douglass hoped that this forced interaction might lay the groundwork for a strong culture of personal and social responsibility. If individuals from diverse backgrounds are educated together they will gain an appreciation for their common humanity. In addition to all the other forms of moral education discussed in previous parts of this chapter, Douglass believed a robust system of universal education was an essential part of a well-ordered political community.

Toward a Free and Virtuous Society: Douglass on the Moral Education of the Citizenry

Although Douglass did not offer an extensive program of moral education, he did discuss a variety of formal and informal mechanisms by which citizens could be "taught" to behave in ways that promote liberal ideals. The first aim of a liberal regime should be to secure the natural rights of all citizens. Douglass believed men could be taught to respect the rights of others by using force against those who violate this fundamental liberal duty. Although this is a rather crude form of education, he thought the security of individual rights was an essential baseline for just political life.

In addition to teaching men to respect the rights of others by threatening and punishing them with force, Douglass believed it was important to send a variety of public messages about the rights and responsibilities of citizenship. The state sends such messages in a formal way through positive law, which he believed ought to be used to communicate moral ideals to which the citizenry should aspire. For example, even though the Civil Rights Bill was not being enforced in the South, Douglass thought it was worth keeping on the books because it offered a clear statement about how individuals *should* behave. He admitted that the aims of the Civil Rights Bill seemed unrealistic at the time of its passage, but this law "did speak" to citizens. The use of positive law to educate citizens, Douglass believed, was an indispensable part of political leadership.

Statesmen use positive law to communicate messages to the citizenry, but they are also able to use the art of rhetoric to "teach" their listeners about the rights and responsibilities of citizenship. Although Douglass theorized quite a bit more on the role played by reformers in promoting social justice, he also reflected on the importance of good statesmanship. While campaigning and serving in positions of power, good statesmen remind citizens about the moral commitments that are supposed to unite the political community and the actions that must be taken to close the gap between those ideals and reality.

A fourth mechanism of moral education that Douglass thought was essential is the celebration of civic ceremonies such as Decoration Day. Although this need not be state-initiated or -supported, it has a slightly more formal character than the matters discussed in the previous chapter. Civic ceremonies provide important "teachable moments." As rational beings capable of reflection and moral understanding, human beings are subject to the influences of habit and ritual. Through the celebration of the lives and deeds of great citizens of the past, Douglass thought, we can deepen our commitment to the ideals that animated them. When we celebrate something like Decoration Day, he argued, we ask ourselves and each other questions about the meaning of our political lives. When we reflect upon these questions and discuss them with our fellow citizens, we engage in an important form of moral education that, at its best, can serve to deepen our commitment to ideals of political morality and to strengthen the bonds of community that support those ideals.

The fifth mechanism of moral education Douglass discussed is a robust system of public and private schools. Universal education is an important part of Douglass's political project for three reasons. First, he believed the practical and intellectual skills developed equip individuals to be free. Because the primary aim of Douglass's political vision was to secure the conditions under which individuals can exercise personal freedom, the education of all citizens is essential. Second, because "ignorance and immorality usually go hand in hand," the process of education can promote the morally responsible behavior that is essential to a free society. For Douglass, the central problem in American political life was the lack of a strong moral atmosphere. Because ignorance and immorality usually go hand in hand, it is crucial to develop a robust system of education. In Douglass's mind, education was linked to both freedom and virtue. In order to achieve freedom, individuals must acquire the intellectual and practical skills provided by a liberal education. In order to develop the moral and civic virtues that are supportive of freedom, individuals must be liberated from the vices of ignorance. Third, because a good education contributes to the intellectual and moral development of individuals, the education of all people has a positive impact on the economic and moral well-being of the community.

Without betraying the fundamental liberal commitment to personal freedom, Douglass offered a strong case that the state had an important role to play in encouraging individuals to be responsible citizens. Through the use of force, the promulgation of law, the rhetoric of statesmen, the celebration of civic holidays, and the promotion of a robust educational system, the state can direct individuals toward the path of personal and social responsibility.

Conclusion

Frederick Douglass in the American Mind

Introduction

What was Frederick Douglass trying to do and how did he try to do it? These are the central questions I seek to answer in this conclusion. In so doing, I hope to provide my contribution to the interpretive questions with which I began: where does my reading fit within the debate over how best to understand Douglass's political thought and what does my reading reveal about the significance of that thought for contemporary political theory and practice?

What Was Frederick Douglass Trying to Do and How Did He Try to Do It?

Douglass's aims were essentially liberal; he sought to achieve a political community in which each individual was free to author his or her own life. He believed this goal could be realized only when limited government was established to protect the rights of all individuals, guarantee equality before the law, and promote fairness in the social and economic spheres. For Douglass, the process of achieving and maintaining this liberal political community was dependent upon the prevalence of a particular set of virtues. What Douglass called "true virtue" was the paramount of these virtues; he used this term to capture the idea that each of us has a moral obligation to combat injustice. Although he did not spell out in great detail precisely what our obligations were to other people in all circumstances, it is clear that he believed we have not satisfied the requirements of morality by simply refraining from violating the rights of others. Instead, the doctrine of true virtue requires us to do what we can to help those who are being denied the basic promises of liberalism. In other words, if the government is failing to protect a person's rights, provide her with equality before the law, or ensure that she is treated fairly in the social and economic spheres, each of us has a responsibility to use the moral and political means available to us to rectify the situation.

In addition to the doctrine of true virtue, which is essential to achieving and maintaining a just society, Douglass believed the virtues embodied in the Self-Made Man were vital to a flourishing community. The ideal type of the Self-Made Man served as a model of personal responsibility in Douglass's thought. He hoped that once set free from the impediments of injustice, inequality, and unfairness, individuals would devote themselves to soulful hard work so that they would be better able to contribute to the well-being of those around them. Although Douglass did not believe material success ought to be the end to which individuals devote themselves, he did believe that economic security was a crucial foundation from which individuals could pursue the higher goal of moral excellence.

Douglass believed the achievement of a just political community requires the leadership of individuals attentive to the moral health of the community. As such, he longed for leaders who would practice the virtues of good statesmanship. A good statesman, from Douglass's perspective, must first and foremost be animated by the principles of justice described above: liberty, equality, and fairness. A good statesman must furthermore be sensitive to the ways in which the moral ecology of the community can impact the realization of those principles of justice. In other words, Douglass longed for political leaders who would not only devote themselves to designing institutions that protect rights, guarantee equality, and promote fairness, but who would also always have an eye toward educating the people about the rights and responsibilities essential to a free society.

Douglass in the American Political Tradition

With this basic summary of my interpretation of Douglass's political thought now on the table, we can return to the question of where his ideas fit within the multiple traditions of American political thought. A consensus of scholars has coalesced around the idea that American political thought is best understood as a "rich tapestry" of multiple traditions including classical liberalism, reform liberalism, republicanism, and inegalitarian ideologies of exclusion.[1] What ground does Douglass occupy in this multiple traditions paradigm?

First, my argument suggests that Douglass fits within the liberal tradition. The more difficult question is whether he is best thought of as a classical or reform liberal. It is on this question that scholars are most deeply split. My interpretation suggests that both the classical and reform liberal readings capture part of the truth and that therefore neither reading captures the whole truth. Douglass was a classical liberal insofar as he was strongly committed to the ideas of universal self-ownership, natural rights, limited government, and an ethos of self-reliance. My arguments have revealed, though, that he had a reform liberal's sensitivity to the ways in which social and economic inequality can undermine the promise of liberty. As such, he defended an active role for the state to combat inequality and promote fairness. We might be tempted to conclude that he advocated the pursuit of classical liberal ends through reform liberal means, but this implies that reform liberal ends are substantially different from those of classical liberals. If anything, we can say that the central difference between classical and reform liberalism is that the former perspective is willing to accept a higher level of inequality if it means more liberty and the latter perspective is willing to accept a greater infringement on liberty if it means less inequality. In the end, Douglass, like many other liberal thinkers, was ambivalent on this point. His message to individuals was to behave as if they would have to go it alone, but he was simultaneously instructing all of us—citizens and statesmen alike—to be animated by an ethos of "each for all and all for each."

It is on this last point that we confront the question of how, if at all, the republican strand of American political thought was part of Douglass's vision. At its most basic level, the republican strand, in the words of political scientist Sue Davis, "moved away from an emphasis on natural rights and equality of individuals to focus on the importance to a successful political community of a body of virtuous citizens who transcend self-interest to participate in public affairs in order to promote the common good."[2] It is clear that Douglass, like those within the republican tradition, emphasized the importance of political participation and he believed that participation ought to be guided not by naked self-interest, but by the ideals of liberty, equality, and fairness for all people. What is less clear is whether or not the tradition of republicanism really captures Douglass's conception of virtue. Recall that in his famous Fourth of July oration of 1852, Douglass seemed to confront the republican conception of virtue directly when he said that the American founders "loved their country more than their private interests." Though "this is not the highest form of human excellence," he continued, "all will concede that it is a rare virtue, and that when it is exhibited, it ought to command respect."[3] Douglass's qualified endorsement of this form of human excellence is telling. It is clear that he admired the republican conception of virtue, but did not consider it the "highest form" of virtue. If the interpretation I have offered in this book is correct, the higher form of virtue he had in mind is the doctrine of true virtue described above. For Douglass, the highest form of virtue would be to love humanity more than your private interests and to be willing to act on that love when the well-being of others is threatened. Douglass's devotion to country was secondary to his devotion to these humanitarian principles. So we might conclude that "republicanism" was a part of Douglass's thought insofar as he shared the republican tradition's emphasis on virtue as essential to the achievement and maintenance of a free society. His conception of virtue, though, was universal and humanitarian (as opposed to nationalist and civic) in nature and he considered it to be a part of, rather than an alternative to, his liberalism.[4]

Perhaps the most important contribution of Rogers Smith's formulation of the multiple traditions paradigm has been its emphasis on the "historical intertwining" of the liberal and republican strands with "inegalitarian" ideologies of exclusion such as racism, sexism, and xenophobia in the history of American "doctrines, institutions and practices."[5] Smith's work has drawn our attention to the ways in which the behavior of Americans has often fallen short of the ideals expressed in documents such as the Declaration of Independence and the Constitution. Smith's focus on ideologies of exclusion can be especially helpful to our attempt to understand Douglass's project. As a former slave and abolitionist, Douglass was especially sensitive to the evils of inegalitarian ideologies. His goal was to purge American doctrines, institutions, and practices of the pernicious influence of these ideologies so that the promises of liberalism could be extended to all people. In order to accomplish this goal, Douglass attempted to convince his audiences that true liberalism was rooted in egalitarian humanism and that the realization of a free society required a robust commitment to the well-being of others.

Douglass's Legacy for Contemporary Political Theory

My interpretation suggests that Douglass is best understood as a particular kind of liberal. Over the course of my work on this book, I have given his brand of liberalism many labels—civic liberalism and communitarian liberalism come to mind—but in the end, none of these seemed to be a perfect fit. In the language of contemporary political theory, Douglass does seem to occupy a ground somewhere between liberalism and its communitarian and republican critics. According to these critics, classical liberalism is insufficient "because it cannot," in the words of political theorist Michael Sandel, "inspire the moral and civic engagement" necessary to "secure the liberty it promises."[6] In the view of critics like Sandel, the liberal preoccupation with individual rights and freedom from interference has led to a failure to pay adequate attention to the virtues necessary to secure liberty. In response to these criticisms, some scholars have turned to the history of liberal thought in order to counter this claim. In works like Peter Berkowitz's *Virtues and the Making of Modern Liberalism*, James T. Kloppenberg's *The Virtues of Liberalism*, John Patrick Diggins's *The Lost Soul of American Politics*, and J. David Greenstone's *The Lincoln Persuasion*, we see attempts to reconstruct the ideas of great thinkers and statesmen to reveal that within the breadth and depth of the liberal tradition there are indeed voices that have attempted to combine the language of rights and liberty with a robust moral vocabulary of virtue and obligation.[7] If my interpretation in this book is correct, then Douglass should be thought of as part of this strand within the liberal tradition.

According to political theorist Thomas Spragens, one of the best reasons to engage in reconstructive projects like this one is that it might be seen as a "way to revitalize the liberal project" by recovering "the moral complexity found within it" so that we might figure out how to "adapt and apply" what we find "to the demands and constraints of contemporary politics."[8] So, how can Douglass's philosophy be adapted and applied to contemporary politics? This brings us back to the ideological tug-of-war over Douglass's legacy.

Frederick Douglass's Legacy for Contemporary Politics

Aside from the fact that they are the only two African Americans to have served on the U.S. Supreme Court, Thurgood Marshall and Clarence Thomas do not have all that much in common. Marshall is remembered as one of the last great progressive justices whose constitutional vision embraced affirmative action, the abolition of capital punishment, and abortion rights. Thomas is known as one of the most conservative of contemporary justices, reaching conclusions on the opposite side of the constitutional universe from Marshall on just about every hot button issue. And yet if we were able to visit the chambers of either justice, we would find memorials to Douglass central to the décor and if we were able to ask these men to name their heroes, it is almost certain that Douglass would be near the top of both their lists.[9] Indeed, I believe it is fair to say that both men would describe themselves as the legitimate heirs of the spirit of Douglass's political philosophy. For Thomas, Douglass's life and thought provide us with a powerful defense of the laissez-faire individualism at the core of classical liberalism. "Leave us alone!" and "Work!" are the mantras that ring in Thomas's ears when he thinks of Douglass. For Marshall, Douglass's life and thought provide us with a powerful defense of the egalitarianism and humanitarianism at the core of reform liberalism. "Agitate!" and "each for all and all for each!" are the mantras that rang in Marshall's ears when he thought of Douglass. This disagreement between Marshall and Thomas is but one prominent example of the divergent versions of Douglass's legacy that reside in the minds of Americans.

Thomas's understanding of Douglass's relevance to contemporary politics is revealed by two of the most provocative instances in which he has cited the great abolitionist in his decisions. In two recent ideologically charged cases: *Zelman v. Simmons-Harris*, which dealt with the constitutionality of the Cleveland school voucher program, and *Grutter v. Bollinger*, which dealt with the constitutionality of the University of Michigan Law School's affirmative action program, Thomas has appealed to the words of Douglass in order to support his conservative opinions.[10] In both cases, Thomas implied that if Douglass was alive today, he would align himself with conservatives in favor of school voucher programs and against affirmative action. In *Zelman*, Thomas began his concurring opinion with this: "Frederick Douglass once said that '[e]ducation . . . means emancipation. It means light and liberty. It means the uplifting of the soul of man into the glorious light of truth, the light by which men can only be made free.' Today many of our inner-city public schools deny emancipation to urban minority students."[11] Thomas went on to defend the constitutionality and wisdom of the school voucher program before returning to Douglass's words in conclusion: "As Frederick Douglass poignantly noted, 'no greater benefit can be bestowed upon a long benighted people, than giving to them, as we are here earnestly this day endeavoring to do, the means of an education.'"[12] By beginning and concluding his opinion with Douglass's words, the reader is left with the impression that Douglass's ideas have a direct bearing on this late-twentieth-century legal dispute and that his commitments would place him squarely in the conservative camp.

In *Grutter v. Bollinger*, a case in which the Court upheld the University of Michigan Law School's affirmative action program, Thomas began his dissenting opinion with Douglass's words: "Frederick Douglass, speaking to a group of abolitionists almost 140 years ago, delivered a message lost on today's majority:

[I]n regard to the colored people, there is always more that is benevolent, I perceive, than just, manifested towards us. What I ask for the negro is not benevolence, not pity, not sympathy, but simply *justice*. The American

people have always been anxious to know what they shall do with us. . . .
I have had but one answer from the beginning. Do nothing with us! Your
doing with us has already played the mischief with us. Do nothing with us!
If the apples will not remain on the tree of their own strength, if they are
worm-eaten at the core, if they are early ripe and disposed to fall, let them
fall! . . . And if the negro cannot stand on his own legs, let him fall also. All
I ask is, give him a chance to stand on his own legs! Let him alone! . . . [Y]
our interference is doing him positive injury.[13]

Like Douglass, I believe blacks can achieve in every avenue of American
life without the meddling of university administrators."[14] If Thomas is to be
believed, Douglass is best understood as an anti-paternalist libertarian; his
message to would-be benefactors is: leave us alone!

Justice Thurgood Marshall did not cite Douglass in his judicial opinions,
but he said he reread Douglass's autobiographies often as a source of inspiration. What was it about Douglass that so inspired the first African American Supreme Court Justice? Marshall's response to this question is telling:
"because I don't know of a Negro today, or later than Douglass, who had the
courage he had, in the things he said."[15] Marshall's emphasis on the things
Douglass said is an indication that he was moved not just by the dramatic
physical courage he displayed during his life as a slave and reformer, but also
by his intellectual courage. Although Marshall could have had many things
in mind when he uttered these words, I think it is safe to conclude that what
he found inspiring was Douglass's willingness to stand up for egalitarianism
in the face of a political culture that was profoundly racist and sexist and his
willingness to tell his audiences that they had extensive moral obligations to
assist those who were being oppressed.

What does my study reveal about the merits of each side in this interpretive dispute between Justices Thomas and Marshall? Is Justice Thomas right
to suggest that if Douglass was alive today, he would join him in his classical liberal (or conservative) stance in opposition to affirmative action and in
favor of school vouchers? Or is Justice Marshall correct to suggest that Douglass would be a natural fit with the reform liberalism of contemporary progressives? If my argument is correct, then it is fair to say that Justices Thomas
and Marshall are both right and they are both wrong.

First, it is worth pointing out that any attempt to apply Douglass's ideas to
contemporary debates must be chastened by a heavy dose of humility. More
than a century has passed since Douglass died and we cannot know how the
events of the twentieth century would have altered his views. As we attempt

to determine the significance of Douglass's legacy for contemporary politics, then, we seek nothing more than to capture how the core principles of his thought might inform us as we reflect upon our problems.

With this in mind, I would like to suggest that Justice Thomas's classical liberal interpretation is true to the spirit of Douglass's thought insofar as it draws on the philosophy of self-reliance at its core. Like Thomas, Douglass had a deep faith in the power of the individual to *make* himself successful through hard work and virtuous behavior. Furthermore, Thomas is right to say that Douglass did indeed often say that what black people needed more than anything else was the simple justice of being left alone. In his command to "let them alone," Douglass trumpeted perhaps the central tenet of classical liberalism.

What Thomas's interpretation misses, though, reveals one of the ways in which Marshall's reform liberal reading is closer to the truth. A more careful consideration of Douglass's language leads us to conclude that Thomas fundamentally misunderstands his message. In the passages relied upon by Thomas in his critique of affirmative action, Douglass makes clear what he means by "let him alone": "If you see a negro wanting to purchase land, let him purchase it. If you see him on the way to school, let him go; don't say he shall not go into the same school with other people. . . . If you see him on his way to the workshop, let him alone; let him work."[16] When Douglass said "let him alone," he was demanding that both state and nonstate actors refrain from preventing African Americans from exercising their legitimate rights. This is not quite the same as what Thomas has in mind. When Thomas and other advocates of the classical liberal interpretation cite this passage, they make it seem as though Douglass is talking about paternalistic government officials like those meddlesome admissions officers at the University of Michigan Law School. In fact, Douglass's attitude toward active government involvement in social and economic life differs in significant ways from the views of contemporary conservatives and libertarians. Indeed, Douglass almost always coupled his "let them alone" arguments with a demand for "fair play." When Douglass talked about fair play, he had two ideas in mind that we associate with the reform liberalism of the progressive view in contemporary American politics.

First, for Douglass, fair play meant that government had to play an important role in order to ensure that the social and economic rules were not rigged in favor of or against any particular group. In other words, he believed that government has a vital role to play in ensuring that individuals are relatively free to participate in the marketplace and to make sure that no systematic attempts are being made to prevent individuals from making economic progress (i.e., sharecropping). At a certain level of abstraction, both classical and reform liberals accept the idea that government should play this role, but differ on precisely how this role should be carried out. It is the second idea encapsulated in Douglass's understanding of fair play that does the most to undermine a purely classical liberal reading.

The second component of Douglass's understanding of fair play is his belief that government should take aggressive action to level the playing field. In the speech on "Self-Made Men," which is a favorite of contemporary conservatives, Douglass makes this point clear:

> I have said 'Give the negro fair play and let him alone.' I meant all that I said and a good deal more than some understand by fair play. It is not fair play to start the negro out in life, from nothing and with nothing, while others start with the advantage of a thousand years behind them. . . . Should the American people put a school house in every valley of the South and a church on every hillside and supply the one with teachers and the other with preachers, for a hundred years to come [this was in 1894], they would not then have given fair play to the negro. The nearest approach to justice to the negro for the past is to do him justice in the present.[17]

The spirit of Douglass's language makes clear that contrary to those who wish to argue that he fits neatly into a laissez-faire view of social affairs, he was in fact quite attentive to the problem of inequality and believed that government had an important role to play in combating it. At the core of the arguments offered by contemporary conservatives like Thomas is a belief that government programs to assist those in need—the agenda of what Thomas calls "the benevolent state"—are rooted in "an ideology of victimhood" that undermines the dignity and self-respect of those they are intended to help.[18] Although Douglass was always sensitive to the impact policies might have on the self-respect of individuals and on the perceptions of those individuals by others, he did not accept this way of thinking. In an address entitled "Strong to Suffer, and Yet Strong to Strive," delivered at the twenty-fourth celebration of emancipation in the District of Columbia in 1886, Douglass reflected on the challenges still confronting blacks in the South. Of the "emancipated class" in Mississippi, he said:

> They need and ought to have material aid of both white and colored people of the free states. A million dollars devoted to this purpose would do

more for the colored people of the south than the same amount expended in any other way. There is no degradation, no loss of self-respect, in asking this aid, considering the circumstances of these people. The white people of this nation owe them this help and a great deal more. The key-note of the future should not be the concentration, but diffusion [and] distribution. This may not be a remedy for all evils now uncured, but it certainly will be a help in the right direction.[19]

It is clear from passages like these that Douglass's sometimes-individualist rhetoric was always coupled with sensitivity to circumstances. In certain contexts, Douglass believed, a purely pull-yourself-up-by-your-bootstraps philosophy was woefully inadequate.

Should these flaws in the classical liberal reading lead us to conclude that Douglass's legacy is easily assimilated into contemporary reform liberalism? I believe this study reveals that this would be a mistake as well because there is an important part of the story that the reform liberal reading gets wrong. There is no question that Douglass offered a strong defense of the idea of "self-reliance," which according to some political theorists (most notably Wilson Carey McWilliams in his discussion of Douglass) is antagonistic to the robust conception of mutual responsibility at the core of the reform liberal view. A careful consideration of Douglass's reflections upon the relationship between self-help and social responsibility reveals that he did not believe these ideas were necessarily in conflict.

Perhaps the most powerful statement of Douglass's individualism is his speech on "Self-Made Men," but even in this speech we must remember that he began with a significant caveat concerning the relationship between the idea of "individual independence" and the ideas of "brotherhood and inter-dependence."[20] Douglass's lecture on the Self-Made Man is a decidedly individualist text, but his discussion of interdependence at the beginning of the speech is an indication that he did not see individualism and a strong sense of interdependence as mutually exclusive:

It must in truth be said though it may not accord well with self-conscious individuality and self-conceit, that no possible native force of character, and no depth or wealth of originality, can lift a man into absolute independence of his fellow-men, and no generation of men can be independent of the preceding generation. The brotherhood and inter-dependence of mankind are guarded and defended at all points. I believe in individuality, but individuals are, to the mass, like waves to the ocean. The highest order of genius is as dependent as is the lowest. It, like the loftiest waves of the sea, derives its power and greatness from the grandeur and vastness of the ocean of which it forms a part. We differ as the waves, but are one as the sea.[21]

Douglass's speech focuses on a class of human beings that seem to embody the virtues of individualism, but he thought exaltation of self-made men was consistent with his belief in interdependence. Rather than seeing self-reliance and interconnection as antagonistic, he saw them as closely related. Douglass believed the practice of the virtues of self-reliance, industriousness, sobriety, integrity, orderliness, and a desire for self-improvement was the most promising path to independence *and*, perhaps paradoxically, assimilation into the community.[22] In an 1886 speech on the "progress of the colored race," he said:

> We have but to toil and trust, throw away whiskey and tobacco, improve the opportunities that we have, put away all extravagance, learn to live within our means, lay up our earnings, educate our children, live industrious and virtuous lives, establish a character for sobriety, punctuality, and general uprightness, and we shall raise up powerful friends who shall stand by us in our struggle for an equal chance in the race of life.[23]

This passage points to the complex relationship between self-reliance and interdependence in Douglass's thought. These passages indicate that Wilson Carey McWilliams, whose interpretation captures the essence of what progressives find so compelling in Douglass's political philosophy, was mistaken when he classified Douglass as a devotee of "fraternity and humanity" *as opposed to* "individualism and the doctrine of self-reliance."[24] Unlike McWilliams, Douglass did not believe these ideas were necessarily irreconcilable. He believed individuals could "raise up powerful friends" by striving to be self-reliant. In other words, rather than thinking of the ethos of self-reliance as deleterious of the bonds of community, Douglass thought of it as a crucial step in building up the respect individuals have for one another.

Where does this leave us? Rather than providing us with a clear lens through which to assess contemporary political controversies, Douglass gives us a complex one. The classical liberal elements in his thought remind us that we ought to encourage individuals to strive to be self-reliant by behaving in virtuous ways, but the reform liberal elements in his thought remind us that we must be sensitive to the ways in which injustice and unfairness threaten the capacity of individuals to flourish. The complexity of this message should lead us to conclude that any contention that Douglass fits neatly into a contemporary ideological category is likely ignoring an important aspect of his political thought. This does not mean that his ideas on rights, the role of government, virtue, and statesmanship are irrelevant to the problems of our time. Instead, it means that as we attempt to draw from Douglass's wisdom to the circumstances of the present moment, we ought to be humble and careful to appreciate the depth and breadth of his thought.

Perhaps Douglass's most powerful legacy for contemporary politics is contained in language from "The Prospect in the Future" essay with which I began this book. Recall that in that 1860 essay, Douglass lamented the fact that "narrow and wicked" selfishness allowed Americans to proclaim their love of liberty while at the same time denying basic rights to so many human beings around them. Douglass's mission was to resolve this "terrible paradox" by convincing Americans to replace this narrowness with egalitarianism and to replace this selfishness with humanitarianism. Perhaps the closest we can come to capturing the spirit of Douglass's political philosophy in the present moment is to ask ourselves the questions he asked in that essay: in what ways is our own love of liberty haunted by narrow and wicked selfishness and how can we close the gaps between the ideal of liberty we claim to love so much and the realities that surround us? It seems to me that in those moments when we are willing to ask ourselves these difficult questions and, when our answers require it, we are moved from "the downy seat of inaction" to close the gaps between our ideals and reality, we come closest to being the legitimate heirs of Frederick Douglass's political project.

Notes

1. Frederick Douglass, in Philip S. Foner, ed., *The Life and Writings of Frederick Douglass,* 5 volumes (New York: International Publishers, 1950–1975), 2: 495. [Hereinafter cited as Foner, *The Life and Writings of Frederick Douglass.*]

2. Ibid., 2: 494–495.

3. Frederick Douglass, "In Law Free; In Fact a Slave," an address delivered in Washington, D.C., on April 16, 1888, in John W. Blassingame, ed., *The Frederick Douglass Papers, Series One: Speeches, Debates, and Interviews,* 5 volumes (New Haven: Yale University Press, 1979–1992), 5: 373. [Hereinafter cited as Blassingame, *The Frederick Douglass Papers.*]

4. Frederick Douglass, "A Friendly Word to Maryland," an address delivered in Baltimore, Maryland, on November 17, 1864, in Blassingame, *The Frederick Douglass Papers,* 4: 42. Emphasis in original. Frederick Douglass, "William the Silent," an address delivered in Cincinnati, Ohio, on February 8, 1869, in Blassingame, *The Frederick Douglass Papers,* 4: 190. Douglass was paraphrasing the words of British abolitionist Charles James Fox.

5. Douglass wrote three autobiographies. These texts have been annotated beautifully by the Frederick Douglass Papers Project in *The Frederick Douglass Papers, Series Two: Autobiographical Writings, Volumes 1, 2, and 3* (New Haven: Yale University Press, 1999, 2003, 2010). There have been several excellent biographies of Douglass. See, e.g., Philip S. Foner, *Frederick Douglass: A Biography* (New York: Citadel Press, 1969), and William McFeely, *Frederick Douglass* (New York: W. W. Norton, 1995). There have also been several recent works by historians that may be of interest to those seeking a greater understanding of Douglass's life. See, e.g., James Colaiaco, *Frederick Douglass and the Fourth of July* (New York: Palgrave Macmillan, 2006); James Oakes, *The Radical and the Republican* (New York: W. W. Norton, 2007); John Stauffer, *Giants: The Parallel Lives of Frederick Douglass and Abraham Lincoln* (New York: Twelve, 2009).

6. For Douglass's description of "city slavery," see Frederick Douglass, *Autobiographies,* Henry Louis Gates, ed. (New York: Library of America, 1994), 218. For a description of life with Covey, see *Autobiographies,* 258–269.

7. Frederick Douglass, *The Life and Times of Frederick Douglass* (Mineola: Courier Dover Publications, 2003), 153.

8. For extensive discussions of the Lincoln-Douglass relationship, see James Oakes, *The Radical and the Republican*; and John Stauffer, *Giants.*

9. William McFeely, *Frederick Douglass,* 381.

10. Garrett Ward Sheldon, *The Political Philosophy of Thomas Jefferson* (Baltimore: Johns Hopkins University Press, 1993), 1–2.

11. By classic interpretations of American political thought, I have in mind books like Louis Hartz, *The Liberal Tradition in America* (New York: Harcourt Brace, 1991); Richard Hofstadter, *The American Political Tradition and the Men Who Made It* (New York: Vintage, 1989); and John Patrick Diggins, *The Lost Soul of American Politics* (Chicago: University of Chicago Press, 1986). My research on this project began in 2005 when I was a graduate student at the University of Southern California. In 2008, political theorist Peter C. Myers published *Frederick Douglass: Race and the Rebirth of American Liberalism* (Lawrence: University Press of Kansas, 2008).

12. Douglass had been the subject of essay-length studies by great scholars of American political thought such as Herbert J. Storing, "Frederick Douglass," in Joseph M. Bessette, ed., *Toward a More Perfect Union* (Washington, D.C.: American Enterprise Institute, 1995), 151–175.

13. Judith Shklar, "The Liberalism of Fear," in *Political Thought and Political Thinkers*, Stanley Kauffman, ed. (Chicago: University of Chicago Press, 1998), 3.

14. Louis Hartz, *The Liberal Tradition in America*.

15. See, e.g., John Patrick Diggins, *The Lost Soul of American Politics*; James T. Kloppenberg, *The Virtues of Liberalism* (New York: Oxford University Press, 2000); J. David Greenstone, *The Lincoln Persuasion* (Princeton: Princeton University Press, 1994); and James P. Young, *Reconsidering American Liberalism* (Boulder, Colo.: Westview Press), 1996.

16. Kenneth Dolbeare, *American Political Thought*, 5th ed. (Washington, D.C.: CQ Press, 2004), xxx.

17. By "classical liberalism," I mean the strand of liberal thought that envisions a free society governed by a "night watchman state." Classical liberals tend to emphasize negative liberty, the sanctity of property rights, and strict limitations on government power.

18. See, e.g., Thomas Sowell, *The Vision of the Anointed* (New York: Basic Books, 1996); John McWhorter, *Winning the Race* (New York: Gotham Books, 2006); Shelby Steele, *The Content of Our Character* (New York: Harper Perennial, 2001).

19. Judith Shklar, *American Citizenship: The Quest for Inclusion* (Cambridge: Harvard University Press, 1998), 96.

20. Ibid.

21. John Patrick Diggins, *On Hallowed Ground: Abraham Lincoln and the Foundations of American History* (New Haven: Yale University Press, 2000), 275.

22. Ibid.

23. Ibid., 277.

24. Wilson Jeremiah Moses, *Creative Conflict in African American Thought* (New York: Cambridge University Press, 2004), 106.

25. See, e.g., ibid., 45.

26. Waldo E. Martin, *The Mind of Frederick Douglass* (Chapel Hill: University of North Carolina Press, 1984).

27. Gayle McKeen, "A 'Guiding Principle' of Liberalism in the Thought of Frederick Douglass and W. E. B. Du Bois," in *The Liberal Tradition in American Politics*, David F. Ericson and Louisa Bertch Green, eds. (New York: Routledge, 1999), 107.

28. Peter C. Myers, *Frederick Douglass*, 7.

29. Ibid., 202–203.

30. Ibid.

31. Wilson Carey McWilliams, *The Idea of Fraternity in America* (Berkeley: University of California Press, 1973), 582.

32. J. David Greenstone, *The Lincoln Persuasion*, 59, 190.

33. Daniel Walker Howe, *Making the American Self* (Cambridge: Harvard University Press, 1997), 155.

34. Ibid.

35. Alan Gibson, *Interpreting the Founding* (Lawrence: University Press of Kansas, 2009), 2.

36. Daniel McInerney, *The Fortunate Heirs of Freedom: Abolition and Republican Thought*, (Lincoln: University of Nebraska Press, 1994), 1.

37. Michael Sandel, *Democracy's Discontent* (Cambridge: Harvard University Press, 1996), 177–181.

38. Robert Gooding-Williams, *In the Shadow of Du Bois* (Cambridge: Harvard University Press, 2009), 192, 194.

39. For another interpretation of Douglass's philosophy as one of regeneration, see Gayle McKeen, "A 'Guiding Principle' of Liberalism in the Thought of Frederick Douglass and W. E. B. Du Bois," 107–108.

40. Derrick Darby, *Rights, Race, and Recognition* (New York: Cambridge University Press, 2009), 168; and Robert Gooding-Williams, *In the Shadow of Du Bois*, 194.

41. During the course of the 2008 campaign for the presidency, Democrat Hillary Clinton called Douglass "one of my heroes" during a debate on January 21, 2008 in South Carolina. A transcript of this debate can be found at http://www.cnn.com/2008/POLITICS/01/21/debate.transcript/index.html. Less than a year later, the Republican National Committee included Douglass on the "American Heroes and Famous Republicans" feature of the RNC website. A visitor to the RNC "American Heroes and Famous Republicans" website could find Douglass's image sandwiched between the images of Barry Goldwater and Ronald Reagan. The RNC's "American Heroes and Famous Republicans" site can be found at: http://www.gop.com/index.php/issues/heroes/. Glenn Beck devoted a significant amount of time to Douglass on the "African-American Founders" episode of his television program on the Fox News Channel on May 30, 2010. Angela Davis served as editor of a recent "critical edition" of Douglass's *Narrative of the Life of Frederick Douglass* in which his work is coupled with her "Lectures on Liberation." See *Narrative of the Life of Frederick Douglass, An American Slave, Written by Himself: A New Critical Edition by Angela Y. Davis* (San Francisco: City Lights Books, 2009). It should be noted that Davis's discussion of Douglass is not entirely celebratory. She expresses concern, for example, with the gendered dimension of his conception of freedom.

42. Frederick Douglass, "The Prospect in the Future," in *Douglass' Monthly*, August 1860, in Foner, *The Life and Writings of Frederick Douglass*, 2: 497.

CHAPTER 2

1. Frederick Douglass, "Santo Domingo," an address delivered in St. Louis, Missouri, on January 13, 1873, in Foner, *The Life and Writings of Frederick Douglass*, 4: 347.

2. For a fabulous discussion of the importance of "negative" foundations in political theory, see Jonathan Allen, "The Place of Negative Morality in Political Theory," *Political Theory* 29, no. 3 (June 2001): 337.

3. Sheldon Wolin, *Politics and Vision* (New York: Little and Brown, 1960), 8.

4. Frederick Douglass, "A Friendly Word to Maryland," an address delivered in Baltimore, Maryland, on November 17, 1864, in Blassingame, *The Frederick Douglass Papers*, 4: 49.

5. Sharon Krause, *Liberalism with Honor* (Cambridge: Harvard University Press, 2002), ix.

6. Frederick Douglass, "The Color Line," from *The North American Review,* June 1881, in Foner, *The Life and Writings of Frederick Douglass,* 4: 347.

7. Frederick Douglass, "Advice to My Canadian Brothers and Sisters," an address delivered in Chatham, Canada West, on August 3, 1854, in Blassingame, *The Frederick Douglass Papers,* 2: 528.

8. Frederick Douglass, "American Slavery, American Religion, and the Free Church of Scotland," an address delivered in London, England, on May 22, 1846, in Blassingame, *The Frederick Douglass Papers,* 1: 273.

9. Ibid., 1: 273.

10. Frederick Douglass, "Advice to My Canadian Brothers and Sisters," an address delivered in Chatham, Canada West, on August 3, 1854, in Blassingame, *The Frederick Douglass Papers,* 2: 528.

11. Frederick Douglass, "Slavery and the Slave Power," an address delivered in Rochester, New York, on December 1, 1850, in Blassingame, *The Frederick Douglass Papers,* 2: 255.

12. Ibid., 2: 254.

13. Frederick Douglass, "International Moral Force Can Destroy Slavery," an address delivered in Paisley, Scotland, on March 17, 1846, in Blassingame, *The Frederick Douglass Papers,* 1:183.

14. Ibid., 1:183; Frederick Douglass, "I Am Here to Spread Light on American Slavery," an address delivered in Cork, Ireland, on October 14, 1845, in Blassingame, *The Frederick Douglass Papers,* 1: 39.

15. Frederick Douglass, "International Moral Force Can Destroy Slavery," an address delivered in Paisley, Scotland, on March 17, 1846, in Blassingame, *The Frederick Douglass Papers,* 1:183.

16. Frederick Douglass, "Advice to My Canadian Brothers and Sisters," an address delivered in Chatham, Canada West, on August 3, 1854, in Blassingame, *The Frederick Douglass Papers,* 2: 528.

17. Frederick Douglass, "An Account of American Slavery," an address delivered in Glasgow, Scotland, on January 15, 1846, in Blassingame, *The Frederick Douglass Papers,* 1: 134–135.

18. William McFeely, *Frederick Douglass* (New York: W. W. Norton, 1991), 79.

19. Frederick Douglass, *My Bondage and My Freedom* (New York: Penguin Books, 2003), 256–257.

20. Frederick Douglass, "An Account of American Slavery," an address delivered in Glasgow, Scotland, on January 15, 1846, in Blassingame, *The Frederick Douglass Papers,* 1: 134–135.

21. Ibid., 1: 135.

22. Frederick Douglass, "Slavery and America's Bastard Republicanism," an address delivered in Limerick, Ireland, on November 10, 1845, in Blassingame, *The Frederick Douglass Papers,* 1: 78.

23. Frederick Douglass, "Slavery and the Slave Power," an address delivered in Rochester, New York, on December 1, 1850, in Blassingame, *The Frederick Douglass Papers,* 2: 258.

24. Ibid.

25. Frederick Douglass, "Is Civil Government Right?" from *Frederick Douglass' Paper,* October 23, 1851, in Foner, *The Life and Writings of Frederick Douglass,* 5: 209.

26. Ibid., 5: 212.

27. Frederick Douglass, "Pioneers in a Holy Cause," an address delivered in Canandaigua, New York, on August 2, 1847, in Blassingame, *The Frederick Douglass Papers*, 2: 73.

28. Frederick Douglass, "Slavery and Slave Power," an address delivered in Rochester, New York, on December 1, 1850, in Blassingame, *The Frederick Douglass Papers*, 2: 254.

29. Frederick Douglass, "The Labor Question," from *The New National Era*, October 12, 1871, in Foner, *The Life and Writings of Frederick Douglass*, 4: 282.

30. Frederick Douglass, "Who and What Is Woman?" an address delivered in Boston, Massachusetts, on May 24, 1886, in Blassingame, *The Frederick Douglass Papers*, 5: 252.

31. Frederick Douglass, "In Law Free; In Fact a Slave," an address delivered in Washington, D.C., in Blassingame, *The Frederick Douglass Papers*, 5: 360.

32. Frederick Douglass, "Is Civil Government Right?" from *Frederick Douglass' Paper*, October 23, 1851, in Foner, *The Life and Writings of Frederick Douglass*, 5: 212–213.

33. Frederick Douglass, "Aggressions of the Slave Power," an address delivered in Rochester, New York, on May 22, 1856, in Blassingame, *The Frederick Douglass Papers*, 3: 127.

34. Frederick Douglass, "Santo Domingo," an address delivered in St. Louis, Missouri, on January 13, 1873, in Blassingame, *The Frederick Douglass Papers*, 4: 344.

35. Josh Gottheimer, ed., *Ripples of Hope: Great American Civil Rights Speeches* (New York: Basic Civitas, 2003), 87. For characteristic statements against Chinese immigration, see James Harvey Slater and James Zachariah George, "Speeches on Chinese Immigration," reprinted in Isaac Kramnick and Theodore Lowi, eds., *American Political Thought: A Norton Anthology* (New York: W. W. Norton, 2009): 893–901.

36. Frederick Douglass, "We Must Not Abandon the Observance of Decoration Day," an address delivered in Rochester, New York, on May 30, 1882, in Blassingame, *The Frederick Douglass Papers*, 5: 51. Italics mine.

37. Frederick Douglass, "Strong to Suffer, and Yet Strong to Strive," an address delivered in Washington, D.C., on April 16, 1886, and "In Law Free; In Fact a Slave," an address delivered in Washington, D.C., on April 16, 1888, both in Blassingame, *The Frederick Douglass Papers*, 5: 213–214, 5: 360.

38. Frederick Douglass, "The Claims of the Negro Ethnologically Considered," an address delivered in Hudson, Ohio, on July 12, 1854, in Blassingame, *The Frederick Douglass Papers*, 2: 507.

39. This distinction is discussed by Mark Blitz, "Liberal Freedom and Responsibility," in T. William Boxx and Gary M. Quinlivan, eds., *Public Morality, Civic Virtue, and the Problem of Modern Liberalism* (Grand Rapids: William B. Eerdmans Publishing, 2000), 110–111.

40. Frederick Douglass, "Slavery Corrupts American Society and Religion," an address delivered in Cork, Ireland, on October 17, 1845, and "The Skin Aristocracy in America," an address delivered in Coventry, England, on February 2, 1847, both in Blassingame, *The Frederick Douglass Papers*, 1: 46, 2: 3.

41. Frederick Douglass, "Slavery and America's Bastard Republicanism," an address delivered in Limerick, Ireland, on November 10, 1845, in Blassingame, *The Frederick Douglass Papers*, 1: 78.

42. Frederick Douglass, "Slavery as It Exists Now in the United States," an address delivered in Bristol, England, on August 25, 1846, in Blassingame, *The Frederick Douglass Papers*, 1: 344.

43. Frederick Douglass, "Pioneers in a Holy Cause," an address delivered in Canandaigua, New York, on August 2, 1847, in Blassingame, *The Frederick Douglass Papers*, 2: 73.

44. Frederick Douglass, "American Religion, and the Free Church of Scotland," an address delivered in London, England, on May 22, 1846, and "An Account of American Slavery," an address delivered in Glasgow, Scotland, on January 15, 1846, both in Blassingame, *The Frederick Douglass Papers*, 1: 273; 1: 135.

45. Frederick Douglass, "An Inside View of Slavery," an address delivered in Boston, Massachusetts, on February 8, 1855, in Blassingame, *The Frederick Douglass Papers*, 3: 11–12.

46. Frederick Douglass, "Slavery and America's Bastard Republicanism," an address delivered in Limerick, Ireland, on November 10, 1845, in Blassingame, *The Frederick Douglass Papers*, 1: 78.

47. Frederick Douglass, "International Moral Force Can Destroy Slavery," an address delivered in Paisley, Scotland, on March 17, 1846, in Blassingame, *The Frederick Douglass Papers*, 1:184.

48. Frederick Douglass, "Slavery, the Free Church, and British Agitation against Bondage," an address delivered in Newcastle-upon-Thyne, England, on August 3, 1846, in Blassingame, *The Frederick Douglass Papers*, 1: 318.

49. Ibid., 1: 321.

50. Frederick Douglass, "American Slavery Is America's Disgrace," an address delivered in Sheffield, England, on March 25, 1847, in Blassingame, *The Frederick Douglass Papers*, 2: 10.

51. Frederick Douglass, "An Inside View of Slavery," an address delivered in Boston, Massachusetts, on February 8, 1855, in Blassingame, *The Frederick Douglass Papers*, 3: 8–9.

52. Frederick Douglass, "International Moral Force Can Destroy Slavery," an address delivered in Paisley, Scotland, on March 17, 1846, in Blassingame, *The Frederick Douglass Papers*, 1:183–184.

53. Frederick Douglass, *My Bondage and My Freedom* (New York: Penguin Books, 2003), 65–66.

54. Ibid., 67.

55. Jenny Franchot, "The Punishment of Esther: Frederick Douglass and the Construction of the Feminine," in Eric J. Sundquist, ed., *Frederick Douglass: New Literary and Historical Essays* (New York: Cambridge University Press, 1990), 141.

56. Peter C. Myers, *Frederick Douglass: Race and the Rebirth of American Liberalism* (Lawrence: University Press of Kansas, 2008), 73–75.

57. Ibid., 70.

58. Frederick Douglass, "The Color Line," a letter from Frederick Douglass Mss., Douglass Memorial home, Anacostia, D.C., in Foner, *The Life and Writings of Frederick Douglass*, 4: 347.

59. Frederick Douglass, "Slavery Corrupts American Society and Religion," an address delivered in Cork, Ireland, on October 17, 1845, in Blassingame, *The Frederick Douglass Papers*, 1: 46.

60. Frederick Douglass, "Slavery and the Slave Power," an address delivered in Rochester, New York, on December 1, 1850, in Blassingame, *The Frederick Douglass Papers*, 2: 255.

61. Frederick Douglass, "Slavery and America's Bastard Republicanism," an address delivered in Limerick, Ireland, in Blassingame, *The Frederick Douglass Papers*, 1: 78, and *My Bondage and My Freedom*, 47.

62. Frederick Douglass, "Slavery and the Slave Power," an address delivered in Rochester, New York, on December 1, 1850, in Blassingame, *The Frederick Douglass Papers*, 2: 255.

63. Frederick Douglass, *My Bondage and My Freedom*, 39.

64. Ibid.

65. Frederick Douglass, "An Inside View of Slavery," an address delivered in Boston, Massachusetts, on February 8, 1855, in Blassingame, *The Frederick Douglass Papers*, 3: 11.

66. Junius P. Rodriguez, ed., *Slavery in the United States: A Social, Historical, and Political Encyclopedia* (Santa Barbara: ABC-CLIO, 2007), 117–118: "Many slaveholding southerners believed that their ownership of slaves was a necessary form of social control rooted in paternalism. . . . The slaveowner was the mentor and teacher, and some would later argue that the plantation or farm was essentially a school where tutelage occurred. A parent-child relationship is marked by genuine bonds of affection and is usually characterized by a sense of mutuality or reciprocity in which both parties to the arrangement comprehend at least some aspect of the benefits that occur."

67. Frederick Douglass, "American Slavery Is America's Disgrace," an address delivered in Sheffield, England, on March 25, 1847, in Blassingame, *The Frederick Douglass Papers*, 2: 10.

68. Frederick Douglass, "An Inside View of Slavery," an address delivered in Boston, Massachusetts, on February 8, 1855, in Blassingame, *The Frederick Douglass Papers*, 3:11–12. Italics mine.

69. Frederick Douglass, "An Antislavery Tocsin," an address delivered in Rochester, New York, on December 8, 1850, in Blassingame, *The Frederick Douglass Papers*, 2: 267.

70. See, e.g., Leo Strauss, *Natural Right and History* (Chicago: University of Chicago Press, 1953), 3–8; and Judith Shklar, "The Liberalism of Fear," in Stanley Hoffmann, ed., *Political Thought and Political Thinkers* (Chicago: University of Chicago Press, 1998), 3.

71. Eric Foner, *Politics and Ideology in the Age of the Civil War* (New York: Oxford University Press, 1980), 64.

72. Paul Sigmund, *Natural Law in Political Thought* (Cambridge: Winthrop Publishers, 1971), v.

73. Sheldon Wolin, *Politics and Vision*, 24.

74. Robert Smallman Taylor, "The Theory and Practice of Self-Ownership," Ph.D. dissertation (University of California, Berkeley, 2002), 10–11.

75. Amy Dru Stanley, *From Bondage to Contract: Wage Labor, Marriage, and the Market in the Age of Slave Emancipation* (Cambridge: Cambridge University Press, 1998), 18.

76. Frederick Douglass, "Eulogy on the Late William Jay," an address delivered in New York, New York, on May 12, 1859, in Foner, *The Life and Writings of Frederick Douglass*, 5: 442.

77. Frederick Douglass, "A Friendly Word to Maryland," an address delivered in Baltimore, Maryland, on November 17, 1864, in Blassingame, *The Frederick Douglass Papers*, 4: 42.

78. Frederick Douglass, "I Am a Radical Woman Suffrage Man," an address delivered in Boston, Massachusetts, on May 28, 1888, and "Who and What Is Woman?" an address delivered in Boston, Massachusetts, on May 24, 1886, in Blassingame, *The Frederick Douglass Papers*, 5: 386, 5: 253.

79. Frederick Douglass, "Woman Suffrage Movement," *The New National Era*, October 20, 1870, in Foner, *The Life and Writings of Frederick Douglass*, 4: 231.

80. Frederick Douglass, "Letter to Thomas Auld," September 3, 1848, in Foner, *The Life and Writings of Frederick Douglass*, 1: 339.

81. Anthony Arblaster, *The Rise and Decline of Western Liberalism* (Oxford: Basil Blackwell, 1984), 25–27.

82. Frederick Douglass, "Who and What Is Woman?" an address delivered in Boston, Massachusetts, on May 24, 1886, in Blassingame, *The Frederick Douglass Papers*, 5: 255.

83. Frederick Douglass, "Letter to Thomas Auld," September 3, 1848, in Foner, *The Life and Writings of Frederick Douglass*, 1: 339.

84. Frederick Douglass, "Woman and the Ballot," from *The New National Era*, October 27, 1870, in Foner, *The Life and Writings of Frederick Douglass*, 4: 238.

85. Frederick Douglass, "Woman Suffrage Movement," from *The New National Era*, October 20, 1870, in Foner, *The Life and Writings of Frederick Douglass*, 4: 232.

86. Frederick Douglass, "The Claims of the Negro Ethnologically Considered," an address delivered at Western Reserve College in July 1854, in Foner, *The Life and Writings of Frederick Douglass*, 2: 307.

87. Frederick Douglass, "An Antislavery Tocsin," an address delivered in Rochester, New York, on December 8,1850, in Blassingame, *The Frederick Douglass Papers*, 2: 261.

88. Ibid., 2: 261. Italics mine.

89. Frederick Douglass, "An Inside View of Slavery," an address delivered in Boston, Massachusetts, on February 8, 1855, in Blassingame, *The Frederick Douglass Papers*, 3: 7.

90. Frederick Douglass, "The Black Man's Future in the Southern States," an address delivered in Boston, Massachusetts, on February 5, 1862, in Blassingame, *The Frederick Douglass Papers*, 3: 505.

91. See generally, Benjamin Quarles, "Frederick Douglass and the Women's Rights Movement," *Journal of Negro History* 25 (January 1940): 35–44.

92. Philip S. Foner, ed. *Frederick Douglass on Women's Rights* (Westport, Conn.: Greenwood Press, 1976), ix.

93. Frederick Douglass, "Who and What Is Woman?" an address delivered in Boston, Massachusetts, on May 24, 1886, in Blassingame, *The Frederick Douglass Papers*, 5: 255.

94. Ibid., 5: 259.

95. Frederick Douglass, "The Present and Future of the Colored Race in America," an address delivered in Brooklyn, New York, on May 15, 1863, in Blassingame, *The Frederick Douglass Papers*, 3: 577.

96. Frederick Douglass, "The Anti-Slavery Movement," an address delivered in Rochester, New York, on March 19, 1855, in Blassingame, *The Frederick Douglass Papers*, 3: 46.

97. Ibid.

98. Frederick Douglass, "Letter to Thomas Auld," September 3, 1848, in Foner, *The Life and Writings of Frederick Douglass*, 1: 339.

99. For a brief discussion of Douglass's views of dependence and interdependence, see Peter C. Myers, *Frederick Douglass*, 146–147.

100. Frederick Douglass, "Advice to My Canadian Brothers and Sisters," an address delivered in Chatham, Canada West, on August 3, 1854, in Blassingame, *The Frederick Douglass Papers*, 2: 536.

101. Charles Taylor, "Atomism," in *Philosophy and the Human Sciences* (New York: Cambridge University Press, 1985), 187.

102. Arnaud Leavelle, and Thomas Cook, "George Fitzhugh and the Theory of American Conservatism," *Journal of Politics* 7 (May 1945): 147. Interested readers may also wish to consult Thomas Schneider's useful comparison of Fitzhugh's ideas with those of Abraham Lincoln in *Lincoln's Defense of Politics: The Public Man and His Opponents in the Crisis over Slavery* (Columbia: University of Missouri Press, 2006), 54–72; and David F. Ericson's counterintuitive interpretation of Fitzhugh as a liberal in *The Debate over Slavery* (New York: NYU Press, 2000), 93–120.

103. George Fitzhugh, *Sociology for the South*, reprinted in *Antebellum: Three Classic Works on Slavery in the Old South* (New York: Capricorn, 1960), 57. Italics mine.

104. Frederick Douglass, "I Am a Radical Woman Suffrage Man," an address delivered in Boston, Massachusetts, on May 28, 1888, in Blassingame, *The Frederick Douglass Papers*, 5: 383.

105. Frederick Douglass, "Freedom in the West Indies," an address delivered in Poughkeepsie, New York, on August 2, 1858, in Blassingame, *The Frederick Douglass Papers*, 3: 222–223.

106. Ibid., 3: 219.

107. Frederick Douglass, "An Antislavery Tocsin," an address delivered in Rochester, New York, on December 8,1850, in Blassingame, *The Frederick Douglass Papers*, 2: 267.

108. It is beyond my scope to take up the question of whether or not these criticisms of Locke and Nozick are sound. I do think it is fair to say, though, that critics are right to say the defenses of self-ownership offered by Locke and Nozick *emphasize* the relationship between this idea and the right to private property.

109. Peter Walker, *Moral Choices: Memory, Desire, and Imagination in Nineteenth Century* Abolition (Baton Rouge: Louisiana State University Press, 1978); Waldo Martin, *The Mind of Frederick Douglass* (Chapel Hill: University of North Carolina Press, 1986); Wilson Jeremiah Moses, *Creative Conflict in African American Thought: Frederick Douglass, Alexander Crummell, Booker T. Washington, W. E. B. Du Bois, and Marcus Garvey* (New York: Cambridge University Press, 2004).

110. Waldo Martin, *The Mind of Frederick Douglass* (Chapel Hill: University of North Carolina Press, 1984), 131–132.

111. The term "moral fences" is taken from Eric Mack, "The State of Nature Has a Law of Nature to Govern It," in Tibor R. Machan, ed., *Individual Rights Reconsidered* (Palo Alto: Hoover Institution Press, 2001), 88.

112. Joyce Appleby, *Capitalism and a New Social Order* (New York: NYU Press, 1984), 85.

113. For discussions of the exclusion of most Americans from the liberal promise of freedom in the eighteenth and nineteenth centuries, see Rogers Smith, *Civic Ideals* (New Haven: Yale University Press, 1999); Mark E. Kann, *On the Man Question* (Philadelphia: Temple University Press, 1991); Mark E. Kann, *A Republic of Men* (New York: NYU Press, 1998); Mark E. Kann, *Punishment, Prisons, and Patriarchy* (New York: NYU Press, 2005).

114. Anthony Arblaster, *The Rise and Decline of Western Liberalism*, 27.

115. Frederick Douglass, "Radical," in *The New National Era*, October 13, 1870. A copy of this document is available at the Frederick Douglass Papers Project at Indiana University-Purdue University Indianapolis, in Indianapolis, Indiana.

116. For a discussion of this conflict, see Sue Davis, *The Political Thought of Elizabeth Cady Stanton: Women's Rights and the American Political Traditions* and Mark Leibovich, "Rights vs. Rights: An Improbable Collision Course," *New York Times*, January 13, 2008.

117. Elizabeth Cady Stanton et al., *History of Woman Suffrage: 1861–1876* (Salem: Ayer Publishers, 1985), 383.

118. Leslie Friedman Goldstein, "Morality and Prudence in the Statesmanship of Frederick Douglass," *Polity* 16 (Summer 1984): 614.

CHAPTER 3

1. Louis Hartz, *The Liberal Tradition in America* (New York: Harcourt Brace, 1991).

2. Lewis Perry, "Versions of Anarchism in the Antislavery Movement," *American Quarterly* 20, no. 4 (Winter 1968): 768–782. It is worth noting that Garrison himself resisted this label because he believed in the "government of God," who has final authority over human affairs. Thanks to an anonymous reviewer for emphasizing this point.

3. See generally, John Humphrey Noyes, *History of American Socialisms* (Philadelphia: J. B. Lippincott, 1870); and Carl J. Guarneri, *The Utopian Alternative: Fourierism in Nineteenth-Century America* (Ithaca: Cornell University Press, 1994), 255.

4. Ronald Dworkin, "Rights as Trumps," in Jeremy Waldron, ed., *Theories of Rights* (Oxford: Oxford University Press, 1984), 153–167.

5. Kenneth Dolbeare, "Introduction: American Liberalism—An Overview," in *American Political Thought* (Chatham: Chatham House Publishers, 1996), 5.

6. For an interesting discussion of the variety that exists within American liberalism, see generally, Peter Berkowitz, "The Liberal Spirit in America," *Policy Review*, no. 120 (2003).

7. Judith Shklar, "The Liberalism of Fear," in Stanley Hoffmann, ed., *Political Thought and Political Thinkers* (Chicago: University of Chicago, 1998), 5.

8. Judith Shklar, *Legalism* (Cambridge: Harvard University Press, 2006), 6.

9. Judith Shklar, "The Liberalism of Fear," 5–6.

10. Ibid.

11. Benjamin Barber, *Strong Democracy: Participatory Politics for a New Age* (Berkeley: University of California Press, 1984), 6.

12. Sheldon Wolin, *Politics and Vision* (Boston: Little, Brown, 1960), 306–308.

13. John Locke, *Second Treatise of Civil Government* (New York: Barnes and Noble Press, 2004), 75.

14. James Madison, *Federalist #51*, in *The Federalist Papers* (New York: Classic Books America, 2009), 222.

15. Judith Shklar, "Political Theory and the Rule of Law," in Stanley Hoffmann, ed., *Political Thought and Political Thinkers* (Chicago: University of Chicago Press, 1998), 22.

16. John Locke, *Second Treatise of Civil Government*, chapter 6, Section 57.

17. Judith Shklar, "The Liberalism of Fear," 18.

18. Ibid., 19.

19. Sheldon Wolin, "The Liberal-Democratic Divide: On Rawls's *Political Liberalism*," *Political Theory* 24, no. 1 (February 1996): 97.

20. Judith Shklar, *Legalism*, 66.

21. Frederick Douglass, "Slavery, Freedom, and the Kansas-Nebraska Act," an address delivered in Chicago, Illinois, on October 30, 1854, in Blassingame, *The Frederick Douglass Papers*, 2: 557.

22. Frederick Douglass, "I Am a Radical Woman Suffrage Man," an address delivered in Boston, Massachusetts, on May 28, 1888, in Blassingame, *The Frederick Douglass Papers*, 5: 384.

23. As quoted in Allen Guelzo, "Apple of Gold and the Picture of Silver," in *The Lincoln Enigma: The Changing Faces of an American Icon*, ed. Gabor Boritt (New York: Oxford University Press, 2001), 88.

24. Frederick Douglass, "The Shame of America," in *Frederick Douglass' Paper*, June 27, 1856. A copy of this document is available at the Frederick Douglass Papers Project at Indiana University-Purdue University Indianapolis, in Indianapolis, Indiana.

25. Frederick Douglass, "We Ask Only for Our Rights," an address delivered in Troy, New York, on September 4, 1855, in Blassingame, *Frederick Douglass Papers*, 3: 91–92.

26. Frederick Douglass, "In Law Free; In Fact, a Slave," an address delivered in Washington, D.C., on April 16, 1888, in Blassingame, *The Frederick Douglass Papers*, 5: 373.

27. Frederick Douglass, "Resolutions Proposed for Anti-Capital Punishment Meeting, Rochester, New York, October 7, 1858," in *The Liberator*, October 7, 1858, in Foner, The *Life and Writings of Frederick Douglass*, 5: 418.

28. Frederick Douglass, "American Civilization," from *Douglass' Monthly*, October, 1859, in Foner, *The Life and Writings of Frederick Douglass*, 5: 456.

29. Frederick Douglass, "An Antislavery Tocsin," an address delivered in Rochester, New York, on December 8, 1850, in Blassingame, *The Frederick Douglass Papers*, 2: 261.

30. Ibid.

31. Frederick Douglass, "Is It Right and Wise to Kill a Kidnapper?" from *Frederick Douglass' Paper*, June 2, 1854, in Foner, *The Life and Writings of Frederick Douglass*, 2: 285.

32. John Stuart Mill, *On Liberty* (New York: Oxford University Press, 1991), 15; and Frederick Douglass, "The Kansas-Nebraska Bill," speech at Chicago, October 30, 1854, from *Frederick Douglass' Paper*, November 24, 1854, in Foner, *The Life and Writings of Frederick Douglass*, 2: 317.

33. John Locke, *Second Treatise on Civil Government*, chapter 2, Section 6.

34. Robert P. George, *Making Men Moral* (New York: Oxford University Press, 1995), 19–20.

35. Frederick Douglass, "Too Much Religion, Too Little Humanity," an address delivered in New York, New York, on May 9, 1849, in Blassingame, *The Frederick Douglass Papers*, 2: 182–183.

36. For discussion of this "doctrine of separate spheres," see, e.g., Carl Degler, *At Odds: Women and Family in American History* (New York: Oxford University Press, 1980), 9.

37. Frederick Douglass, "Who and What Is Woman?" an address delivered in Boston, Massachusetts, on May 24, 1886, in Blassingame, *The Frederick Douglass Papers*, 5: 257–258.

38. Frederick Douglass, "I Am a Radical Woman Suffrage Man," an address delivered in Boston, Massachusetts, on May 28, 1888, in Blassingame, *The Frederick Douglass Papers*, 5: 382.

39. "Frederick Douglass on Prohibition," letter to the editor of *The Issue*, republished in *The Washington Bee*, April 24, 1886. A copy of this document can be found at The Frederick Douglass Papers Project, Indiana University-Purdue University Indianapolis, in Indianapolis, Indiana.

40. Frederick Douglass, "Temperance and Anti-Slavery," an address delivered in Paisley, Scotland, on March 30, 1846, in Blassingame, *Frederick Douglass Papers*, 1: 207.

41. Ibid.

42. Frederick Douglass, "Colonizationist Measures," an address delivered in New York, New York, on April 24, 1849, in Blassingame, *The Frederick Douglass Papers*, 2: 165. This

similarity was recognized by Leslie Friedman Goldstein, "The Political Thought of Frederick Douglass," Ph.D. dissertation, Department of Political Science, Cornell University, 1974, 55.

43. Frederick Douglass, "Politics an Evil to the Negro," from *The New National Era*, August 24, 1871, in Foner, *The Life and Writings of Frederick Douglass*, 4: 271–272.

44. Carl J. Guarneri, *The Utopian Alternative*, 17, xii.

45. Ibid., 18.

46. Ibid., 256.

47. Ibid., 255.

48. Frederick Douglass, "Property in Soil and Property in Man," from *The North Star*, November 24, 1848, in Foner, *The Life and Writings of Frederick Douglass*, 5: 105.

49. Frederick Douglass, "The Labor Question," from *The New National Era*, October 12, 1871, in Foner, *The Life and Writings of Frederick Douglass*, 4: 282.

50. Ibid.

51. Ibid.

52. Ibid., 4: 283.

53. Ibid.

54. See Eric Foner, *Politics and Ideology in the Age of the Civil War* (New York: Oxford University Press, 1980), 57–76; Eric Foner, *The Story of American Freedom* (New York: W. W. Norton, 1998), 69–114; Carl J. Guarneri, *The Utopian Alternative*.

55. Judith Shklar, *Legalism*, 5.

56. John Rawls, *Political Liberalism* (New York: Columbia University Press, 2005), 37.

57. Frederick Douglass, "Who and What Is Woman?" an address delivered in Boston, Massachusetts, on May 24, 1889, in Blassingame, *The Frederick Douglass Papers*, 5: 247.

58. See generally, Sasha Tarrant et al., *Antifeminism in America: A Historical Reader* (New York: Routledge, 2000).

59. Frederick Douglass, "Who and What Is Woman?" an address delivered in Boston, Massachusetts, on May 24, 1886, in Blassingame, *The Frederick Douglass Papers*, 5: 260.

60. Ibid., 5: 261.

61. Ibid.

62. Ibid.

63. Ibid.

64. Ibid. Italics mine.

65. John Rawls, *Political Liberalism*, 4.

66. Frederick Douglass, "Letter to William Lloyd Garrison," in *The Liberator*, June 26, 1846, in Foner, *The Life and Writings of Frederick Douglass*, 1: 167–168.

67. Frederick Douglass, "Preface: The Fifteenth Amendment," in Foner, *The Life and Writings of Frederick Douglass*, 4: 48. For more on this controversy, see William L. Van Deburg, "Frederick Douglass: Maryland Slave to Religious Liberal," in *By These Hands: A Documentary History of African American Humanism*, Anthony B. Pinn, ed. (New York: NYU Press, 2001), 92.

68. Frederick Douglass, "A Public Letter by Frederick Douglass to Editor," in *Philadelphia Press*, July 14, 1870. A copy of this document is available at the Frederick Douglass Papers Project at Indiana University-Purdue University Indianapolis, in Indianapolis, Indiana.

69. Frederick Douglass, "Antislavery Meeting," in *Frederick Douglass' Paper*, November 20, 1851. A copy of this document is available at the Frederick Douglass Papers Project at Indiana University-Purdue University Indianapolis, in Indianapolis, Indiana.

70. Frederick Douglass, "St. Paul's Bachelor Views," in *The New National Era*, November 24, 1870. A copy of this document is available at the Frederick Douglass Papers Project at Indiana University-Purdue University Indianapolis, in Indianapolis, Indiana.

71. Frederick Douglass, "An Attempt against Religious Liberty," *The New National Era*, January 19, 1871. A copy of this document is available at the Frederick Douglass Papers Project at Indiana University-Purdue University Indianapolis, in Indianapolis, Indiana.

72. Frederick Douglass, "Dark Prospects," in *The New National Era*, May 4, 1871. A copy of this document is available at the Frederick Douglass Papers Project at Indiana University-Purdue University Indianapolis, in Indianapolis, Indiana.

73. Josh Gottheimer, ed. *Ripples of Hope: Great American Civil Rights Speeches* (New York: Basic Civitas, 2003), 87. For characteristic statements against Chinese immigration, see James Harvey Slater and James Zachariah George, "Speeches on Chinese Immigration," reprinted in Isaac Kramnick and Theodore Lowi, eds. *American Political Thought: A Norton Anthology* (New York: W. W. Norton, 2009): 893–901.

74. Frederick Douglass, "Our Composite Nationality," an address delivered in Boston, Massachusetts, on December 7, 1869, in Blassingame, *The Frederick Douglass Papers*, 4: 258.

75. Ibid. Italics mine.

76. Frederick Douglass, Review of "A Discourse, Delivered before the Historical Society of Pennsylvania" by Thomas Kane, published in *The North Star*, October 3, 1850. A copy of this document is in the archives of the Frederick Douglass Papers Project at Indiana University-Purdue University Indianapolis, in Indianapolis, Indiana. For more on Kane's pamphlet, see Donald Q. Cannon, "Thomas L. Kane Meets the Mormons," *BYU Studies* 18, no. 1 (1977): 1–3.

77. Frederick Douglass, "Toleration and Indifference," in *The New National Era*, May 11, 1871. A copy of this document is available at the Frederick Douglass Papers Project at Indiana University-Purdue University Indianapolis, in Indianapolis, Indiana.

78. Frederick Douglass, "Is Civil Government Right?" from *Frederick Douglass' Paper*, October 23, 1851, in Foner, *The Life and Writings of Frederick Douglass*, 5: 209.

79. See generally, Lewis Perry, *Radical Abolitionism: Anarchy and the Government of God in Antislavery Thought* (Ithaca: Cornell University Press, 1973).

80. Henry C. Wright, "Anthropology" (Boston: E. Seepard, 1850), 68–69.

81. Ibid., 69.

82. Lewis Perry, "Versions of Anarchism in the Antislavery Movement," 770, 772.

83. Frederick Douglass, "Is Civil Government Right?" in *Frederick Douglass' Paper*, October 23, 1851, in Foner, *The Life and Writings of Frederick Douglass*, 5: 209.

84. Frederick Douglass, "American Civilization," in *Douglass' Monthly*, October 1859, in Foner, *The Life and Writings of Frederick Douglass*, 5: 457; Frederick Douglass, "Shalt Thou Steal?" an address delivered in New York, New York, on May 8, 1849, in Blassingame, *The Frederick Douglass Papers*, 2: 175; Frederick Douglass, "The Fugitive Slave Law," speech to the National Free Soil Convention at Pittsburgh, August 11, 1852," in *Frederick Douglass' Paper*, August 1852, in Foner, *The Life and Writings of Frederick Douglass*, 2: 207.

85. Frederick Douglass, "Will Non-Resistance Keep Slavery Out of Kansas?" in *Frederick Douglass' Paper*, March 21, 1856. A copy of this document is available at the Frederick Douglass Papers Project at Indiana University-Purdue University Indianapolis, in Indianapolis, Indiana.

86. Frederick Douglass, "Is Civil Government Right?" from *Frederick Douglass' Paper*, October 23, 1851, in Foner, *The Life and Writings of Frederick Douglass*, 5: 210.

87. Ibid., 5: 210.

88. Frederick Douglass, "Let All Soil Be Free Soil," an address delivered in Pittsburgh, Pennsylvania, on August 11, 1852, in Blassingame, *The Frederick Douglass Papers*, 2: 392.

89. Frederick Douglass, "Freedom in the West Indies," an address delivered in Poughkeepsie, New York, on August 2, 1858, in Blassingame, *The Frederick Douglass Papers*, 3: 223.

90. For Douglass's views of capital punishment, see Frederick Douglass, "The Colored People and Our Paper," from *Frederick Douglass' Paper*, November 27, 1851, in Foner, *The Life and Writings of Frederick Douglass*, 5: 218.

91. Frederick Douglass, "Is Civil Government Right?" from *Frederick Douglass' Paper*, October 23, 1851, in Foner, *The Life and Writings of Frederick Douglass*, 5: 213–214.

92. Ibid., 214.

93. Frederick Douglass, "Is It Right and Wise to Kill a Kidnapper?" in *Frederick Douglass' Paper*, June 2, 1854, in Foner, *The Life and Writings of Frederick Douglass*, 2: 286.

94. Frederick Douglass, Review of *Selections from the Writings of William Lloyd Garrison*, in *Frederick Douglass' Paper*, January 29, 1852. A copy of this document is available at the Frederick Douglass Papers Project at Indiana University-Purdue University Indianapolis, in Indianapolis, Indiana.

95. Frederick Douglass. "In Law Free; In Fact, a Slave," an address delivered in Washington, D.C., on April 16, 1888, in Blassingame, *The Frederick Douglass Papers*, 5: 369.

96. Frederick Douglass, "Is Civil Government Right?" from *Frederick Douglass' Paper*, October 23, 1851, in Foner, *The Life and Writings of Frederick Douglass*, 5: 212.

97. Ibid., 5: 211.

98. Ibid., 5: 212.

99. Frederick Douglass, "The Constitution of the United States: Is It Pro-Slavery or Anti-Slavery?" speech delivered in Glasgow, Scotland, on March 26, 1860, in Foner, *The Life and Writings of Frederick Douglass*, 2: 480.

100. Frederick Douglass, "The Kansas-Nebraska Bill, speech at Chicago, October 30, 1854," from *Frederick Douglass' Paper*, November 24, 1854, in Foner, *The Life and Writings of Frederick Douglass*, 5: 328.

101. Frederick Douglass, " Our Composite Nationality," an address delivered in Boston, Massachusetts, on December 7, 1869, in Blassingame, *The Frederick Douglass Papers*, 4: 251.

102. Frederick Douglass, "Is Civil Government Right?" from *Frederick Douglass' Paper*, October 23, 1851, in Foner, *The Life and Writings of Frederick Douglass*, 5: 212.

103. *The Life and Writings of Frederick Douglass*, 5: 210–211.

104. Ibid., 5: 212–213; Frederick Douglass, "Nobody Can Be Represented by Anybody Else," an address delivered in Boston, Massachusetts, on December 15, 1873, in Foner, *The Frederick Douglass Papers*, 4: 396.

105. Frederick Douglass, "Is Civil Government Right?" from *Frederick Douglass' Paper*, October 23, 1851, in Foner, *The Life and Writings of Frederick Douglass*, 5: 210–211.

106. Frederick Douglas, "I Am a Radical Woman Suffrage Man," an address delivered in Boston, Massachusetts, on May 28, 1888, in Blassingame, *The Frederick Douglass Papers*, 5: 387.

107. Ibid.

108. Frederick Douglass, "Politics an Evil to the Negro?" from *The New National Era*, August 24, 1871, in Foner, *The Life and Writings of Frederick Douglass*, 4: 271–272.

109. Frederick Douglass, "Who and What Is Woman?" an address delivered in Boston, Massachusetts, on May 24, 1886, in Blassingame, *The Frederick Douglass Papers*, 5: 253.

110. Frederick Douglass, "Slavery and America's Bastard Republicanism," an address delivered in Limerick, Ireland, on November 10, 1845, in Blassingame, *The Frederick Douglass Papers*, 1: 81, and "Equal Rights for All," an address delivered in New York, New York, on May 14, 1868, in Blassingame, *The Frederick Douglass Papers*, 4: 174.

111. Frederick Douglass, "Sources of Danger to the Republic," an address delivered in St. Louis, Missouri, on February 7, 1867, in Blassingame, *The Frederick Douglass Papers*, 4: 158.

112. Frederick Douglass, "Compulsory Voting," *New National Era*, July 20, 1871. A copy of this document is available at the Frederick Douglass Papers at Indiana University-Purdue University Indianapolis, in Indianapolis, Indiana.

113. Frederick Douglass, "Woman and the Ballot," from *The New National Era*, October 27, 1870, in Foner, *The Life and Writings of Frederick Douglass*, 4: 236.

114. Frederick Douglass, "Who and What Is Woman?" an address delivered in Boston, Massachusetts, on May 24, 1886, in Blassingame, *The Frederick Douglass Papers*, 5: 262.

115. Frederick Douglass, "Equal Rights for All: Addresses Delivered in New York, New York, on 14 May 1868," in Blassingame, *The Frederick Douglass Papers*, 4: 175.

116. Frederick Douglass, "Woman and the Ballot," from *The New National Era*, October 27, 1870, in Foner, *The Life and Writings of Frederick Douglass*, 4: 238.

117. Frederick Douglass, "Sources of Danger to the Republic," an address delivered in St. Louis, Missouri, on February 7, 1867, in Blassingame, *The Frederick Douglass Papers*, 4: 165.

118. Frederick Douglass, "The Present and Future of the Colored Race in America," an address delivered in Brooklyn, New York, on May 15, 1863, in Blassingame, *The Frederick Douglass Papers*, 3: 575.

119. Ibid., 3: 578–579.

120. Frederick Douglass, "The Opening Campaign for the Presidency," in *Frederick Douglass' Paper*, June 3, 1852. A copy of this document is available at the Frederick Douglass Papers Project at Indiana University-Purdue University Indianapolis, in Indianapolis, Indiana.

121. Daniel McInerney, *The Fortunate Heirs of Freedom: Abolition and Republican Thought* (Lincoln: University of Nebraska Press, 1994), 43.

122. Frederick Douglass, "Woman and the Ballot," from *The New National Era*, October 27, 1870, in Foner, *The Life and Writings of Frederick Douglass*, 4: 237–238.

123. Judith Shklar, *American Citizenship: The Quest for Inclusion* (Cambridge: Harvard University Press, 1998).

124. For a discussion of the "protective" model of democracy, see Donald Hudson, *Democracy in Peril* (Washington, D.C.: CQ Press, 2010), 8–10.

125. Frederick Douglass, "Is It Right and Wise to Kill a Kidnapper?" from *Frederick Douglass' Paper*, June 2, 1854, in Foner, *The Life and Writings of Frederick Douglass*, 2: 288.

126. Frederick Douglass, "Slavery, Freedom, and the Kansas-Nebraska Act," an address delivered in Chicago, Illinois, on October 30, 1854, in Blassingame, *The Frederick Douglass Papers*, 2: 556.

127. Ibid., 2: 557.

128. Ibid.

129. Ibid., 2: 557–558.

130. Frederick Douglass, "The Presidential Campaign of 1860," from *Douglass' Monthly*, September 1860, in Foner, *The Life and Writings of Frederick Douglass*, 2: 516. Italics in original.

131. Frederick Douglass, "Comments on Gerrit Smith's Address," from *The North Star*, March 30, 1849, in Foner, *The Life and Writings of Frederick Douglass*, 1: 375.

132. Frederick Douglass, "Sources of Danger to the Republic," an address delivered in St. Louis, Missouri, on February 7, 1867, in Blassingame, *The Frederick Douglass Papers*, 4: 167.

133. Frederick Douglass, "Is Civil Government Right?" from *Frederick Douglass' Paper*, October 23, 1851, in Foner, *The Life and Writings of Frederick Douglass*, 5: 210–211.

134. Frederick Douglass, "Our Composite Nationality," an address delivered in Boston, Massachusetts, on December 7, 1869, in Foner, *The Life and Writings of Frederick Douglass*, 4: 255.

CHAPTER 4

1. Frederick Douglass, "We Are Not Yet Quite Free," an address delivered in Medina, New York, on August 3, 1869, in Blassingame, *The Frederick Douglass Papers*, 4: 233.

2. Frederick Douglass, "The Dred Scott Decision," an address delivered in New York, New York, in May 1857, in Blassingame, *The Frederick Douglass Papers*, 3: 173.

3. Ibid.

4. In all fairness to Garrison, it should be noted that he believed disunion would leave slaveholders more susceptible to slave revolts and therefore force them to consider emancipation more seriously. Thanks to an anonymous reviewer for emphasizing this point.

5. When Douglass used the term "human brotherhood" he intended women to be included. An incident from Douglass's career as a newspaper editor reveals his sensitivity to the gendered reading of these terms. When Douglass was thinking of changing the name of his newspaper, one of the possibilities was "The Brotherhood," but he rejected this name because he worried it might lead some to mistakenly conclude that the paper's agenda "excluded" concern for "the sisterhood." See Frederick Douglass, "Letter to Hon. Gerrit Smith," January 14, 1853, in Foner, *The Life and Writings of Frederick Douglass*, 2: 223.

6. Frederick Douglass, *My Bondage and My Freedom* (New York: Penguin Books, 2003), 113. Goldstein calls this the "Divinely or naturally implanted sentiment of human brotherly love." See Leslie Friedman Goldstein, "The Political Thought of Frederick Douglass," Ph.D. dissertation, Department of Political Science, Cornell University, 1974, 60–61.

7. Ibid., 115–116.

8. Ibid., 105.

9. Ibid., 107.

10. Frederick Douglass, "Did John Brown Fail?" an address delivered in Harper's Ferry, West Virginia, on May 30, 1881, in Blassingame, *The Frederick Douglass Papers*, 5: 10.

11. Frederick Douglass, "Is It Right and Wise to Kill a Kidnapper?" in *Frederick Douglass' Paper*, June 2, 1854, in Foner, *The Life and Writings of Frederick Douglass*, 2: 284–285.

12. Frederick Douglass, "The Significance of Emancipation in the West Indies," an address delivered in Canandaigua, New York, on August 3, 1857, in Blassingame, *The Frederick Douglass Papers*, 3:195.

13. Frederick Douglass, "The Blessings of Liberty and Education," an address delivered in Manassas, Virginia, on September 3, 1894, in Blassingame, *The Frederick Douglass Papers*, 5: 625.

14. Frederick Douglass, "'It Moves,' or the Philosophy of Reform," an address delivered in Washington, D.C., on November 20, 1883, in Blassingame, *The Frederick Douglass Papers*, 5: 129.

15. Frederick Douglass, "The Antislavery Tocsin," an address delivered in Rochester, New York, on December 8, 1850, in Blassingame, *The Frederick Douglass Papers*, 2: 264–265. Douglass was paraphrasing the words of British abolitionist Charles James Fox's "Abolition of the Slave Trade," *Speeches of the Right Honourable Charles James Fox in the House of Commons* (London, 1815), 4: 190.

16. Frederick Douglass, "The Prospect in the Future," in *Douglass' Monthly*, August 1860, in Foner, *The Life and Writings of Frederick Douglass*, 2: 494.

17. Samuel Huntington, *Who Are We? Challenges to American National Identity* (New York: Simon and Schuster, 2005), xv.

18. Frederick Douglass, "The American Apocalypse," an address delivered in Rochester, New York, on June 16, 1861, in Blassingame, *The Frederick Douglass Papers*, 3: 444.

19. Frederick Douglass, "Fighting the Rebels with One Hand," an address delivered in Philadelphia, Pennsylvania, on January 14, 1862, in Blassingame, *The Frederick Douglass Papers*, 3: 480.

20. For a discussion of the irrational element of many theories of community, see Robert Booth Fowler, *The Dance with Community* (Lawrence: University Press of Kansas, 1993), 3.

21. Frederick Douglass, "The Anti-Slavery Movement," an address delivered in Rochester, New York, on March 19, 1855, in Blassingame, *The Frederick Douglass Papers*, 3: 46. See also Leslie Goldstein, "The Political Thought of Frederick Douglass," 41.

22. Frederick Douglass, "The American Apocalypse," an address delivered in Rochester, New York, on June 16, 1861, in Blassingame, *The Frederick Douglass Papers*, 3: 437.

23. Frederick Douglass, "The Proclamation and a Negro Army," an address delivered in New York, New York, on February 6, 1863, in Blassingame, *The Frederick Douglass Papers*, 3: 553.

24. Philip S. Foner, "Frederick Douglass," *The Life and Writings of Frederick Douglass*, 2: 54.

25. Although I think this is beyond the scope of this particular argument, I do not think this is unimportant. Douglass's decision to accept the legitimacy of the Constitution and the propriety of political action was an enormously important one. This decision transformed his political identity and opened up a wide array of arguments previously unavailable to him.

26. As quoted in Philip S. Foner, "Frederick Douglass," *The Life and Writings of Frederick Douglass*, 2: 54.

27. Alexis de Tocqueville, *Democracy in America*, Harvey Mansfield and Delba Winthrop, eds. (Chicago: University of Chicago Press, 2000), 501.

28. For Douglass's discussions of "the slave power," see "The Encroachment of Slave Power," an address delivered in Troy, New York, on September 5, 1855, and "Aggressions of the Slave Power," an address delivered in Rochester, New York, on May 22, 1856, in Blassingame, *The Frederick Douglass Papers*, 3: 97, 3: 114.

29. Frederick Douglass, "The Ballot and the Bullet," *Frederick Douglass' Paper*, September 30, 1859. A copy of this document can be found at the Frederick Douglass Papers Project at Indiana University-Purdue University Indianapolis, in Indianapolis, Indiana.

30. Frederick Douglass, "We Are Not Yet Quite Free," an address delivered in Medina, New York, on August 3, 1869, in Blassingame, *The Frederick Douglass Papers*, 4: 232–233.

31. Frederick Douglass, "The Suffrage Question," *Frederick Douglass' Paper*, April 25, 1856. A copy of this document can be found at the Frederick Douglass Papers Project at Indiana University-Purdue University Indianapolis, in Indianapolis, Indiana.

32. Frederick Douglass, "The Nation's Problem," an address delivered in Washington, D.C., on April 16, 1889, in Blassingame, *The Frederick Douglass Papers*, 5: 424.

33. Ibid., 5: 424–425.

34. Frederick Douglass, *Autobiographies*, ed. Henry Louis Gates (New York: Library of America, 1994), 256.

35. Ibid., 65.

36. Ibid., 286. Emphases in original.

37. Ibid., 274–275.

38. For an excellent discussion of the relationship between protest and self-respect in Douglass's thought (as well as that of W. E. B. Du Bois), see Bernard Boxill, "Self-Respect and Protest," *Philosophy and Public Affairs* 6, no. 1 (1976): 58–69.

39. Frederick Douglass, "The Prospect in the Future," in *Douglass' Monthly*, August 1860, in Foner, *The Life and Writings of Frederick Douglass*, 2: 494.

40. Ibid., 2: 495.

41. Ibid.

42. Ibid., 2: 496.

43. Ibid., 2: 496–497.

44. Ibid., 2: 497.

45. In philosophical terms, sympathy from brotherhood is an a priori view of human dignity and sympathy from merit is an a posteriori view of human dignity.

46. Frederick Douglass, "The Prospect in the Future," in *Douglass' Monthly*, August 1860, in Foner, *The Life and Writings of Frederick Douglass*, 2: 497.

47. Ibid., 2: 497.

48. Frederick Douglass, "Citizenship and the Spirit of Caste," an address delivered in New York, New York, on May 11, 1858, in Blassingame, *The Frederick Douglass Papers* 3: 210.

49. For an extensive discussion of Douglass's evolving attitudes toward black enlistment, see David Blight, *Frederick Douglass' Civil War: Keeping Faith in Jubilee* (Baton Rouge: LSU Press, 1991).

50. William McFeely, *Frederick Douglass* (New York: W. W. Norton, 1991) 223–224.

51. This matter is discussed in Samuel Huntington, *Who Are We?* 198.

52. Frederick Douglass, "Why Should a Colored Man Enlist?" from *Douglass' Monthly*, April 1863, in Foner, *The Life and Writings of Frederick Douglass*, 3: 342.

53. Ibid., 3: 342–343.

54. Frederick Douglass, "Advice to My Canadian Brothers and Sisters," an address delivered in Chatham, Canada West, on August 3, 1854, in Blassingame, *The Frederick Douglass Papers*, 2: 536.

55. Frederick Douglass, "Learn Trades or Starve!" in *Frederick Douglass' Paper*, March 4, 1853, in Foner, *The Life and Writings of Frederick Douglass*, 2: 224.

56. Frederick Douglass, "Trust: The Basis of Charity," an address delivered in Rochester, New York, on January 5, 1854, in Blassingame, *The Frederick Douglass Papers*, 2: 453. Emphasis in original.

57. Ibid., 2: 451.

58. Ibid., 2: 452. Emphasis in original.

59. Ibid., 2: 453.

60. Frederick Douglass, "The American Apocalypse," an address delivered in Rochester, New York, on June 16, 1861, in Blassingame, *The Frederick Douglass Papers*, 3: 437–438.

61. Frederick Douglass, "America's Compromise with Slavery and the Abolitionists'
Work," an address delivered in Paisley, Scotland, on April 6, 1846, in Blassingame, *The
Frederick Douglass Papers*, 1: 210.

62. Frederick Douglass, "Parties Were Made for Men, Not Men for Parties," an address
delivered in Louisville, Kentucky, in Blassingame, *The Frederick Douglass Papers*, 5: 89.

63. Frederick Douglass, "The Slave Democracy Again in the Field," from *Douglass'
Monthly*, November 1862, in Foner, *The Life and Writings of Frederick Douglass*, 3: 292.

64. Frederick Douglass, "Letter to Major Delany," from *The New National Era*, August
31, 1871, in Foner, *The Life and Writings of Frederick Douglass*, 4: 279.

65. Frederick Douglass, "America's Compromise with Slavery and the Abolitionists'
Work," an address delivered in Paisley, Scotland, on April 6, 1846, in Blassingame, *The
Frederick Douglass Papers*, 1: 210.

66. Frederick Douglass, "The Prospect in the Future," from *Douglass' Monthly*, August
1860, in Foner, *The Life and Times of Frederick Douglass* 2: 497.

67. Frederick Douglass, "Our Composite Nationality," an address delivered in Boston,
Massachusetts, on December 7, 1869, in Blassingame, *The Frederick Douglass Papers*, 4: 251.

68. Frederick Douglass, "To Gerrit Smith," from the Gerrit Smith Papers, Syracuse Uni-
versity, September 24, 1874, in Foner, *The Life and Writings of Frederick Douglass*, 4: 308;
Frederick Douglass, "We Are Confronted by a New Administration," an address delivered
in Washington, D.C., on April 16, 1885; "Lessons of the Hour," an address delivered in
Washington, D.C., on January 6, 1894; and "Country, Conscience, and the Antislavery
Cause," an address delivered in New York, New York, on May 11, 1847, in Blassingame, *The
Frederick Douglass Papers*, 5: 191, 5: 596, 2: 61.

CHAPTER 5

1. As quoted in Reginald F. Davis, *Frederick Douglass: A Precursor to Liberation Theology*
(Atlanta: Mercer University Press, 2004), ix.

2. Frederick Douglass, "Self-Made Men," an address delivered in Carlisle, Pennsylvania,
in March 1894, in Blassingame, *The Frederick Douglass Papers*, 5: 545. The precise date on
which Douglass delivered this address is unknown.

3. Robert Bellah et al., *Habits of the Heart* (Berkeley: University of California Press,
1985) , 284.

4. Michael Novak, *Cultivating Liberty: Essays on Moral Ecology* (New York: Rowan and
Littlefield, 1999).

5. Frederick Douglass, "The Prospect in the Future," from *The Douglass Monthly*, August
1860, in Foner, *The Life and Writings of Frederick Douglass*, 2: 497.

6. Frederick Douglass, "Self-Made Men," an address delivered in Carlisle, Pennsylvania,
in March 1894, in Blassingame, *The Frederick Douglass Papers*, 5: 548.

7. Douglass uses the phrase "simple justice" to describe a basic framework of society in
which the rights of all individuals are respected and all individuals are treated fairly. See

Frederick Douglass, "The Black Man's Future in the Southern States," an address delivered in Boston, Massachusetts, on February 5, 1862, in Blassingame, *The Frederick Douglass Papers*, 3: 499.

8. Frederick Douglass, "'It Moves,' or the Philosophy of Reform," an address delivered in Washington, D.C., on November 20, 1883, in Blassingame, *The Frederick Douglass Papers*, 5: 129.

9. Frederick Douglass, "The Antislavery Tocsin," an address delivered in Rochester, New York, on December 8, 1850, in Blassingame, *The Frederick Douglass Papers*, 2: 264. Douglass was paraphrasing the words of British abolitionist Charles James Fox's "Abolition of the Slave Trade," *Speeches of the Right Honourable Charles James Fox in the House of Commons* (London, 1815), 4:190.

10. Frederick Douglass, "'It Moves,' or the Philosophy of Reform," an address delivered in Washington, D.C., on November 20, 1883, in Blassingame, *The Frederick Douglass Papers*, 5: 139.

11. Ibid., 5: 127.

12. Frederick Douglass, "The Anti-Slavery Movement," an address delivered in Rochester, New York, on March 19, 1855, in Blassingame, *The Frederick Douglass Papers*, 3: 45.

13. Ibid., 3: 45–46.

14. Frederick Douglass, "The Skin Aristocracy in America," an address delivered in Coventry, England, on February 2, 1847, in Blassingame, *The Frederick Douglass Papers*, 2: 6.

15. Frederick Douglass, "Did John Brown Fail?" an address delivered in Harper's Ferry, West Virginia, on May 30, 1881, in Blassingame, *The Frederick Douglass Papers*, 5: 13.

16. Ibid.

17. Frederick Douglass, "The Proclamation and a Negro Army," an address delivered in New York, New York, on February 6, 1862, in Blassingame, *The Frederick Douglass Papers*, 3: 553.

18. As quoted in David S. Reynolds, *John Brown, Abolitionist: The Man Who Killed Slavery, Sparked the Civil War, and Seeded Civil Rights* (New York: Vintage: 2005), ix.

19. Frederick Douglass, "Did John Brown Fail?" an address delivered in Harper's Ferry, West Virginia, on May 30, 1881, in Blassingame, *The Frederick Douglass Papers*, 5: 22.

20. Ibid., 5: 14–15.

21. I discuss Douglass's views of good statesmanship in the next chapter.

22. Frederick Douglass, "The American Apocalypse," an address delivered in Rochester, New York, on June 16, 1861, in Blassingame, *The Frederick Douglass Papers*, 3: 437.

23. Frederick Douglass, "'It Moves,' or the Philosophy of Reform," an address delivered in Washington, D.C., on November 20, 1883, in Blassingame, *The Frederick Douglass Papers*, 5: 137.

24. Frederick Douglass, "Is Civil Government Right?" from *Frederick Douglass' Paper*, October 23, 1851, in Foner, *The Life and Writings of Frederick Douglass*, 5: 209.

25. Frederick Douglass, "The American Apocalypse," an address delivered in Rochester, New York, on June 16, 1861, in Blassingame, *The Frederick Douglass Papers*, 3: 437–438.

26. Frederick Douglass, "Great Britain's Example Is High, Noble, and Grand," an address delivered in Rochester, New York, on August 6, 1885, *The Frederick Douglass Papers*, 5: 200.

27. Frederick Douglass, "The Significance of Emancipation in the West Indies," an address delivered in Canandaigua, New York, on August 3, 1857, in Blassingame, *The Frederick Douglass Papers*, 3: 204.

28. For more on Douglass's lobbying efforts, see generally David Blight, *Frederick Douglass' Civil War: Keeping Faith in Jubilee* (Baton Rouge: LSU Press, 1991).

29. Frederick Douglass, "The Slaveholders' Rebellion," an address delivered in Himrod's, New York, on July 4, 1862, in Blassingame, *The Frederick Douglass Papers*, 3: 532–533.

30. Wilson Jeremiah Moses, *Creative Conflict in African American Thought* (New York: Cambridge University Press, 2004), 43.

31. Frederick Douglass, "What to the Slave Is the Fourth of July?" an address delivered in Rochester, New York, on July 5, 1852, in Blassingame, *The Frederick Douglass Papers*, 2: 364.

32. Frederick Douglass, "The Antislavery Tocsin," an address delivered in Rochester, New York, on December 8, 1850, in Blassingame, *The Frederick Douglass Papers*, 2: 264.

33. Frederick Douglass, "An Antislavery Tocsin," an address delivered in Rochester, New York, on December 8, 1850, in Blassingame, *The Frederick Douglass Papers*, 2: 270.

34. Frederick Douglass, "American Slavery Is America's Disgrace," an address delivered in Sheffield, England, on March 25, 1847, in Blassingame, *The Frederick Douglass Papers*, 2: 11.

35. Frederick Douglass, "Country, Conscience, and the Anti-Slavery Cause," an address delivered in New York, New York, on May 11, 1847, in Blassingame, *The Frederick Douglass Papers*, 2: 61. Emphasis in original.

36. Frederick Douglass, "Fighting the Rebels with One Hand," an address delivered in Philadelphia, Pennsylvania, on January 14, 1862, in Blassingame, *The Frederick Douglass Papers*, 3: 473–474.

37. Frederick Douglass, "Sources of Danger to the Republic," an address delivered in St. Louis, Missouri, in February 7, 1867, in Blassingame, *The Frederick Douglass Papers*, 4: 152.

38. Frederick Douglass, "R. D. Webb—George Thompson and the Liberty Party," in *Frederick Douglass' Paper*, October 16, 1851. A copy of this document is available at the Frederick Douglass Papers Project at Indiana University-Purdue University Indianapolis, in Indianapolis, Indiana.

39. Frederick Douglass, "What Is My Duty as an Anti-Slavery Voter?" in *Frederick Douglass' Paper*, April 25, 1856. A copy of this document is available at the Frederick Douglass Papers Project at Indiana University-Purdue University Indianapolis, in Indianapolis, Indiana.

40. Frederick Douglass, "Can an Abolitionist Vote for Fremont?" in *Frederick Douglass' Paper*, September 12, 1856. A copy of this document is available at the Frederick Douglass Papers Project at Indiana University-Purdue University Indianapolis, in Indianapolis, Indiana.

41. See generally Eric Foner, *Free Soil, Free Labor, Free Men: The Ideology of the Republican Party before the Civil War* (New York: Oxford University Press, 1995).

42. Frederick Douglass, "Self-Made Men," an address delivered in Carlisle, Pennsylvania, in March 1894, in Blassingame, *The Frederick Douglass Papers*, 5: 545.

43. Ibid., 5: 575.

44. Ibid., 5: 550.

45. Ibid., 5: 549.

46. Ibid.

47. I will return to this matter in chapter 7.

48. Frederick Douglass, "Self-Made Men," an address delivered in Carlisle, Pennsylvania, in March 1894, in Blassingame, *The Frederick Douglass Papers*, 5: 549–550.

49. Ibid., 5: 550.

50. Ibid., 5: 552.

51. Ibid., 5: 552–553.

52. Ibid., 5: 555.

53. Ibid., 5: 553.

54. Ibid., 5: 556.

55. Ibid. This is reminiscent of the ideas popularized by Horatio Alger.

56. Ibid., 5: 557.

57. Ibid., 5: 561.

58. Ibid., 5: 560.

59. Ibid., 5: 564.

60. Ibid., 5: 562–572.

61. For a detailed account of this philosophy, see Deirdre N. McCloskey, *The Bourgeois Virtues: Ethics for an Age of Commerce* (Chicago: University of Chicago Press, 2006).

62. Frederick Douglass, "Letter to Major Delany," from *The New National Era*, August 31, 1871, in Foner, *The Life and Writings of Frederick Douglass*, 4: 279.

63. Frederick Douglass, "Advice to My Canadian Brothers and Sisters," an address delivered in Chatham, Canada West, on August 3, 1854, in Blassingame, *The Frederick Douglass Papers*, 2: 533.

64. I discuss Douglass's views of the state at length in chapter 6.

65. Frederick Douglass, "The National Labor Convention," in *The New National Era*, January 19, 1871. A copy of this document is available at the Frederick Douglass Papers Project at Indiana University-Purdue University Indianapolis, in Indianapolis, Indiana.

66. Frederick Douglass, "Boyhood in Baltimore," an address delivered in Baltimore, Maryland, on September 6, 1891, in Blassingame, *The Frederick Douglass Papers*, 5: 484.

67. Frederick Douglass, "Self-Made Men," an address delivered in Carlisle, Pennsylvania, in March 1893, in Blassingame, *The Frederick Douglass Papers*, 5: 564.

68. Frederick Douglass, "Agriculture and Black Progress," an address delivered in Nashville, Tennessee, on September 18, 1873, in Blassingame, *The Frederick Douglass Papers*, 4: 393.

69. Frederick Douglass, "Fourteen Days in Ohio," in *Frederick Douglass' Paper*, June 27, 1856. A copy of this document is available at the Frederick Douglass Papers Project at Indiana University-Purdue University Indianapolis, in Indianapolis, Indiana.

70. Frederick Douglass, "Trust: The Basis of Charity," an address delivered in Rochester, New York, on January 5, 1854, in Blassingame, *The Frederick Douglass Papers*, 2:453. Emphasis in original.

71. Gayle McKeen, "A 'Guiding Principle' of Liberalism in the Thought of Frederick Douglass and W. E. B. DuBois," in David F. Ericson and Louisa Bertch Green, eds., *The Liberal Tradition in American Politics* (New York: Routledge, 1999), 104.

72. Frederick Douglass, "The Blessings of Liberty and Education," an address delivered in Manassas, Virginia, on September 3, 1894, in Blassingame, *The Frederick Douglass Papers*, 5: 622.

73. Leo Strauss, *Natural Right and History* (Chicago: University of Chicago Press, 1953), 251.

74. John Stauffer, "Douglass's Self-Making and Abolitionism," in Maurice Lee, ed., *The Cambridge Companion to Frederick Douglass* (New York: Cambridge University Press, 2009), 28.

75. Mary Ann Glendon and David Blankenhorn, eds. *Seedbeds of Virtue: Sources of Competence, Character, and Citizenship in American Society* (New York: Madison Books, 1995).

76. Frederick Douglass, "Slavery, Freedom, and the Kansas-Nebraska Act," an address delivered in Chicago, Illinois, on October 30, 1854, in Blassingame, *The Frederick Douglass Papers,* 2: 544.

77. Frederick Douglass, "Our National Capital," an address delivered in Baltimore, Maryland, on May 8, 1877, in Blassingame, *The Frederick Douglass Papers,* 4: 455.

78. Frederick Douglass, "The Folly of Our Opponents," in *The Liberty Bell,* 1845, in Foner, *The Life and Writings of Frederick Douglass,* 1: 114.

79. Frederick Douglass, "The Work of the Future," in *Douglass' Monthly,* November 1862, in Foner, *The Life and Writings of Frederick Douglass,* 3: 292.

80. Frederick Douglass, "Freedom Has Brought Duties," an address delivered in Washington, D.C., on January 1, 1883, in Blassingame, *The Frederick Douglass Papers,* 5: 57.

81. Frederick Douglass, "Lessons of the Hour," an address delivered in Washington, D.C., on January 9, 1894, in Blassingame, *The Frederick Douglass Papers,* 5: 598.

82. Frederick Douglass, "Our National Capital," an address delivered in Baltimore, Maryland, on May 8, 1877, in Blassingame, *The Frederick Douglass Papers,* 4: 469.

83. Frederick Douglass, "Boyhood in Baltimore," an address delivered in Baltimore, Maryland, on September 6, 1891, in Blassingame, *The Frederick Douglass Papers,* 5: 483.

84. Frederick Douglass, "Of Morals and Men," an address delivered in New York, New York, on May 8, 1849, in Blassingame, *The Frederick Douglass Papers,* 2: 172.

85. Frederick Douglass, "Agitate, Agitate," an address delivered in Salem, Ohio, on August 23, 1853, in Blassingame, *The Frederick Douglass Papers,* 2: 396.

86. Frederick Douglass, "Did John Brown Fail?" an address delivered in Harper's Ferry, West Virginia, on May 30, 1881, in Blassingame, *The Frederick Douglass Papers,* 5: 22.

87. Frederick Douglass, "The Lessons of Emancipation to the New Generation," an address delivered in Elmira, New York, on August 2, 1879, in Blassingame, *The Frederick Douglass Papers,* 4: 570.

CHAPTER 6

1. Frederick Douglass, "Our Composite Nationality," an address delivered in Boston, Massachusetts, on December 7, 1869, in Blassingame, *The Frederick Douglass Papers,* 4: 255.

2. Thomas Spragens, *Civic Liberalism: Reflections on Our Democratic Ideals* (Lanham: Rowman and Littlefield, 1999), 232.

3. Ibid., 234.

4. Frederick Douglass, "The Present and Future of the Colored Race in America," an address delivered in Brooklyn, New York, on May 15, 1863, in Blassingame, *The Frederick Douglass Papers,* 3: 577.

5. Frederick Douglass, "Is Civil Government Right?" from *Frederick Douglass' Paper,* October 23, 1851, in Foner, *The Life and Writings of Frederick Douglass,* 5: 209.

6. Ibid., 5: 212.

7. Frederick Douglass, "The Fugitive Slave Law," from *Frederick Douglass' Paper,* August 1852, in Foner, *The Life and Writings of Frederick Douglass,* 2: 208; Frederick Douglass, "Is Civil Government Right?" from *Frederick Douglass' Paper,* October 23, 1851, in Foner, *The Life and Writings of Frederick Douglass,* 5: 213–214.

8. Ibid., 5: 212–213.

9. Ibid., 5: 212.

10. Frederick Douglass, "The New Party Movement," from *The New National Era*, August 10, 1871, in Foner, *The Life and Writings of Frederick Douglass*, 4: 255.

11. Frederick Douglass, "Is Civil Government Right?" from *Frederick Douglass' Paper*, October 23, 1851, in Foner, *The Life and Writings of Frederick Douglass*, 5: 213.

12. Frederick Douglass, "Selections from the Writings and Speeches of William Lloyd Garrison, by R. F. Wallent," in *Frederick Douglass' Paper*, January 29, 1852, in Foner, *The Life and Writings of Frederick Douglass*, 5: 222.

13. Frederick Douglass, "America's Compromise with Slavery and the Abolitionists' Work," an address delivered in Paisley, Scotland, on April 6, 1846, in Blassingame, *The Frederick Douglass Papers*, 1: 210.

14. Frederick Douglass, "Lessons of the Hour," an address delivered in Washington, D.C., on January 9, 1894, in Blassingame, *The Frederick Douglass Papers*, 5: 590.

15. Frederick Douglass, "The Prospect in the Future," from *Douglass Monthly*, August 1860, in Foner, *The Life and Writings of Frederick Douglass*, 2: 497.

16. Frederick Douglass, "Capital Punishment Is a Mockery of Justice," an address delivered in Rochester, New York, on October 7, 1858, in Blassingame, *The Frederick Douglass Papers*, 3: 244.

17. Ibid., 3: 247.

18. Ibid.

19. Ibid.

20. Frederick Douglass, "Is Civil Government Right?" from *Frederick Douglass' Paper*, October 23, 1851, in Foner, *The Life and Writings of Frederick Douglass*, 5: 213.

21. Frederick Douglass, "The Prospect in the Future," from *Douglass Monthly*, August 1860, in Foner, *The Life and Writings of Frederick Douglass*, 2: 497.

22. Frederick Douglass, "There Was a Right Side in the Late War?" an address delivered in New York, New York, on May 30, 1878, in Blassingame, *The Frederick Douglass Papers*, 4: 487.

23. Philip Harvey, "Aspirational Law," *Buffalo Law Review* 52, 118–119 (2004).

24. Frederick Douglass, "Seeming and Real," in *The New National Era*, October 10, 1870, in Foner, *The Life and Writings of Frederick Douglass*, 4: 227.

25. There has been a significant amount of work done on Douglass's understanding of the Constitution. See, e.g., David Schrader, "Natural Law in Douglass's Constitutional Thought," in Frank M. Kirkland and Bill Lawson, eds., *Frederick Douglass: A Critical Reader* (Malden: Blackwell, 1999), 85–99; Peter C. Myers, *Frederick Douglass: Race and the Rebirth of American Liberalism* (Lawrence: University Press of Kansas, 2008), 83–109; Gregg Crane, "Human Law and Higher Law," in Maurice Lee, ed., *The Cambridge Companion to Frederick Douglass* (New York: Cambridge University Press, 2009), 89–102.

26. David Blight, *Frederick Douglass' Civil War: Keeping Faith in Jubilee* (Baton Rouge: LSU Press, 1991), 115, 106.

27. Frederick Douglass, "This Decision Has Humbled the Nation," an address delivered in Washington, D.C., on October 22, 1883, in Blassingame, *The Frederick Douglass Papers*, 5: 121–122.

28. Frederick Douglass, "The Labor Question," from *The New National Era*, October 12, 1871, in Foner, *The Life and Writings of Frederick Douglass*, 4: 284.

29. Wilson Jeremiah Moses, *Creative Conflict in African American Thought* (New York: Cambridge University Press, 2004), 44–45.

30. Frederick Douglass, "In Law Free; In Fact, a Slave," an address delivered in Washington, D.C., on April 16, 1888, in Blassingame, *The Frederick Douglass Papers*, 5: 369.

31. Ibid.

32. For an excellent discussion of Douglass playing the role of statesman as educator, see Peter C. Myers, "A Good Work for Our Race To-Day: Interests, Virtues, and the Achievement of Justice in Frederick Douglass's Freedmen's Monument Speech," *American Political Science Review* 104, no. 2 (2010): 209–225.

33. Frederick Douglass, "Great Is the Miracle of Human Speech," an address delivered in Washington, D.C., on August 31, 1891, in Blassingame, *The Frederick Douglass Papers*, 5: 476–477.

34. Frederick Douglass, "The Prospect in the Future," from *Douglass Monthly*, August 1860, in Foner, *The Life and Writings of Frederick Douglass*, 2: 494.

35. Frederick Douglass, "An Inspiration to High and Virtuous Endeavor," an address delivered in Syracuse, New York, on October 1, 1884, in Blassingame, *The Frederick Douglass Papers*, 5:164–165.

36. Frederick Douglass, "The Mission of the War," an address delivered in New York, New York, on January 13, 1864, in Blassingame, *The Frederick Douglass Papers*, 4: 12.

37. Ibid., 4: 14.

38. Ibid., 4: 15.

39. Frederick Douglass, "Notes on the War," from *Douglass' Monthly*, July 1861, in Foner, *The Life and Writings of Frederick Douglass*, 3: 116.

40. Frederick Douglass, "Lessons of the Hour," an address delivered in Washington, D.C., on January 9, 1894, in Blassingame, *The Frederick Douglass Papers*, 5: 607.

41. Frederick Douglass, "Weekly Review of Congress," in *The New National Era*, March 15, 1850. A copy of this document is available at the Frederick Douglass Papers Project at Indiana University-Purdue University Indianapolis, in Indianapolis, Indiana.

42. Frederick Douglass, "Great Public Virtues," in *The New National Era*, October 20, 1870. A copy of this document is available at the Frederick Douglass Papers Project at Indiana University-Purdue University Indianapolis, in Indianapolis, Indiana.

43. Douglass uses the term "actuating motives" in "Fighting the Rebels with One Hand," an address delivered in Philadelphia, Pennsylvania, in January 1862, in Blassingame, *The Frederick Douglass Papers*, 3: 480.

44. Frederick Douglass, "The Republican Party," from *Douglass' Monthly*, August 1860, in Foner, The *Life and Writings of Frederick Douglass*, 2: 492.

45. Frederick Douglass, "Our Destiny Is Largely in Our Own Hands," an address delivered in Washington, D.C., on April 16, 1883, in Blassingame, *The Frederick Douglass Papers*, 5: 78.

46. Frederick Douglass, "The Mission of the War," an address delivered in New York, New York, on January 13, 1864, in Blassingame, *The Frederick Douglass Papers*, 4: 12. It is also worth noting that later scholars have argued that Lincoln's letter to Greeley was not nearly as damnable as abolitionists like Douglass believed. William Lee Miller, for example, has argued that what is significant about the letter is *not* that Lincoln wrote what he did about the priority of preserving the Union, but rather that Lincoln adds that he would be willing to pursue emancipation if it would achieve that end. See William Lee Miller,

Lincoln's Virtues: An Ethical Biography (New York: Knopf, 2002), 438–439. Thanks to an anonymous reviewer for suggesting incorporation of Miller's scholarship on this letter.

47. Frederick Douglass, "The Freedmen's Monument to Abraham Lincoln," an address delivered in Washington, D.C., on April 14, 1876, in Blassingame, *The Frederick Douglass Papers*, 4: 436. For extensive discussions of the relationship between Douglass and Lincoln, see James Oakes, *The Radical and the Republican* (New York: W. W. Norton, 2007); and John Stauffer, *Giants: The Parallel Lives of Frederick Douglass and Abraham Lincoln* (New York: Twelve, 2008).

48. Peter C. Myers, "A Good Work for Our Race To-Day," 214.

49. Frederick Douglass, "The Republican Party," from *Douglass' Monthly*, August 1860, in Foner, *The Life and Writings of Frederick Douglass*, 2: 492.

50. Peter C. Myers, "A Good Work for Our Race To-Day," 215.

51. Blair L. M. Kelley, *Right to Ride: Streetcar Boycotts and African American Civil Rights in the Era of Plessy v. Ferguson* (Chapel Hill: University of North Carolina Press, 2010), 71.

52. For an extensive discussion of this speech, see James Colaiaco, *Frederick Douglass and the Fourth of July* (New York: Palgrave Macmillan, 2006).

53. Frederick Douglass, "We Must Not Abandon the Observance of Decoration Day," an address delivered in Rochester, New York, on May 30, 1881, in Blassingame, *The Frederick Douglass Papers*, 5: 38. For a history of Decoration Day, see David Blight, "Decoration Days: The Origins of Memorial Day in the North and South," in Alice Fahs and Joan Waugh, eds., *The Memory of the Civil War in American Culture* (Chapel Hill: University of North Carolina Press, 2003), 94.

54. Frederick Douglass, "We Must Not Abandon the Observance of Decoration Day," an address delivered in Rochester, New York, on May 30, 1881, in Blassingame, *The Frederick Douglass Papers*, 5: 38.

55. Ibid., 5: 42.

56. Ibid.

57. Ibid., 5: 43.

58. Ibid., 5: 44.

59. Ibid., 5: 44–45.

60. David Blight, *Race and Reunion: The Civil War in American Memory* (Cambridge: Belknap Press, 2002), 15.

61. Frederick Douglass, "We Must Not Abandon the Observance of Decoration Day," an address delivered in Rochester, New York, on May 30, 1881, in Blassingame, *The Frederick Douglass Papers*, 5: 51–52.

62. Gene Andrew Jarrett, "Douglass, Ideological Slavery, and Postbellum Racial Politics," in Maurice Lee, ed., *The Cambridge Companion to Frederick Douglass* (New York: Cambridge University Press, 2009), 167.

63. Ibid., 160.

64. Ibid., 167.

65. Frederick Douglass, "We Must Not Abandon the Observance of Decoration Day," an address delivered in Rochester, New York, on May 30, 1881, in Blassingame, *The Frederick Douglass Papers*, 5: 45. The "great poet" is William Shakespeare.

66. Ibid.

67. Ibid., 5: 48.

68. Frederick Douglass, *My Bondage and My Freedom* (New York: Penguin, 2003), 109.

69. Frederick Douglass, "Agriculture and Black Progress," an address delivered in Nashville, Tennessee, on September 18, 1873, in Blassingame, *The Frederick Douglass Papers*, 4: 390–391.

70. Frederick Douglass, "Parties Were Made for Men, Not Men for Parties," an address delivered in Louisville, Kentucky, on September 25, 1883, in Blassingame, *The Frederick Douglass Papers*, 5: 102–103.

71. Frederick Douglass, "The Blessings of Liberty and Education," an address delivered in Manassas, Virginia, on September 3, 1894, in Blassingame, *The Frederick Douglass Papers*, 5: 622.

72. Frederick Douglass, "Letter to Capt. Thomas Auld, Formerly My Master," in *The Liberator*, September 14, 1849, in Foner, *The Life and Writings of Frederick Douglass*, 1: 404.

73. Frederick Douglass, "The Suffrage Question," in *Frederick Douglass' Paper*, April 25, 1856. A copy of this document is available at the Frederick Douglass Papers Project at Indiana University-Purdue University Indianapolis, in Indianapolis, Indiana.

74. Frederick Douglass, "Learn Trades or Starve!" from *Frederick Douglass' Paper*, March 4, 1853, in Foner, *The Life and Writings of Frederick Douglass*, 2: 224.

75. Frederick Douglass, "Letter to Harriet Beecher Stowe," from *Proceedings of the Colored National Convention*, July 1853, in Foner, *The Life and Writings of Frederick Douglass*, 2: 235.

76. Frederick Douglass, "The Blessings of Liberty and Education," an address delivered in Manassas, Virginia, on September 3, 1894, in Blassingame, *The Frederick Douglass Papers*, 5: 621.

77. Frederick Douglass, "Advice to My Canadian Brothers and Sisters," an address delivered in Chatham, Canada West, on August 3, 1854, in Blassingame, *The Frederick Douglass Papers*, 2: 536.

78. Frederick Douglass, "Boyhood in Baltimore," an address delivered in Baltimore, Maryland, on September 6, 1891, in Blassingame, *The Frederick Douglass Papers*, 5: 483.

79. Frederick Douglass, "Curing Symptoms," in *The New National Era*, November 10, 1870. A copy of this document is available at the Frederick Douglass Papers Project at Indiana University-Purdue University Indianapolis, in Indianapolis, Indiana.

80. Frederick Douglass, "Editorial Correspondence," in *The North Star*, April 7, 1848, in Foner, *The Life and Writings of Frederick Douglass*, 1: 302–303.

81. Frederick Douglass, "The Blessings of Liberty and Education," an address delivered in Manassas, Virginia, on September 3, 1894, in Blassingame, *The Frederick Douglass Papers*, 5: 621.

82. Ibid., 5: 623.

83. Frederick Douglass, "Parties Were Made for Men, Not Men for Parties," an address delivered in Louisville, Kentucky, on September 25, 1883, in Blassingame, *The Frederick Douglass Papers*, 5: 103.

84. Frederick Douglass, "A Progressive State," in *The New National Era*, May 18, 1871. A copy of this document is available at the Frederick Douglass Papers Project at Indiana University-Purdue University Indianapolis, in Indianapolis, Indiana.

85. Frederick Douglass, "Lessons of the Hour," an address delivered in Washington, D.C., on January 9, 1849, in Blassingame, *The Frederick Douglass Papers*, 5: 596.

86. Frederick Douglass, "The Negro Problem," an address delivered in Washington, D.C., on October 21, 1890, in Blassingame, *The Frederick Douglass Papers*, 5: 454–455.

87. Frederick Douglass, "The Blessings of Liberty and Education," an address delivered in Manassas, Virginia, on September 3, 1894, in Blassingame, *The Frederick Douglass Papers*, 5: 623.

CHAPTER 7

1. Rogers Smith, *Civic Ideals* (New Haven: Yale University Press, 1999); and Sue Davis, *The Political Thought of Elizabeth Cady Stanton* (New York: NYU Press, 2008).

2. Sue Davis, *The Political Thought of Elizabeth Cady Stanton*, 2.

3. Frederick Douglass, "What to the Slave Is the Fourth of July?" an address delivered in Rochester, New York, on July 5, 1852, in Blassingame, *The Frederick Douglass Papers*, 2: 364.

4. Douglass's emphasis on virtue without abandoning the core principles of liberalism lends support to those scholars of American political thought who have argued that republicanism and liberalism should not be thought of as separate traditions. See, e.g., David F. Ericson, *The Shaping of American Liberalism: The Debates over Ratification, Nullification, and Slavery* (Chicago: University of Chicago Press, 1993), 10–26.

5. Rogers Smith, "Understanding the Symbiosis of American Rights and American Racism," in Mark Hulliung, ed., *The American Liberal Tradition Reconsidered: The Contested Legacy of Louis Hartz* (Lawrence: University of Kansas Press, 2010), 55.

6. Michael Sandel, *Democracy's Discontent* (Cambridge: Harvard University Press, 1996), 323.

7. Peter Berkowitz, *Virtue and the Making of Modern Liberalism* (Princeton: Princeton University Press, 2000); James T. Kloppenberg, *The Virtues of Liberalism* (New York: Oxford University Press, 2000); John Patrick Diggins, *The Lost Soul of American Politics* (Chicago: University of Chicago Press, 1986); J. David Greenstone, *The Lincoln Persuasion* (Princeton: Princeton University Press, 1994).

8. Thomas Spragens, *Civic Liberalism: Reflections on Our Democratic Ideals* (Lanham: Rowman and Littlefield, 1999), xvi.

9. For discussions of Douglass's "presence" in the chambers of Marshall and Thomas, see Juan Williams, *Thurgood Marhsall: American Revolutionary* (New York: Three Rivers Press, 2000), 386; and Andrew Peyton Thomas, *Clarence Thomas: A Biography* (New York: Encounter Books, 2002), 458.

10. *Zelman v. Simmons Harris*, 536 U.S. 639 (2002); *Grutter v. Bollinger*, 539 U.S. 306 (2002).

11. *Zelman* at 657.

12. *Zelman* at 676.

13. Thomas is citing Frederick Douglass, "What the Black Man Wants," an address delivered in Boston, Massachusetts, on January 26, 1865, in Blassingame, *Frederick Douglass Papers*, 4: 68.

14. *Grutter* at 349–350.

15. Mark V. Tushnet and Randall Kennedy, eds., *Thurgood Marshall: His Speeches, Writings, Arguments, Opinions, and Reminiscences* (Chicago: Lawrence Hill Books, 2001), 420.

16. Frederick Douglass, "Let the Negro Alone," an address delivered in New York, May 1869, in Blassingame, *The Frederick Douglass Papers*, 4: 202.

17. Ibid., 5:549. Parenthetical note added by me.

18. Clarence Thomas, "Personal Responsibility," 12 *Regent U.L. Rev.* 317 (2000).

19. Frederick Douglass, "Strong to Suffer, and Yet Strong to Strive," an address delivered in Washington, D.C., on April 16, 1886, in Blassingame, *The Frederick Douglass Papers,* 5: 233.

20. Frederick Douglass, "Self-Made Men," an address delivered in Carlisle, Pennsylvania, March 1893, in Blassingame, *The Frederick Douglass Papers,* 5: 549.

21. Ibid.

22. Frederick Douglass, "Advice to My Canadian Brothers and Sisters," an address delivered in Chatham, Canada West, on August 3, 1854, in Blassingame, *The Frederick Douglass Papers,* 2: 534.

23. Frederick Douglass, "Strong to Suffer, and Yet Strong to Strive," an address delivered in Washington, D.C., on April 16, 1886, in Blassingame, *The Frederick Douglass Papers,* 5: 237–238.

24. Wilson Carey McWilliams, *The Idea of Fraternity in America* (Berkeley: University of California Press, 1973), 573.

Bibliography

Allen, Jonathan. "The Place of Negative Morality in Political Theory." *Political Theory* 29, no. 3 (June 2001): 337.

Appleby, Joyce. *Capitalism and a New Social Order*. New York: NYU Press, 1984.

Arblaster, Anthony. *The Rise and Decline of Western Liberalism*. Oxford: Basil Blackwell, 1984.

Attas, Daniel. "Freedom and Self-Ownership." *Social Theory and Practice* 26 (Spring 2000): 1.

Bailyn, Bernard. *The Ideological Origins of the American Revolution*. Cambridge: Belknap Press, 1992.

Barber, Benjamin. *Strong Democracy: Participatory Politics for a New Age*. Berkeley: University of California Press, 1984.

Barnett, Randy E. *Restoring the Lost Constitution: The Presumption of Liberty*. Princeton: Princeton University Press, 2004.

Bellah, Robert, et al. *Habits of the Heart*. Berkeley: University of California Press, 1985.

Berkowitz, Peter. "The Liberal Spirit in America." *Policy Review*, no. 120 (2003).

———. *Virtue and the Making of Modern Liberalism*. Princeton: Princeton University Press, 2000.

Blight, David. "Decoration Days: The Origins of Memorial Day in the North and South." In Alice Fahs and Joan Waugh, eds., *The Memory of the Civil War in American Culture*. Chapel Hill: University of North Carolina Press, 2003.

———. *Frederick Douglass' Civil War: Keeping Faith in Jubilee*. Baton Rouge: LSU Press, 1991.

———. *Race and Reunion: The Civil War in American Memory*. Cambridge: Belknap Press, 2002.

Blitz, Mark. "Liberal Freedom and Responsibility." In T. William Boxx and Gary M. Quinlivan, eds., *Public Morality, Civic Virtue, and the Problem of Modern Liberalism*. Grand Rapids: William B. Eerdmans Publishing, 2000.

Bork, Robert. *Slouching towards Gomorrah*. New York: Regan Books, 1996.

Boxill, Bernard. "Self-Respect and Protest." *Philosophy and Public Affairs* 6, no.1 (1976): 58.

Cannon, Donald Q. "Thomas L. Kane Meets the Mormons." *BYU Studies* 18, no. 1 (1977): 1–3.

Cohen, G. A. *Self-Ownership, Freedom, and Equality*. Cambridge: Cambridge University Press, 1995.

Colaiaco, James. *Frederick Douglass and the Fourth of July*. New York: Palgrave Macmillan, 2006.

Crane, Gregg. "Human Law and Higher Law." In Maurice Lee, ed., *The Cambridge Companion to Frederick Douglass*. New York: Cambridge University Press, 2009.

Dagger, Richard. *Civic Ideals*. New York: Oxford University Press, 1997.

Darby, Derrick. *Rights, Race, and Recognition*. New York: Cambridge University Press, 2009.

Davis, Angela. *Narrative of the Life of Frederick Douglass, An American Slave, Written by Himself: A New Critical Edition by Angela Y. Davis*. San Francisco: City Lights Books, 2009.

Davis, Reginald F. *Frederick Douglass: A Precursor to Liberation Theology*. Atlanta: Mercer University Press, 2004.

Davis, Sue. *The Political Thought of Elizabeth Cady Stanton*. New York: NYU Press, 2008.

Degler, Carl. *At Odds: Women and Family in American History*. New York: Oxford University Press, 1980.

Diggins, John Patrick. *On Hallowed Ground: Abraham Lincoln and the Foundations of American History*. New Haven: Yale University Press, 2000.

———. *The Lost Soul of American Politics*. Chicago: University of Chicago Press, 1986.

Dolbeare, Kenneth. "Introduction: American Liberalism—An Overview." In *American Political Thought*. Chatham: Chatham House Publishers, 2004.

Douglass, Frederick. *Autobiographies*. Ed. Henry Louis Gates. New York: Library of America, 1994.

———. *My Bondage and My Freedom*. New York: Penguin Books, 2003.

———. *The Frederick Douglass Papers*. 5 volumes. Ed. John Blassingame. New Haven: Yale University Press, 1979–1992.

———. *The Life and Times of Frederick Douglass*. Mineola: Courier Dover Publications, 2003.

———. *The Life and Writings of Frederick Douglass*. 5 volumes. Ed. Philip S. Foner. New York: International Publishers, 1950–1975.

Dworkin, Ronald. "Rights as Trumps," in Jeremy Waldron, ed., *Theories of Rights*. Oxford: Oxford University Press, 1984.

Ericson, David F. *The Debate over Slavery*. New York: NYU Press, 2000.

———.*The Shaping of American Liberalism: The Debates over Ratification, Nullification, and Slavery*. Chicago: University of Chicago Press, 1993.

Etzioni, Amitai. *The New Golden Rule*. New York: Basic Books, 1998.

Fitzhugh, George. *Sociology for the South*, reprinted in *Antebellum: Three Classic Works on Slavery in the Old South*. New York: Capricorn, 1960.

Foner, Eric. *Free Soil, Free Labor, Free Men: The Ideology of the Republican Party before the Civil War*. New York: Oxford University Press, 1995.

———. *Politics and Ideology in the Age of the Civil War*. New York: Oxford University Press, 1980.

———. *The Story of American Freedom*. New York: W. W. Norton, 1998.

Foner, Philip S. *Frederick Douglass: A Biography*. New York: Citadel Press, 1969.

———, ed. *Frederick Douglass on Women's Rights*. Westport: Greenwood Press, 1976.

Fowler, Robert Booth. *The Dance with Community*. Lawrence: University Press of Kansas, 1993.

Fox, Charles James. "Abolition of the Slave Trade." *Speeches of the Right Honourable Charles James Fox in the House of Commons*. London, 1815.

Franchot, Jenny. "The Punishment of Esther: Frederick Douglass and the Construction of the Feminine." In Eric J. Sundquist, ed. *Frederick Douglass: New Literary and Historical Essays*. New York: Cambridge University Press, 1990.

Frisch, Morton, and Richard Stevens, eds. *American Political Thought: The Philosophic Dimension of American Statesmanship*. Dubuque: Kendall-Hunt Publishing, 1976.

Galston, William. *Liberal Purposes*. Cambridge: Cambridge University Press, 1991.

George, Robert P. *Making Men Moral*. New York: Oxford University Press, 1995.

Gibson, Alan. *Interpreting the Founding*. Lawrence: University Press of Kansas, 2009.

Glendon, Mary Ann. *Rights Talk*. New York: Free Press, 1993.

Glendon, Mary Ann, and David Blankenhorn, eds. *Seedbeds of Virtue: Sources of Competence, Character, and Citizenship in American Society*. New York: Madison Books, 1995.

Goldstein, Leslie Friedman. "Morality and Prudence in the Statesmanship of Frederick Douglass." *Polity* 16 (Summer 1984): 614.

———. "The Political Thought of Frederick Douglass." Ph.D. dissertation, Department of Political Science, Cornell University, 1974.

Gooding-Williams, Robert. *In the Shadow of Du Bois*. Cambridge: Harvard University Press, 2009.

Gottheimer, Josh, ed. *Ripples of Hope: Great American Civil Rights Speeches*. New York: Basic Civitas, 2003.

Greenstone, J. David. *The Lincoln Persuasion*. Princeton: Princeton University Press, 1994.

Guarneri, Carl J. *The Utopian Alternative: Fourierism in Nineteenth-Century America*. Ithaca: Cornell University Press, 1994.

Guelzo, Allen. "Apple of Gold and the Picture of Silver." In Gabor Boritt, ed., *The Lincoln Enigma: The Changing Faces of an American Icon*. New York: Oxford University Press, 2001.

Hartz, Louis. *The Liberal Tradition in America*. New York: Harcourt Brace, 1991.

Harvey, Philip. "Aspirational Law." *Buffalo Law Review* 52 (2004): 118.

Hertzke, Allen D. "The Concept of Moral Ecology." *Review of Politics* 60, no. 4 (Autumn 1998): 629.

Hofstadter, Richard. *The American Political Tradition and the Men Who Made It*. New York: Vintage, 1989.

Howe, Daniel Walker. *Making the American Self*. Cambridge: Harvard University Press, 1997.

Hudson, Donald. *Democracy in Peril*. Washington, D.C.: CQ Press, 2010.

Hulliung, Mark. *The American Liberal Tradition Reconsidered*. Lawrence: University Press of Kansas, 2010.

Huntington, Samuel. *Who Are We? Challenges to American National Identity*. New York: Simon and Schuster, 2005.

Jaffa, Harry. *Crisis over a House Divided*. Chicago: University of Chicago Press, 1999.

Jarrett, Gene Andrew. "Douglass, Ideological Slavery, and Postbellum Racial Politics." In Maurice Lee, ed., *The Cambridge Companion to Frederick Douglass*. New York: Cambridge University Press, 2009.

Kann, Mark E. *On the Man Question*. Philadelphia: Temple University Press, 1991.

———. *Punishment, Prisons, and Patriarchy*. New York: NYU Press, 2005.

———. *A Republic of Men*. New York: NYU Press, 1998.

Kautz, Steven. *Liberalism and Community*. Ithaca: Cornell University Press, 1995.

Kelley, Blair L. M. *Right to Ride: Streetcar Boycotts and African American Civil Rights in the Era of Plessy v. Ferguson*. Chapel Hill: University of North Carolina Press, 2010.

Kloppenberg, James T. *The Virtues of Liberalism*. New York: Oxford University Press, 2000.

Krause, Sharon. *Liberalism with Honor*. Cambridge: Harvard University Press, 2002.

Lawson, Bill E. "Frederick Douglass and Social Progress." In Frank M. Kirkland and Bill Lawson, eds., *Frederick Douglass: A Critical Reader*. Malden: Blackwell Publishers, 1999.

Leibovich, Mark. "Rights vs. Rights: An Improbable Collision Course." *New York Times*, January 13, 2008.

Leavelle, Arnaud, and Thomas Cook. "George Fitzhugh and the Theory of American Conservatism." *Journal of Politics* 7 (May 1945): 147.

Locke, John. *Second Treatise of Civil Government*. New York: Barnes and Noble Press, 2004.

Macedo, Stephen. *Diversity and Distrust*. Cambridge: Harvard University Press, 2003.

———. *Liberal Virtues*. Oxford: Clarendon Press, 1990.

MacIntyre, Alasdair. *After Virtue*. South Bend: University of Notre Dame Press, 1984.

Mack, Eric. "The State of Nature Has a Law of Nature to Govern It." In Tibor R. Machan, ed. *Individual Rights Reconsidered*. Palo Alto: Hoover Institution Press, 2001.

Macpherson, C. B. *The Political Theory of Possessive Individualism*. Oxford: Oxford University Press, 1962.

Madison, James. *Federalist #51*. In *The Federalist Papers*. New York: Classic Books America, 2009.

Martin, Waldo E. *The Mind of Frederick Douglass*. Chapel Hill: University of North Carolina Press, 1984.

McCloskey, Deirdre. *The Bourgeois Virtues: Ethics for an Age of Commerce*. Chicago: University of Chicago Press, 2006.

McFeely, William. *Frederick Douglass*, New York: W. W. Norton, 1995.

McInerney, Daniel. *The Fortunate Heirs of Freedom: Abolition and Republican Thought*. Lincoln: University of Nebraska Press, 1994.

McKeen, Gayle. "A 'Guiding Principle' of Liberalism in the Thought of Frederick Douglass and W. E. B. Du Bois." In David F. Ericson and Louisa Bertch Green, eds., *The Liberal Tradition in American Politics*. New York: Routledge, 1999.

McKeen, Gayle. "Whose Rights? Whose Responsibility? Self-Help in African-American Thought." *Polity* XXXIV, no. 3 (Summer 2002): 417.

McWhorter, John. *Winning the Race*. New York: Gotham Books, 2006.

McWilliams, Wilson Carey. *The Idea of Fraternity in America*. Berkeley: University of California Press, 1973.

———. "Ironies and Ambiguities." In Andrew R. Cecil and W. Lawson Taitte, eds. *Moral Values in Liberalism and Conservatism*. Austin: University of Texas Press, 1995.

Mill, John Stuart. *On Liberty*. New York: Oxford University Press, 1991.

Miller, William Lee. *Lincoln's Virtues: An Ethical Biography*. New York: Knopf, 2002.

Moses, Wilson Jeremiah. *Creative Conflict in African American Thought*. New York: Cambridge University Press, 2004.

Myers, Peter C. "Frederick Douglass' Natural Rights Constitutionalism: The Postwar, Pre-Progressive Period." In John Marini and Ken Masugi, eds., *The Progressive Revolution in Politics and Political Science*. Lanham: Rowman and Littlefield, 2005.

———. *Frederick Douglass: Race and the Rebirth of American Liberalism*. Lawrence: University Press of Kansas, 2008.

———. "A Good Work for Our Race To-Day: Interests, Virtues, and the Achievement of Justice in Frederick Douglass's Freedmen's Monument Speech." *American Political Science Review* 104, no. 2 (2010): 209–225.

Novak, Michael. *Cultivating Liberty: Essays on Moral Ecology.* New York: Rowan and Littlefield, 1999.

Noyes, John Humphrey. *History of American Socialisms.* Philadelphia: J. B. Lippincott, 1870.

Nozick, Robert. *Anarchy, State, and Utopia.* New York: Basic Books, 1974.

Oakes, James. "Radical Liberals, Liberal Radicals: The Dissenting Traditions in American Political Culture." *Reviews in American History* 27, no. 3 (1999): 508.

———. *The Radical and the Republican.* New York: W. W. Norton, 2007.

Palmer, Tom. "Saving Rights Theory from Its Friends." In Tibor Machan, ed., *Individual Rights Reconsidered.* Stanford: Hoover Institution Press, 2001.

Perry, Lewis. *Radical Abolitionism: Anarchy and the Government of God in Antislavery Thought.* Ithaca: Cornell University Press, 1973.

———. "Versions of Anarchism in the Antislavery Movement." *American Quarterly* 20, no. 4 (Winter 1968): 770.

Pocock, J. G. A. *The Machiavellian Moment.* Princeton: Princeton University Press, 2003.

Quarles, Benjamin. "Frederick Douglass and the Women's Rights Movement." *Journal of Negro History* 25 (January 1940): 35.

Rawls, John. *Political Liberalism.* New York: Columbia University Press, 2005.

Reynolds, David S. *John Brown, Abolitionist: The Man Who Killed Slavery, Sparked the Civil War, and Seeded Civil Rights.* New York: Vintage, 2005.

Rodriguez, Junius P., ed. *Slavery in the United States: A Social, Historical, and Political Encyclopedia.* Santa Barbara: ABC-CLIO, 2007.

Sandel, Michael. *Democracy's Discontent.* Cambridge: Harvard University Press, 1996.

———. *Public Philosophy: Essays on Morality and Politics.* Cambridge: Harvard University Press, 2006.

Schneider, Thomas. *Lincoln's Defense of Politics: The Public Man and His Opponents in the Crisis over Slavery.* Columbia: University of Missouri Press, 2006.

Schrader, David. "Natural Law in Douglass's Constitutional Thought." In Frank M. Kirkland and Bill Lawson, eds., *Frederick Douglass: A Critical Reader.* Malden: Blackwell, 1999.

Schwarzenbach, Sibyl. "On Civic Friendship." *Ethics* 107 (October 1996): 99.

Sheldon, Garrett Ward. *The Political Philosophy of Thomas Jefferson.* Baltimore: Johns Hopkins University Press, 1993.

Shklar, Judith. *American Citizenship: The Quest for Inclusion.* Cambridge: Harvard University Press, 1998.

———. *Legalism.* Cambridge: Harvard University Press, 2006.

———. "The Liberalism of Fear." In Stanley Hoffmann, ed., *Political Thought and Political Thinkers.* Chicago: University of Chicago Press, 1998.

———. *Ordinary Vices.* Cambridge: Harvard University Press, 1984.

———. "Political Theory and the Rule of Law." In Stanley Hoffmann, ed., *Political Thought and Political Thinkers.* Chicago: University of Chicago Press, 1998.

Sigmund, Paul. *Natural Law in Political Thought,* Cambridge: Winthrop Publishers, 1971.

Slater, James Harvey, and James Zachariah George. "Speeches on Chinese Immigration." Reprinted in Isaac Kramnick and Theodore Lowi, eds., *American Political Thought: A Norton Anthology.* New York: W. W. Norton, 2009.

Smith, Rogers. *Civic Ideals.* New Haven: Yale University Press, 1999.

—————. "Understanding the Symbiosis of American Rights and American Racism." In Mark Hulliung, ed., *The American Liberal Tradition Reconsidered: The Contested Legacy of Louis Hartz*. Lawrence: University Press of Kansas, 2010.

Sowell, Thomas. *The Vision of the Anointed*. New York: Basic Books, 1996.

Spragens, Thomas. *Civic Liberalism: Reflections on our Democratic Ideals*. Lanham: Rowman and Littlefield, 1999.

Stanley, Amy Dru. *From Bondage to Contract: Wage Labor, Marriage, and the Market in the Age of Slave Emancipation*. Cambridge: Cambridge University Press, 1998.

Stanton, Elizabeth Cady, et al. *History of Woman Suffrage: 1861–1876*. Salem: Ayer Publishers, 1985.

Stauffer, John. "Douglass's Self-Making and Abolitionism." In Maurice Lee, ed., *The Cambridge Companion to Frederick Douglass*. New York: Cambridge University Press, 2009.

—————. *Giants: The Parallel Lives of Frederick Douglass and Abraham Lincoln*. New York: Twelve, 2008.

Steele, Shelby. *The Content of Our Character*. New York: Harper Perennial, 2001.

Storing, Herbert J. "Frederick Douglass." In Joseph M. Bessette, ed. *Toward a More Perfect Union*. Washington, D.C.: American Enterprise Institute, 1995.

Strauss, Leo. *Natural Right and History*. Chicago: University of Chicago Press, 1953.

Tarcov, Nathan. *Locke's Education for Liberty*. Chicago: University of Chicago Press, 1989.

Tarrant, Sasha, et al. *Antifeminism in America: A Historical Reader*. New York: Routledge, 2000.

Taylor, Charles. "Atomism." In *Philosophy and the Human Sciences*. New York: Cambridge University Press, 1985.

—————. *The Ethics of Authenticity*. Cambridge: Harvard University Press, 1991.

—————. *Sources of Self*. Cambridge: Harvard University Press, 1992.

Taylor, Robert S. "A Kantian Defense of Self-Ownership." *Journal of Political Philosophy* 12 (March 2004): 65.

—————. "The Theory and Practice of Self-Ownership." Ph.D. dissertation, University of California, Berkeley, 2002.

Thomas, Andrew Peyton. *Clarence Thomas: A Biography*. New York: Encounter Books, 2002.

Thomas, Clarence. "Personal Responsibility." 12 *Regent U.L. Rev.* 317 (2000).

Thompson, C. Bradley. "Introduction." *Antislavery Political Writings, 1833–1860*. Armonk: M. E. Sharpe, 2004.

Tocqueville, Alexis de. *Democracy in America*. Eds. Harvey Mansfield and Delba Winthrop. Chicago: University of Chicago Press, 2000.

Tushnet, Mark V., and Randall Kennedy, eds. *Thurgood Marshall: His Speeches, Writings, Arguments, Opinions, and Reminiscences*. Chicago: Lawrence Hill Books, 2001.

Van Deburg, William L. "Frederick Douglass: Maryland Slave to Religious Liberal." In Anthony B. Pinn, ed., *By These Hands: A Documentary History of African American Humanism*. New York: NYU Press, 2001.

Walker, Peter. *Moral Choices:Memory, Desire, and Imagination in Nineteenth Century Abolition*. Baton Rouge: Louisiana State University Press, 1978.

Williams, Juan. *Thurgood Marshall: American Revolutionary*. New York: Three Rivers Press, 2000.

Wolin, Sheldon. *Politics and Vision*. Boston: Little, Brown, 1960.

———. "The Liberal/Democratic Divide: On Rawls's *Political Liberalism.*" *Political Theory* 24, no.1 (February 1996): 97.

Wood, Gordon. *The Creation of the American Republic.* Chapel Hill: University of North Carolina Press, 1998.

Wright, Henry C. "Anthropology." Boston: E. Seepard, 1850.

Yarbrough, Jean. *American Virtues: Thomas Jefferson on the Character of a Free People.* Lawrence: University Press of Kansas, 1998.

Young, James P. *Reconsidering American Liberalism.* Boulder, Colo.: Westview Press, 1996.

Zuckert, Michael. *Natural Rights and the New Republicanism.* Princeton: Princeton University Press, 1998.

Index

religious liberty: denial under slavery, 17; Douglass's support of, 30, 56–59; diversity as protective of, 60

Republican National Committee, 173n41

Republican Party, 113, 140

Reynolds, David S., 190n18

Rhode Island Anti-Slavery Society, 53

Rodriguez, Junius P., 177n66

rule of law, 44; Douglass's embrace of, 74–75

Sandel, Michael, critique of liberalism, 161, 173n37, 198n6

Schneider, Thomas, 179n102

Schrader, David, 194n25

"Self-Made Men," 114–27; good luck theory of, 116; superior mental endowment theory of, 116; supernatural intervention theory of, 116

self-ownership: as central idea in Douglass's thought, 1, 9, 14; conventional history of, 29; definition of, 2, 28; Douglass's defense of, 28–40; emphasis on economic dimension of, 38; relationship to the right to property in Douglass's thought, 52

self-reliance: classical liberal commitment to, 6; Douglass's commitment to, 94; in Douglass's idea of the "Self-Made Man," 102, 114, 115, 117, 119; tension with the idea of fraternity, 9; in Clarence Thomas's interpretation of Douglass, 165

selfishness: in American political culture, 1, 61, 72, 86, 87, 92, 97, 108, 169; as motivation for slavery, 19–22

Seneca Falls Convention of 1848, 33

sharecropping, 136, 166

Sheldon, Garret Ward, 5, 171n10

Shklar, Judith: on the importance of toleration in liberalism 43; interpretation of Douglass as a member of the "party of individual effort," 5–6; on the liberal commitment to democracy, 45, 55, 72, 75, 172nn13, 19, 177n70, 180nn7, 8, 9, 10,

17, 18, 20, 185n123; on the rule of law in liberalism, 44

Sigmund, Paul, 177n72

Slater, James Harvey, 175n35

slavery: cruelties of, 22–28; definition of, 16–17, 28; equation with deprivation of rights, 18–19; equation with drunkenness, 19; equation with poverty, 19; as an illiberal institution, 22; misuse of term, 17–19; possibility of benevolent, 27–28

Smith, Gerrit, 85, 142

Smith, Rogers, 161, 179n113, 198nn1, 5

socialism: Douglass's rejection of, 52–54; as ideological strand in American antislavery movement, 41; tension with the idea of self-ownership in Douglass's thought, 38

Sowell, Thomas, 6, 7, 172n18

Spooner, Lysander, 85, 142

Spragens, Thomas, 129, 162, 193n2, 198n8

Stanley, Amy Dru, 177n75

Stanton, Elizabeth Cady, 33, 180n117; dispute with Douglass over Fifteenth Amendment, 39

Stauffer, John, 171nn5, 8, 192n74, 196n47

Steele, Shelby, 6, 7, 172n18

Stevens, Thaddeus, 154

Storing, Herbert, 172n12

Stout, Ira, 132

Stowe, Harriet Beecher, 26

Strauss, Leo, 122, 177n70, 192n73

Sumner, Charles, 139, 154

Taylor, Charles, 178n101

Taylor, Robert S., 29, 177n74

Temperance movement, 50

Thirteenth Amendment, 134

Thomas, Andrew Peyton, 198n9

Thomas, Clarence, 6, 9, 198n9, 199n18; appeal to Douglass's ideas in his opinions, 162–64

Thompson, George, 112

Tocqueville, Alexis de, 86, 187n27

toleration, 43; Douglass's views of, 55–60

virtue, 125; as basis for community, 77, 89–96; bourgeois doctrine of, 114–15, 119, 123; relationship to liberty, 49–51; true, doctrine of, 1, 103, 110, 158

About the Author

NICHOLAS BUCCOLA is Associate Professor and Founding Director of the Frederick Douglass Forum on Law, Rights, and Justice at Linfield College. His essays have appeared in a number of journals, including the *Review of Politics* and the *Journal of Social Philosophy*.